D0869947

SKIM, DIVE, SURFACE

TEACHING AND LEARNING IN HIGHER EDUCATION

James M. Lang, Series Editor

A list of titles in this series appears at the end of this volume.

SKIM, DIVE, SURFACE

TEACHING DIGITAL READING

JENAE COHN

West Virginia University Press · Morgantown

Copyright © 2021 by West Virginia University Press
All rights reserved
First edition published 2021 by West Virginia University Press
Printed in the United States of America

ISBN 978-1-952271-03-8 (cloth) / 978-1-952271-04-5 (paperback) /
978-1-952271-05-2 (ebook)

Library of Congress Cataloging-in-Publication Data
Names: Cohn, Jenae, author.
Title: Skim, dive, surface : teaching digital reading / Jenae Cohn.
Description: First edition. | Morgantown : West Virginia University Press,
        2021. | Series: Teaching and learning in higher education | Includes
        bibliographical references and index.
Identifiers: LCCN 2020051360 | ISBN 9781952271038 (cloth) | ISBN
        9781952271045 (paperback) | ISBN 9781952271052 (ebook)
Subjects: LCSH: Computers and literacy. | Reading comprehension. |
        Electronic information resources. | Digital media. | Education,
        Higher—Effect of technological innovations on.
Classification: LCC LC149.5 .C625 2021 | DDC 371.33/4—dc23
LC record available at https://lccn.loc.gov/2020051360

Book and cover design by Than Saffel / WVU Press

CONTENTS

PART 1. SKIM
Understanding Historical, Affective, and Neurological
Perspectives on Reading Technologies

PART 2. DIVE
Exploring the Digital Reading Framework to Promote
Deep Reading Practices

PART 3. SURFACE

Critically Approaching the Adoption and Use of Digital
Reading Technologies

ACKNOWLEDGMENTS

Writing is a conversation, and this particular piece of writing has emerged from an invaluable number of conversations. First, I couldn't have imagined a better editorial team to usher me through my first book than Derek Krissoff and James Lang. Derek, your ongoing enthusiasm for this book's concept, your generous engagement with my questions, and your trust in my vision gave me the confidence to complete this book. Jim, you helped me make this book an immeasurably better final product, and your casual side comments about how much content I could convert into a next book really empowered me to see myself as a writer. Thanks also to my two peer reviewers, Ellen Carillo and Dana Gierdowski, who offered thoughtful and encouraging feedback on the full manuscript. The entire editorial team at West Virginia University Press has been kind, patient, and helpful through this whole process.

The earliest vision of this book was crafted during my participation in the National Endowment for the Humanities Summer Institute on The Book: Material Histories and Digital Futures in Summer 2018. Thank you to the institute's organizers, Melissa Helquist, Lisa Bickmore, and Charlotte Howe, for giving me the opportunity and space to think about books critically (what the hell is a book indeed!). Many conversations with other institute attendees offered much-needed inspiration and encouragement at a pivotal early moment.

Many members of my academic community supported me in reading early drafts of this book. Michael Greer was my first reader of this full manuscript and I cannot thank him enough for many lively conversations about book history and digital pedagogy. Carl Whithaus, thank you for always being a supportive and engaged reader of my work for so many years. Sarah Pittock and Michal Reznizki, thank you for early reads on initial chapter drafts and for helping me understand how my work would be understood for my primary audience of scholar-practitioners.

Norah Fahim, thanks for making "Writing Wednesdays" in the Hume Center a reality. Christine Alfano, thank you for your flexibility and encouragement through this process.

I'm grateful for the love and kindness of my friends. Cindy Nguyen, thank you so much for your ongoing "turbo thoughts" and for indulging me in long conversations about this book's vision. Andy Weiner, thanks for being one of my most enduring writing friends and for sharing tips and motivation. Christine Smith, thanks for inquiring about an autographed copy before this book was even finished and for listening as I made my way through a consuming process. Jenny March, thanks for giving me a gigantic hug when I showed you the full, printed-out version of the manuscript. Other friends who often asked about and rooted for this: Sarah, Glenn, Kathleen, Noah, Bri, Yoni, George, Jyoti, Boaz, Mary, Andy, and the virtual short story club.

Most of this book was composed in the following coffee-shops: Philz Coffee (on Forest Avenue), Red Rock Coffee,

Blue Bottle Coffee (in Hanahaus, Palo Alto), and Backyard Brew. Thank you to the baristas and proprietors of these establishments for creating creative space.

My family was remarkably patient and enthusiastic about this project. My parents read the first chapter and called it "surprisingly folksy," so if that's not an endorsement for readability, I don't know what it is! Thank you to Shara, Josh, Henry, Izzy, and Lily for offering love and support the whole way through. Finally, congratulations to my mom for winning the family bet on when I'd finish the manuscript and how long it would be!

Finally, I couldn't have completed this book without the support of my husband, Kevin. Kevin, your belief in me, your unconditional willingness to offer time, space, and a listening ear when I needed it, and your unabashed enthusiasm for just sitting next to me and writing with me for so many weekends in a row (and for hours on end) meant more than I can express. You are the best.

. . . .

WHY TEACH DIGITAL READING?

Stacks of articles towered over my desk. As I sat there with a pink highlighter brandished in my hand, a pencil behind my ear, and a box of Band-Aids at the ready for the inevitable paper-cuts, it hit me: this way of reading was not sustainable. It wasn't just the unwieldy setup that was the issue. As a first-year PhD student, I had hundreds of pages of reading to complete each week—much more than I had ever been asked to do as an undergraduate. Not only did the quantity of reading increase, but the difficulty of it increased too. One hundred pages of critical theory here, another hundred pages of eighteenth-century pamphlets there, and yet another hundred pages of empirical educational research left my head spinning. But every technique I had learned in college for reading, from note-taking in the margins to dog-earing important pages, felt entirely inadequate. It wasn't just close reading at the detail level I had to do: I now had to contextualize those close reading moments to make theoretical claims, to situate the reading in a larger scholarly conversation.

The cognitive load of putting texts into these conversations and, beyond that, considering how these texts might inform an independent research project felt overwhelming. Plus, as a student bridging coursework across the humanities and social sciences and pursuing an interdisciplinary degree, I had to toggle back and forth between the sources I read in ways I never had to do before. My confidence shaken, I realized that I could no longer read well. I had to learn to read all over again.

I know now that I wasn't alone in this struggle, but at the time, I felt very alone. No one talked about reading academic texts at the college or graduate school level. In fact, the last time I had even thought about reading comprehension was during high school, and even then, the conversation was cursory at best. The assumption remained that we would figure out how to read challenging texts on our own. It took my mother's intervention to help me understand that I could use a highlighter judiciously to identify the *truly* important points and not just consider everything on the page valuable (and dye all of my textbooks neon yellow). These home-taught strategies got me through much of my schooling, but as the stakes for my reading got higher, the more lost I became. I didn't feel I could ask anyone for help either, not when I was in college, when I felt like I should know what I was doing, and certainly not in graduate school when I *really* felt like I should know what I was doing. Maura Smale (2020) interviewed several undergraduate students within the City University of New York (CUNY) system and similarly found that students "seemed embarrassed when asked whether they sought support with challenging reading assignments. Students . . . have internalized that reading is something they should know how to do already—as one student told me, in college 'reading is your problem' " (p. 6). When reading becomes the student's "problem," a variety of choices for reading remain in front of them, which can be overwhelming.

When digital reading comes into the equation too, the options become even more dizzying. As Douglas Hartman and Paul Morsink assert, a twenty-first-century reading landscape puts readers at a "crossroads" where they face "a bewildering—or exhilarating—array of choices about what to read, how to read, what reading-assistive technologies to use, how to document or archive their reading, with whom to share their reading (synchronously or asynchronously) and how to (re)conceive the very idea of reading" (2015, p. 75). What might these changes mean for our teaching and for our students' reading practices?

I began to grapple with this question after completing a few quarters of teaching first-year composition. When I taught first-year students, I saw my own struggles reflected in their experiences: we were all wrestling with reading well and grappling with the variety of reading choices available. My first-year undergraduate students struggled not only to comprehend texts, but also to analyze them and contextualize them alongside the rhetorical theories and concepts that undergirded our class discussions. During this time, I tried to reproduce the same reading techniques I had learned as an undergraduate: highlight the important parts. Draw stars next to the main ideas. Draw question marks next to the places of confusion. But I soon realized that my students couldn't employ these techniques successfully because most of them did not ever print hard copies of their texts. For the sake of reducing textbook and/or course reader costs, I picked readings from open source textbooks or chose articles that could be circulated under the fair use clause, which meant that I distributed all of the reading through our course management system for free. So, if students wanted to do annotations on hard copy, they needed to print out the readings themselves. Self-printing proved to be a high barrier for participating in hard-copy annotation: if students lived in dormitories, the printing costs were often prohibitively expensive. If they lived off campus, they often did not have easy access to printers. Plus, many of my students, both those who lived on and those who lived off campus, worked multiple jobs to cover their tuition expenses, and through office-hour conversations and email exchanges, I learned that, to accommodate their many commitments, many of them did their readings on their phones during the bus ride to campus or on their laptops in between classes, perched in a hallway or at the campus cafeteria. We all had lots of choices for how, when, and where to read, but we weren't talking explicitly about how to navigate these choices.

It turns out that my students are not an anomaly in the diverse ways that they read, including accessing their readings on the go. A multiyear study at the University of Central Florida found that 66% of surveyed (n=796) students used a mobile app for learning at least once a week (Chen, Seilhamer, Bennett, & Bauer, 2015). In a 2019 study of community college students and their uses of educational technology for learning, EDUCAUSE researcher Dana Gierdowski found that more students own smartphones than laptops, though ownership for both kinds of devices is high (99% of community college students own smartphones while 97% own laptops) (p. 9, 2019a). These percentages representing device ownership are consistent with a 2018 EDUCAUSE survey of students from across community colleges and four-year institutions (Galanek, Gierdowski, & Brooks p. 7). In the 2018 EDUCAUSE survey, however, one key difference about device usage was clear: students who associated device usage with success differed depending on race, gender, and class. That is, "women, students of color, students with disabilities, first-generation students, students who are independent (with or without dependents of their own), and students who come from disadvantaged socioeconomic backgrounds see their devices as significantly more important to their success than do their counterparts" (p. 5). This key finding suggests that as our student populations grow more diverse, mobile device usage becomes an increasingly critical part of understanding how our students access their learning experiences. Mobile devices, once considered a luxury, are now more commonplace and accessible than other technologies and tools for learning.

What I realized was that my students were doing all of their reading in digital spaces and I was not offering them techniques that would work in those spaces. So, while I was offering some guidance and explicit instruction around reading, it was not going to be actionable without the proper tools. After hearing the same stories and seeing my students read on all of their various screens, it hit me: we needed new techniques that would align with the material conditions of students' lives.

It became my goal not only to find the proper tools, but also to adapt the strategies that I knew could work to scale them up to the levels of critical thinking required in a moment when students had to interpret vast amounts of information on the web. I didn't think I needed to abandon tried and true reading techniques; rather, I realized that what all of us needed was an *expansion* of those techniques. We needed to understand and summarize not only what was on the page but also contextualize that information. We needed techniques that would help us locate that page within a larger dialogue, within a larger network of ideas that would help us situate one perspective among many. What better place to do that than online, where networks of conversations are at our fingertips?

It wasn't easy to figure out how to teach reading in digital spaces explicitly, but what doing so showed me was that reading well involves not only critical inquiry and thought, but also paying acute attention to the materials we use and the spaces we are in. The platforms for our reading—from a printed, bound book to our glowing screens—are not invisible. If we are to improve as readers, we have to bring our attention to these different spaces in order to determine the best ways to retain, comprehend, and analyze the ideas we get from them.

This book emerges from these years of exploration, from finding ways to teach reading with an attention to form, material, media, and, of course, content. I opened this book with a personal story about my own reading experiences, and whether that story resonated with you or not, what I hope it convinced you of is just one thing: we need to draw explicit attention to the act of reading. This need becomes all the more acute in a historical moment when many of our students have already made the choice to read on the most portable, accessible spaces available to them: their laptops and phones.

For many, the idea of reading well on a screen seems impossible. However, I think when we encourage thoughtful engagement and attention to how, when, where, and why we read, reading well in a variety of spaces is more than just possible; when we all make intentional choices about where our reading takes place, our process may be even stronger.

From an equity perspective, considering where and how reading on screens can happen may help us design more inclusive classrooms. After all, we cannot disparage our students for completing their schoolwork in the ways that work best for maintaining their working lives. College is more expensive than it ever has been, and as of the moment of this writing, few signs indicate that it will become significantly more affordable. According to a 2017 study from the Institute for College Access and Success, "In 41 states and the District of Columbia, net prices at public four-year colleges represent more than one-fifth of total incomes for families making up to $75,000 per year. Yet in all 50 states plus the District of Columbia, the net price of going to a public four-year college is more than half of total income for those families making $30,000 or less" (Cochrane & Ahlman, p. 1). I believe it is our responsibility as educators to meet our students where they are and challenge ourselves to consider how the materials of our teaching impact our students' abilities to learn.

The more flexible our range of teaching techniques can be, the more we can reach a broader range of students. In so doing, we may even learn a few things ourselves. Learning to read well is a lifelong journey, one that does not end at basic literacy acquisition. Just as our students continuously encounter new texts in college (and throughout their lives for that matter), so do we. In those situations, we may have to rethink the methods, models, and means of engagement that we use for reading. We cannot assume that print-based literacy always gives us the best tools with which to read; in many ways, what digital reading allows us to do is rethink, reconsider, and expand upon the reading practices that we may have taken for granted.

This book will help us work to expand our methods, models, and means of engagement. But first, it is important to understand the fuller context of what reading looks like in college today and to go back historically to consider how students' ability to learn content has always been influenced by their material conditions for accessing that content. In this next section, I trace how colleges' increased adoption of digital textbooks and materials makes the need to incorporate instructional strategies for digital reading all the more pressing. I then go on to trace the historical roots of conversations about the impact of materiality on understanding and shaping media. I close this introduction with some notes on what to expect from the rest of this book.

Open Educational Resources, Digital Textbooks, and Online Courses: Why We Should Pay Attention to Digital Reading Now

Many college instructors expect their students to begin college able to read not only for basic comprehension but also for critical analysis and engagement (Kerr & Frease, 2017; Sweeney & McBride 2015; Bunn 2013; Hoeft 2012; Lei, Bartlett, Gorney, & Herschbach, 2010; Brost & Bradley, 2006). This assumption is not entirely ungrounded: the Common Core State Standards Initiative, which dictates the content students are taught in the United States K–5 educational system, emphasizes critical reading as a core competency. By the end of fifth grade, all students, according to the Common Core State Standards, should be able not only to read and understand content from fiction and informational texts but also to interpret these texts and use them to inform their own opinions, analyses, and conclusions. If we assume elementary school students are inculcated with these skills, assuming that students continue to strengthen these skills in the years to follow makes perfect sense. With an education grounded in critical reading, why wouldn't students be able to navigate texts successfully at increasingly complicated levels in college?

The Common Core standards frame reading in a particular set of ways that may not necessarily align with the ways we might support in college. Although not all states implement the Common Core specifically, most states implement standards for reading that narrow students' understandings of what's possible in the reading experience. For example, composition scholar Ellen Carillo (2019) offers the critique that the Common Core standards privilege written text as the primary arbiter of meaning without considering what the reader brings to an understanding of the text. Carillo argues that "the standards' conception of reading is an unfortunate throwback to a time when texts were situated as stable repositories of meaning, and by extension, teachers were cast as the masters and safeguards of these meanings" (p. 140). The implications of this positioning are tremendous for students learning in college environments: if students do not see the importance of tapping into their prior knowledge or experiences as part of the reading process and, instead, they rely primarily on the text itself to arbitrate meaning, they may not fully understand how audience impressions can shape the work that a reading does. Specifically, a reader's understanding of their own positionality impacts their interpretation of the text. If students focus primarily on summarizing, analyzing, or investigating a text for isolated sets of claims, they may not understand the full context of what they're reading. In Carillo's (2019) words, "students may come to *know* texts, but not *understand* them" (p. 142). Understanding as a process can only occur when the student engages in reflection as an authentic reader of the text itself.

When students enter college environments, they also

encounter texts and readings that they have never seen before. Regardless of how much fantastic instruction students may have received in their K–12 education, they will likely not have experienced exposure to the kinds of rigorous texts that define learning in higher education. From peer-reviewed research articles to white papers and policy briefs, students in college encounter new genres of reading, both within their majors and in first-year writing courses before they declare a major. Yet they may not necessarily have accumulated the experiences to help them approach and respond to these readings with clarity. Furthermore, adult learners are enrolling in college courses at increasingly high rates; the kinds of texts they are apt to have encountered up to this point may also be distant from the textbooks and peer-reviewed scholarship that are commonly brought into college classes. Even though adult learners may have had access to a wide range of professional texts, they may need new strategies to adjust to the kinds of readings that they will likely encounter in college.

Students may also be asked to read these texts in a variety of forms and media. For the past two decades, college instructors have increasingly offered mandatory course readings in the forms of electronic books (e-books) or digital open educational resources (OERs). According to Babson Survey Research (Seaman & Seaman, 2019), 40% of college instructors surveyed prefer using digital teaching materials as opposed to 25% that prefer print teaching materials and 36% who have a neutral perspective on the media for their teaching materials (p. 23). The Babson study finds, on average, that older faculty tend to prefer print materials, but that, over the years they have been conducting the survey, preferences are shifting toward digital materials; these shifts do not suggest that younger faculty with digital preferences are displacing older faculty, but that faculty of all ages are coming to adopt digital materials more readily.

Although many instructors still require students to purchase hard-copy editions of books, the costs of those books grow increasingly expensive, and students have difficulty accommodating the expense. According to *Inside Higher Ed*'s 2018 Survey of Faculty Attitudes on Technology (Lederman, 2018, published in collaboration with Gallup), 83% of faculty members surveyed agreed that college textbook prices are too expensive for their students. In response, many pioneering faculty members have established robust initiatives for providing access to a variety of scholarly texts and experiences for free (Jhangiani & Jhangiani, 2017; DeRosa & Robison, 2017; Wiley Webb, Weston, & Tonks, 2017). According to the 2019 Babson study, the most common reason that instructors do not adopt textbooks is because of the cost to students (Seaman & Seaman, 2019, p. 26), suggesting that instructors are increasingly cognizant of their students' financial needs and limitations.

As university enrollments swell, especially at community colleges and online institutions, we must take into consideration the greater diversity of students' economic circumstances. Greater economic diversity means that we cannot necessarily assume that all students can always afford the prices that textbooks demand (DeMartini, Marshall, & Chew, 2018; Goldrick-Rab, 2016). E-books and OERs are often lower price and more easily accessible than print books (Ainsworth et. al 2020; Seaman & Seaman, 2020). To emphasize the increasing ubiquity of digital device access, fewer than 1% of the participants surveyed claimed that they had no access to digital devices at all. Although this does not mean that the digital divide no longer exists, it does suggest that the gap is shrinking, a figure worth being attentive to as we consider how students may be apportioning their college budgets. If increasing numbers of students are carrying around devices that allow them to access readings and resources directly on their mobile, connected, digital devices, then why would students see the benefit in purchasing additional, costly, heavy textbooks?

Accessing course content in digital forms may seem like a win-win for everyone involved in higher education: as more texts become digitized, instructors can give their students a diversity of texts to access and students can save money on course materials. However, we should not see digital texts as important to consider only because of their cost, convenience, and efficacy. As we move students increasingly toward reading from digital texts, we need, at the very least, to take their *learning needs* into consideration. How might reading texts on-screen change the ways that students respond to, annotate, and investigate texts? How might accessing readings from networked devices, like phones and laptops, affect how students are navigating, accessing, and engaging with course material? To what extent does the form of the text itself impact students' understanding of the content?

We already know the simple answer to this last question: an awful lot. Educational researchers have conducted numerous studies around the retention of reading material delivered from a screen and from a paper page and the findings are significant (Baron, 2015; Myrberg & Wiberg, 2015; Mangen, Walgermo, & Bronnick, 2013; Daniel & Woody, 2013; Kretzschmar et al., 2013; Ackerman & Goldsmith, 2011; Coiro & Dobler, 2007; Liu, 2005). On the whole, these studies consistently conclude that students retain, remember, and comprehend information more thoroughly when reading on paper than on a screen. Yet although these kinds of findings have grabbed newspaper headlines, researchers have qualified their studies with the important note that they did not control for attitude, motivation, or prior student habits. As Kretzschmar et al. (2013) express, "The present findings thereby suggest that the skepticism towards digital reading media . . . may reflect a general cultural attitude towards reading in this manner rather than measurable cognitive effort during reading" (p. 8). This cultural attitude may be due to a flat understanding of the work that reading involves, too; *reading*, in this case, may very well be conceived of solely as a way to collect and remember information, but it may also include the processes of searching, analyzing, summarizing, and responding to text itself. We might say that an inertia gap is at play in reading at the college level: we keep trying to apply print-based reading strategies to digital reading spaces, but upon realizing those strategies don't work, we move toward blaming the digital space itself.

That's not to say that digital spaces are particularly well designed for effective reading strategies, even those that are attentive to the benefits of the digital space, but we've jumped so quickly to lay blame on the space itself that we have not made room to reform either the digital spaces or the strategies we use to navigate those spaces as readers. As Ziming Liu (2004) points out, "printed media and digital media have their own advantages and limitations. The challenge is to determine the applicability of a particular medium in a given context or process" (p. 701). This challenge should not just be one we ask students to take on for themselves, but one that institutions of higher education and instructors should partner on with students. If we approach reading at the college level with a spirit of openness and awareness of how reading in different spaces may create new possibilities for understanding and interpreting information, we can close the inertia gap around approaching reading at the college level across the curriculum.

Clearly, we still have to learn a lot about students' motivation to read in different spaces and the strategies they've acquired as they move across reading in these spaces. Researchers also acknowledge that we still have much to learn from a neurological perspective (a perspective that we will explore more in later chapters). Yet one finding is obvious: we have enough evidence to suggest that reading from a screen changes students' perceptions and comprehension of source content. But what about students who grew up with these screens around them? Won't reading in these spaces be natural to them?

Moving Beyond Myths: Dispelling Digital Native Assumptions and Supporting Generation Z

Today's college students are not "digital natives," or naturally fluent users of digital technology, for several reasons (Prensky, 2001). First, not all college students are the same age. When we think of college students, we tend to think of teenagers fresh out of high school. But the fastest growing population of students enrolling in college is actually made up of adult learners returning to school to earn additional credentials. According to the National Center for Educational Statistics (2017), the enrollment of students age 25 and over has increased by 13% over the last decade, a substantial increase to consider. This population did not grow up with iPhones and laptops, and their usage of these tools may differ dramatically from that of younger students. Second, it is fallacious to assume that even the students who *did* grow up swiping through apps on touch screens are all well versed in how to use all of the applications on any digital device. Just because an eighteen-year-old can figure out how to garner hundreds of likes on a photo uploaded to a social network doesn't mean that the same eighteen-year-old understands how to identify effective keywords for conducting research on a search engine. That same eighteen-year-old may not know anything about PDF editors or how to use the functionality within them to mark up readings they may receive. And yes, that very same eighteen-year-old also may not understand the diversity of ways to read beyond annotation because they may never have been exposed to reading as a component of an intellectual (and affective) *conversation* with other voices.

I facilitate workshops for undergraduate students at a residential four-year university, one primarily populated by students of traditional college age. Whenever I ask students how many of them use a tool like a PDF editor to mark up articles, it is usually only one-third of the room that has any familiarity with that approach to reading online articles. That percentage always surprises me, as many of these students also came from high schools increasingly equipped with Chromebook laptops, iPads, or other classroom-wide digital devices intended for learning (Singer, 2017; Swartz, 2016). These devices can get used in a number of innovative and compelling ways, and it is clear that strategies used across K–12 schools can differ dramatically. I am not criticizing K–12 institutions for not introducing students to PDF editors; on the contrary, it is possible that this introduction has happened in many places, but students do not remember the intervention. Regardless of *what* students are being taught, what's clear is that when they encounter new texts in a new environment, they may need reminding about what tools are at their disposal to break down those tasks, interpret them, and analyze them from their own perspectives.

The digital native myth impacts many of the ways that college educators discuss uses of digital devices. As administrators grow increasingly interested in understanding Generation Z, others still refer to their students as millennials, engrossed in their smartphones and obsessed with their selfies (Rees, 2018; Qadir, 2018; Gose, 2017; Cunningham, 2007; Lieberman, 2017; Zimmerman, 2016; Gulliver, 2014). Never mind the fact that the bulk of millennials are now old enough to be forming new cohorts of assistant professors, assumptions about how youth use their devices often drive a common solution for how college instructors approach discussions of digital device usage in class: bans. The reasons for banning digital devices in classrooms of all kinds are myriad. They are distractions foremost, but they also impair learning and discourage verbal conversation (Glass and Kang 2019; Ravizza, Hambrick, & Fenn, 2014). By implementing a device ban, instructors are suggesting that they do not see pedagogical potential to device use and, instead, see the device as a barrier to learning because of its potential for distraction. Instructors who implement device bans also tend to claim that a ban encourages students to take notes by hand, a practice that some educational studies have suggested improves retention, memory, and comprehension of course content (Mueller and Oppenheimer, 2014).

Although it is possible that a neurotypical student may benefit from handwriting as a cognitive practice, not all brains are wired in precisely the same way. Comparative studies of note-taking by hand and on the computer tend to exclude examination of people with disabilities, while they also test knowledge recall for only one particular learning situation: a large class lecture. The contexts in which students read on digital devices are diverse, from the small seminar to the large lecture, and every class context in between. Claims about how attention is gathered and memory is retained cannot easily take into account the diversity of learning situations and students that enter our college classrooms. Plenty of others have responded to calls for laptop bans with attentiveness to the limitations of laptop bans. For example, many educators have argued that laptop bans can unfairly punish students who may want to use laptops for their learning, can problematically reveal which students have disabilities in their classes, and ultimately, can reveal the power differential between students and teachers in classes (Elliott-Dorans, 2018; Pryal and Jack, 2017; Lang, 2016; Berry and Westfall, 2015; Weimer, 2015; Aguilar-Roca, Williams, & O'Dowd, 2012; Kim, 2010).

Even if the most effective and memorable note-taking happened by hand both from lectures and course readings, the fact is that not all of our students (much less instructors!) really know how to take notes. Sure, a computer makes it materially easier for students to practically transcribe lecture-based content, thereby bypassing the important process of deciding which information is most critical to their engagement, but knowing what content is most important to write down by hand is not a process that is innately understood either. That is, even *with* the material constraints of writing by hand, students still may not know what to write down in the first place. To that same end, students' understanding of how to take notes on readings may shape their orientation to what they retain and understand more than the media for the act of note-taking.

Basically, study skills are not necessarily improved by material condition alone; study skills still must be acquired through the students' development of metacognitive thought. Effective note-taking in any form or media requires student awareness of what they need to learn, how they learn best, and what media will best suit their conditions for learning. That might mean that some students eventually discover that writing by hand is best for them. Others may discover that note-taking on their laptops is best for them. Others still may come to recognize that note-taking on their mobile phones or tablets is the best option. The point is that if we don't give students options for making these choices, we potentially limit what is possible for them in the first place.

We should recognize that some students don't have a choice about which devices they use for their learning, particularly for their reading. In fact, many students often conceive of their phones as the more affordable reading option for their learning (Gierdowski, 2019a; Smale & Regaldo, 2017; Baron 2015). Buying a single book is, of course, on the whole, less expensive than paying off the steep monthly charges for a smartphone and its data plan. And yet some students have to decide where to spend their monthly budgets and, for many of them, the most economical choice is to buy a phone because of its multipurpose usage: it allows them to make phone calls, maintain engagement in digital life, pay bills, maintain work schedules, complete schoolwork, and the list goes on. A book can really only accomplish one of these uses. Although these economic conditions will not be the case for every student, the real fact of the matter is that many students will bring a digital device with them to an in-person classroom and, as a result, likely use it at some point during the classroom session no matter what. Further, as students move toward taking more online and hybrid courses in their college careers, they will become increasingly comfortable with using those devices as their primary media for learning (Allen & Seamen, 2017). In March 2020, when all institutions experienced an emergency move to remote instruction due to the COVID-19 pandemic, many students relied upon their phones as their primary devices, especially if they lived in homes with unreliable or nonexistent Wi-Fi. Although it is unlikely that institutions will implement remote learning at such speed and with such ubiquity as we experienced it in the immediate aftermath of pandemic shelter-in-place orders, the flexible learning options during the pandemic may yet open up even greater demand for flexible and remote learning situations (as of this book's writing, the long-term ramifications of the pandemic on student interests in hybrid and online enrollments remains unclear). We can no longer deny that we live in a society that increasingly requires students to participate in civic action through digital portals, regardless of their age, exposure, or experience with these devices.

Rather than resisting or rejecting these devices as spaces where students do important work, we need to evolve our own teaching and learning practices to make room for the critical differences of reading in these spaces. Although we cannot eliminate the distractions these devices may provide for our students, we can help them see the affordances of these spaces and leverage those affordances to engage critically in texts. Just because our media for learning is different than it was before, we should not assume that our learning has to be diminished. The ubiquity of digital devices as part and parcel of a learning experience, whether those are remote or in-person, will not spell the end of learning itself. All it demands is that we change our approaches to elevate the ways of learning that we know work. That means diversifying our conception of how people learn and expanding our thinking beyond the conception that learners' abilities can be pegged into individual, narrow learning styles (Alzain, Ireson, & Jwaid, 2018; Kirschner, 2017; Ambrose, Bridges, DiPietro, Lovett, & Norman, 2010).

What this also demands is the ability of instructors to be flexible in their teaching approaches and of educators to educate themselves on how and why digital devices can impact students' understanding of reading in a digital age. Indeed, we can benefit from thinking broadly about who digital learners are in this space. I pick up Thomas Tobin and Kirsten Behling's definition of the *digital generation*, to say that "all people who use mobile technology on a daily basis for problem solving, information gathering, and social purposes—regardless of their age—are mobile learners. This definition allows for variation among the skill sets, background knowledge, and breadth of application that we all possess" (2018, p. 79). This is where this book comes in: I'm writing this book to explore why we should be attuned to the material differences of digital reading and to offer concrete strategies and approaches that you can take to respond to these acute and evolving reader needs.

What's Old Is New Again: A (Brief) Historical Interlude

In 1964, Marshall McLuhan taught students only a few years younger than himself at the University of Toronto. He wondered what made his students' worldviews and learning experiences so different than his own, perhaps in the same way that many teacher-scholars now are thinking about what their students come into the classroom with and how their media might shape their own impressions of content. McLuhan came to realize that the streaming, circulation, and production of media had a tremendous impact on how people saw themselves and the world around them. Indeed, McLuhan claimed that "when our central nervous system is technologically extended to involve us in the whole of mankind and to incorporate the whole of mankind in us, we necessarily participate, in depth, in the consequences of our every action" (1964, p. 4). In contrast to the supposed passivity of reading static text from the pages of a bound book, McLuhan suggested that listening to the radio and watching television demanded instant and immediate response from the viewer. These claims all came before the internet was invented.

Engaging in the consequences of our every action has some challenging implications. First, McLuhan (1964) was just as alarmed by what he saw as the addictive potential of radio and television as we are with the addictive realities of engaging on social networks, games, and apps. The cavalcade of an attentional apocalypse followed McLuhan's theorizing through the subsequent decades with warnings from the likes of Neil Postman (1992) and Sven Birkerts (1994), all equally concerned with the ways that media itself may distract from civic life or engagement.

Little did they know that our media would go on to invite all the more engagement and endorphin-driven action with responses to notifications and the instant ability to like and comment on content. Writers like Sherry Turkle (2015), Adam Alter (2018), Andrew Keen (2012), Jaron Lanier (2010), and Jean Twenge (2017) have pointed out the dangers of so called addictive media and the responsibilities that media developers have to consider the long-term impacts of engaging in digital spaces for our relationships and the formation of our public institutions. Computer scientist Ge Wang (2018) advocates for an artful design of new media devices that considers the ethical implications of networked, online engagement, a call that emerges on the heels of all the very public dangers of online participation, from online harassment to fake news. We are, in other words, both concerned with the monumental impact of new media and also calling distinctly for answers to its absorptive potential.

In spite of all the ways we can worry about social media's all-absorbing demand for our participation, we can often perceive of engagement in these spaces as passive, mindless, and dangerous not because we are *participating*, but because we are simply *lurking*. Digital device users can mindlessly scroll through bottomless feeds, and endlessly swim through photos, status updates, short videos, and waves of text without really processing or remembering any of it. The ability to get absorbed quickly into the vast ocean of online information can feel like the most passive experience of all, one that might recall overwhelming experiences or utter absorption. These experiences can feel anything but active or in depth. And yet these online spaces make it possible to dive deeply into this content; we just have to know how to use the tools effectively and to be mindful of our use.

The feeling of information overload or the temptation to fall into addictive behavior may, in some ways, be unique to our present moment, insofar as there have not been any other moments, historically, in which we have had access to so much information so readily. However, imagine how a nineteenth-century student must have felt accessing a library for the first time or even going to the newsstand at the train station: the volumes of books on the shelves or leaflets on racks may have felt just as intensely overwhelming as the way that we feel when we complete a Google search and find ourselves with millions of results.

We have always needed to be able to curate and discern

content across media. The need to do so just grows more immediately centered in our consciousness when the various options for reading, writing, and communicating with each other are easily accessible to us. We can curb the potential for addictive tendencies, we can find calm in the overwhelming sea of stimulation, if we equip ourselves with the strategies and behaviors that allow us to explore and regulate our options for different purposes and situations. In the subsequent chapters of this book, the ways we teach these strategies and behaviors will be our focus.

Looking Ahead: How Do You Teach Digital Reading?

We've spent a lot of time at this point situating the conversation about digital reading into larger debates about distraction, addiction, and the other concerns that educators have when students adopt digital devices for learning. When it comes to teaching these concepts, however, we can often get absorbed in our own preferences, ideologies, and dispositions about using digital tools for readings. In fact, whenever I've shared that my research and writing is focused on exploring teaching approaches to reading on-screen and on paper, I'm often asked one question: "What do *you* prefer to read on?" My answer is perhaps unsatisfying, but it's always the same: it depends on what I'm reading. If it's an article in *The New Yorker*, I prefer the paper magazine. If it's an article in *College, Composition, and Communication*, the flagship journal for rhetoric and composition scholars, I prefer to read online with my PDF editor and my citation management tool of choice, Zotero. If it's a long novel, I like my e-reader. At this point in the conversation, the person I'm talking to suddenly realizes they're in for a longer conversation than they expected. What

I typically then pivot to is this: that my choice for reading also depends on how I'm being perceived. For example, if I'm reading from a paperback novel on the airplane, I'm far more likely to be asked a question about how I'm enjoying my book than if I'm reading from my e-reader or smartphone. Sometimes, I feel a lot of pride when I'm carrying around a paperback or hardback book that clearly shows whatever I'm reading, especially if it's something that I think makes me look erudite. By contrast, when *Fifty Shades of Grey*, the tawdry romance novel, peaked in its popularity, many readers were grateful to be able to read the book on Kindles or smartphones because they felt embarrassed to be seen reading the book in public (Richards, 2015). It is impossible to escape these ideological charges of what we're reading and what that communicates to other people about us.

Class and university policy can, unfortunately, reinforce many of these implicit biases around what it means to be a reader and a learner. Even though we may not be thinking about what our book covers say about us as readers and learners, how we adhere to and perform other sets of university norms reinforces assumptions about our students' abilities and interests. For example, verbally disparaging how students can possibly read on a mobile phone may seem like an off-hand comment, but it may also unintentionally shame those students who find that reading on a mobile phone is their only option when they're trying to complete requisite homework assignments on a bus ride between campus and their job. When we can develop greater awareness of the diverse ways that we can read and write, we can work to avoid using language to describe reading that may malign certain behaviors as less valuable than others. As Deborah L. Wolter (2018) suggests, "Viewing people through a deficit lens leads to erroneous assumptions about their ability to learn language and literacy and unwittingly creates a vicious cycle of opportunity gaps, which in turn, creates achievement gaps in our schools and employment gaps in our workplaces" (p. 107). When it comes to reading across print and digital spaces, we risk falling into the same kinds of opportunity gaps that Wolter describes.

Part of our job as educators is to empower students to make their own choices about where and how they read. Ideally, we want our students to make choices about when, how, and why they read that are not driven by fears of distraction or fears of judgment, but, instead, are driven by an understanding of what circumstances help them accomplish work thoughtfully and with focus.

To teach digital reading, then, we must stray away from sticking doggedly to our personal preference, personal belief, and personal ideology toward developing an understanding of students' individual learning experiences. Just to reiterate, this is not to say that all students' individual learning experiences are the same. On the contrary, students themselves express a wide range of preferences around how they use technology for their learning and for their personal lives. This book is not advocating for turning all reading experiences into digital ones, since that choice may not necessarily be right for the diversity of students that walk through our doors. What this book advocates for is an awareness of our choices, choices that involve not just relying on convenience or habit but that are shaped by thoughtful interrogation of the learning activity and what we want our students to gain from the activity in different sets of material spaces.

We have established our present conditions of reading at the university level in a digital age, we have skimmed the surface of what media change has looked like in the past, but we have not yet thought ahead to the future. The subsequent sections of this book, therefore, spend a bit more time in the past, and then look ahead to the future.

Part 1, "Skim: Understanding Historical, Affective, and Neurological Perspectives on Reading Technologies," contextualizes our reasons for exploring digital reading now. In Chapter 1, we look to the past by examining the history of the university itself and considering how Western university education has historically responded to the changing material conditions of student access to content and learning materials. I focus on Western institutions here primarily because Western schooling has had the most direct impact on American university education today, and it is the space I know best for analyzing this problem since I have worked exclusively in American institutions. I am sensitive to the fact that in book history as a discipline, Asian and African innovations and legacies around printing have often been elided or ignored. In my discussion of Western institutions, therefore, I acknowledge where and when particular printing and material techniques had been appropriated from other cultures or countries and note the influences on Western education that may have come from the non-Western world. I dedicate the bulk of Chapter 1 to the argument that pedagogy and materiality have always been inextricably linked and that our concerns about evolving reading technology often reiterate centuries of concerns about effective learning.

Chapter 2 explores how reading is an experience deeply rooted in how we feel about books as objects. This chapter starts by briefly connecting the history described in Chapter 1 to the conversation about feelings for reading, showing that books as objects have long signified class and educational status. I argue that we tend to make choices about our learning that feel good for us, since learning is motivated by what we enjoy. This chapter explores how we might help students identify their own emotional attachments to what or how they read, and how those attachments may (or may not) impact what they're willing or unwilling to do as readers. This chapter contrasts much of the affective language used around print books with digital books to consider its impact upon our emotional ties to reading practice.

Chapter 3 contextualizes the importance of exploring digital reading from a neuroscience and learning science perspective. I examine the current research on how the brain reads and what neuroscientists, psychologists, and educators have discovered about the plasticity of the brain in a digital age. Although new scientific observations continue to be made, the one fact that has conclusively emerged from the neuroscientific exploration of the brain is that reading on a screen *is* affecting neurological pathways; however, as educators, we can work to have an impact on the formation of important connective pathways. Specifically, through scaffolding, framing, and guiding reading tasks in digital media, instructors can help students alter the ways that they approach digital texts to help them become more thoughtful, attentive consumers.

Part 2, "Dive: Exploring the Digital Reading Framework to Promote Deep Reading Practices," is the start of our futures-facing content. A brief opening chapter introduces the digital reading framework I've established to show which categories for reading engagement are critical to readers in a digital age. Building on the historical look at the materiality of reading, I share the digital reading framework I've established and explain how the five categories for engagement that I've identified respond directly to the material conditions of a digital reading life. I then devote each of the subsequent chapters (Chapters 4–8) to one of these categories for engagement within the digital reading framework. In each of the chapters corresponding to the five categories for engagement, readers will get a deeper understanding of what each category of engagement means and how they can cultivate and practice each one. I then discuss methods for teaching each category of engagement and provide a cluster of example activities to engage student reading experiences. Although some of these examples may refer to particular kinds of tools that are current as of this writing, I mostly avoid in-depth tool discussions because I did not want the material in this book to become (too) dated by technological obsolescence. I cannot predict which tools or software will remain relevant or usable in the years to come after this book is published. In the appendix of this book, I offer some relevant tool examples, but I suspect that this appendix will continually need to be updated as digital tools tend to become outdated quickly.

Although I cannot necessarily predict what kinds of digital devices may be developed in the years to come, I can tell you that the devices we currently have aren't going away any time soon. And even if the technical specifications of laptops, smartphones, and other mobile digital devices change dramatically in the next few years, the logic of how these devices will display text and how students will receive and understand text likely will not change dramatically. As long as linear, alphabetic texts are the primary way we communicate information, this book will remain a relevant resource for helping instructors help their students have conversations about how the form of what they're reading impacts the content. Even if particular apps are no longer relevant for completing the activities, the workflows and frames of mind that these activities inspire should be transferable to a variety of contexts.

Part 3, "Surface: Critically Approaching the Adoption and Use of Digital Reading Technologies," briefly brings the historical insight of Part 1 and the actionable suggestions of Part 2 together so we can engage in a conversation about how the digital reading framework I developed in Part 2 can be understood in conversation with key digital learning debates. Specifically, Chapter 9 considers how instructors can help their students navigate the complexities of archiving evidence of their digital reading practices while also protecting their privacy online. Digital preservation remains a challenging problem to solve, especially insofar as particular pieces of software and hardware can quickly go unsupported. At the same time, students should have the right to decide when they are actively preserving evidence of their reading. Much online software keeps track of users' reading behaviors through online cookies and data storage, which leads users to create passive archives of their online reading and writing behaviors. What Chapter 9 helps instructors become more mindful of is how to engage students in conversations about when and how to archive their work when they want to and also how to question and critique software so that their reading behaviors are not tracked and surveilled without their knowing consent.

This book's conclusion finally attempts to negotiate a critical tension that is at the heart of this book: the tension between adapting to the conditions of our constantly changing technologies and teaching the habits of mind that remain critical to knowledge consumption and analysis. With this in mind, I end this book with several key principles for managing this balance, leaving readers with a few more actionable items to consider as we all remain flexible to the changes we may yet encounter for future reading experiences.

If we want students to be reading between the lines,

reading with each other, and reading thoughtfully, we have to pay attention to *how* reading happens and where our understandings of reading come from. Reading is a complex process, and if we neglect to consider the conditions that impact how reading happens, we overlook a critical way in which our students access content in their college classes. Even if we can't anticipate the impacts of new technology fully, we can at least offer our students metacognitive frameworks so that each of them can assess how they read in their own ways, with a mindset geared toward developing a clearer understanding of their own practices and ideologies toward reading.

Some may argue that it is a bit too late to look at reading since students are now accessing ample content through video. However, reading is not going anywhere, and even if the lengths or forms of our texts change, text is still everywhere and it still must be interpreted. On the contrary, we now have even more reason to examine processes for reading we may have taken for granted, since our students face increasing choices for how and why they access content in particular forms.

Understanding what digital reading offers, both as an affordance and as a limitation, will help us help our students make the best choices for themselves, whether that is through skimming the surface of or diving deeply into their texts. When we invite moments for students to surface from their reading experiences, and when we, as instructors, find the opportunity to surface ourselves and recognize the diverse reading landscape in front of us, we can see reading in all of the spaces available to us as what it always has been: not a barrier, but an opportunity.

PART 1

SKIM

UNDERSTANDING HISTORICAL,
AFFECTIVE, AND NEUROLOGICAL
PERSPECTIVES ON READING
TECHNOLOGIES

CHAPTER 1

THE CHAINED BOOK:

A HISTORICAL OVERVIEW OF READING

TECHNOLOGY IN HIGHER EDUCATION

In Henry Boughton's 1878 painting *The Waning Honeymoon*, he depicts a melancholy scene of a couple sitting together, but very much in their own worlds. The woman and man sit together on a park bench, but far apart from each other. The woman glances sadly over at the man while he reads, calmly

---

Above: George Henry Boughton, *The Waning Honeymoon*, 1878, oil on canvas (Courtesy of the Walters Art Museum)

absorbed in the book that he holds in front of him. While he absentmindedly pats his dog on the head, the woman seems strikingly, utterly alone. Behind the man and the woman, the painting illustrates two diverging paths, a visual metaphor that isn't too promising for the couple's future. Within the woman's eyes, we see a sense of longing, an image of many things she may want to say but is unable to as her husband escapes into the world of his book. The book might not have caused the rift in their relationship, but the reading technology here certainly isn't helping matters and, in fact, the distraction it provides might make things worse.

You've likely seen comics, illustrations, and photos that have portrayed this familiar phenomenon of people who are longing to converse, but who are unable to because technology is in the way. Whether it's of a group of friends who are sitting in a restaurant but not speaking with each other because they are all on their phones, or of a couple sitting on the bleachers at a sports event, ignoring the action in front of them by staring deeply into their phones, these images tend to show people out of touch, all glued to their devices. Sherry Turkle describes such a scene in her book *Alone Together* (2011) and explains how, when people glance at their phones during a social interaction, they "signal their departure" from the conversation at hand (p. 155). Indeed, she wonders what a place for belonging even means anymore "if those who are physically present have their attention on the absent?" (p. 155). Just as in Boughton's painting, where the woman is "absented" from her distanced partner, Turkle surmises that places aren't meaningful unless those physically present give them their full attention. From these examples, we can determine that over the past hundred years, similar anxieties around reading have been with us: when reading technologies make information accessible constantly, they fracture the relationships and the connections that bring people together.

Books and smartphones are both reading technologies that fundamentally changed how people access information and engage as readers. Regardless of the technology itself, we have long wondered how changing communication technologies impact how we relate to and understand each other. Although our concerns with the distraction of a book may seem quaint in comparison to the intensely interactive pull of the smartphone, seeing this one example of historical comparison shows us that our contemporary concerns with reading are not completely unique to our cultural and historical moment. By seeing how historical precedents compare to our present moment, we have an opportunity to identify what we value in our reading practice and how the materials for reading themselves can align with those values.

There are a lot of ways to tell historical stories of reading technologies. Reading is often metonymic for the acquisition of human knowledge, and many readers worry that when the delivery mechanisms for understanding that knowledge change, the perception of human knowledge-making also shifts. With each shift in reading technology, the ways that human knowledge may be understood thereafter can also change in unexpected and unpredictable ways. This chapter, therefore, explores how particular assumptions, ideologies, and anxieties about what literacy is (or should be) have often shaped the ways we understand the impacts of reading technologies on readers and reading practice.

This chapter explores how shifts in reading technologies over time have surfaced concerns with three main aspects of the reading experience: (1) memory loss, (2) unreliable or unauthoritative sources, and (3) information overload. While focusing on these three main concerns, we'll move back and forth across time, mapping out how these concerns have been expressed, particularly in Western educational contexts. By organizing this chapter thematically rather than purely chronologically, I illustrate the value of the historical intervention here; by placing emphasis on repeated themes of anxiety with reading technologies, I show that history has, indeed, repeated itself when it comes to readerly responses to and concerns with changing reading technologies.

To tell these stories of concerns with shifting reading technology, I'm relying upon a broad swath of scholarship. There are volumes of books about the history of the book, and I simply can't do justice here to the full work of book and media historians. This chapter offers a brief primer so that readers can understand the historical contexts that have inevitably shaped modern debates about reading, particularly when it comes to the impact of digital technologies on reading. In the process, I acknowledge that much of book history reifies White and Western experiences of reading while also obfuscating the influence of people of color in the manufacturing and inventing of print technology. Although it is common knowledge that the technology we now know as the modern printing press was invented by a German printer, Johannes Gutenberg, Gutenberg's legacy was only possible because of the influence of inventions from China and nations in the Ottoman Empire. Plus, access to both print's raw materials and printing technology itself emerges from long legacies of colonization, ones that undermined the material and intellectual labor of people of color. For example, the first materials for writing technology, stone and papyrus, came from Sumer and Egypt, while paper was invented in China between 140 and 86 BCE. According to historian Nicole Howard (2009), papermaking technology only made its way to the Western world when Chinese papermakers were taken captive by Arab armies, and then European crusaders conquered the Muslim world and brought paper to Spain (p. 6). Down to the acquisition of materials and approaches to the manufacturing processes themselves then, histories of oppression affect what we think of when we think of the book today. The material, the social, and the educational are fully intertwined.

We may still worry about how access to information distracts, absorbs, and disconnects us, but our goal here is to take one step back from those concerns to acknowledge that we've always valued the same things: learning from and listening to each other.

Echoes across Time: Grounding Stories of Readers and Reading Practice in Book History

Historian Robert Darnton (1982) suggested that book history cannot just be about the object of the book itself. Rather, if we are going to study books and their impact on intellectual thought, we have to see the book produced as part of a larger network of relationships: between readers, writers, booksellers, book traders, book manufacturers, and everyone in between (including educators). Darnton (1982) created a famous network model, known as the *communication circuit*, that showed the interplay of all the relationships between the agents of reading, writing, and manufacturing to help scholars understand the significance of particular texts in particular times for particular people. Materials are not divorced from their peoples and environments, and if we are to think about the history of how the book has been treated in higher education, we have to go back—way back—to consider the various agents and places that made the printed book the precious object that it has become in our conversations about deep and effective reading today.

The contemporary concept that reading from paper is most effective for learning emerged over a long period of time. This is not to say that paper, as a reading technology, is not important for learning. Paper is an accessible technology insofar as it is lightweight, flexible, and portable. Yet silent reading from some pieces of paper bound together by glue and massively printed is actually not the way that people practiced, recognized, or understood "deep reading" even just two hundred years ago. As historian Roger Chartier establishes, "reading is not uniquely an abstract operation of the intellect: it brings the body into play, it is inscribed in a space and a relationship with oneself or with others. This is why special attention should be paid to ways of reading that have disappeared in our contemporary world" (Chartier, 1994, p. 8). Chartier goes on to describe how, in the sixteenth and seventeenth centuries, works were written with the knowledge that readers would likely vocalize the text by reading aloud, suggesting that our understanding of lived practices impacts how we analyze or understand what deep and sustained engagement with a book looks like. Although it is easy to take for granted that paper books have always facilitated what we might consider deep reading, it is perhaps sobering to recognize that we once thought that reading aloud facilitated deep reading more readily than silent reading.

To understand our present concerns with reading from a screen, let's destabilize the assumption that any one technology or practice can necessarily facilitate deep reading for everyone. Because reading histories are deeply interconnected, fluid, and recursive, historians tend to periodize stages of literacy development by device and technology. For example, media historian and semiotician Walter Ong names three major eras that define how people have engaged with acts of reading and writing: primary orality, print literacy, and secondary orality (1982, p. 134). Ong posits that, in the early twenty-first century, we have entered our era of *secondary orality*, an era that privileges oral communication via the proliferation of audio and video in everyday communications.

Juxtaposing primary and secondary orality, Ong describes how the proliferation of print literacy changed communicators' orientations to literate acts. Specifically, he explains that, prior to the invention of print, audiences needed to communicate orally in order to convey ideas to a group. However, he says in an era of secondary orality, the impulse to communicate orally comes not from a particular *need* to communicate to a larger audience, but rather, out of a reaction to the inward thinking that print reading encourages (p. 134). The affordances of print, in Ong's words, are what have changed communicators' behaviors over time. Other thinkers have built off of Ong's periodization of how technology and literacy practices have intertwined. For example, Gregory Ulmer (2003) has theorized that we can periodize literacy and technology movements in terms of orality, literacy, and, with the proliferation of digital technologies for reading and writing, *electracy*. The concept of electracy can be defined as the new sets of skills and strategies necessary for a communicator to convey their meaning effectively with digital technologies. Ulmer sees electracy as requiring a full-scale shift in pedagogical practice for educators, claiming that the characteristics of electronic communication contexts (as scattered, networked, and global) require full-scale adaptation in reading and writing practices.

Frameworks like Ong's and Ulmer's have helpfully pointed out major ways in which media architecture has affected meaning-making work. However, these frameworks have also had the unintended consequence of simplifying reading praxis across time. We did not necessarily abandon orality entirely when words on paper became more readily available nor have we rid ourselves of paper when so much more information has been digitized today (Sellen and Harper, 2002). Whereas networked publics may bring orality and oral practices to the fore once more, we arguably write more than we speak or read today, given the infrastructures and ecologies of online communications (Brandt, 2015). No single writing technology has necessarily sublimated another, and when we periodize reading technologies by different moments of literacy development, we, unintentionally, flatten the diversity of practices available to us throughout time. Our materials, our practices, and our choices for reading in different environments have always, necessarily, been fluid and interconnected. What happens when we see this interconnection, however, are also moments of tension, moments when we wonder or worry about what a range of practices may do to our understanding of what reading is and when it happens. These are the kinds of concerns we'll address in the subsequent sections of this chapter.

A Fear of Forgetting: Will Shifting Reading Technologies Lead to Memory Loss?

One of the most common measures for assessing whether we read something or how carefully we read it is by testing our memory. Memory is, after all, rather easy to measure: Can you paraphrase, repeat, or articulate a concept from what you read? If so, congratulations! You remembered the thing that you read. We can't build upon any new knowledge if we can't remember the foundation of our knowledge. Even when we're thinking about reading for entertainment, we often have to remember prior information—or at least understand references we might have acquired from other contexts—in order to appreciate what we're reading fully. As we consider reading technologies, we often consider the role that such technologies play in helping us to remember what we've read. We know that the stakes of our ability to retain knowledge from reading are high, so it's no wonder that, over time, some of our biggest worries about reading technologies have had to do with how much they help or hinder our ability to remember and retain what we've read.

One of the oldest and most famous examples of a scholar worrying about the impact of writing technologies on the ability of people to remember and retain knowledge comes from Socrates, as recorded by Plato in the *Phaedrus*. Although ancient societies frequently used writing technologies, like clay tablets and styluses, to retain records of financial transactions (think ancient grocery receipts), much deep and humanistic inquiry was conveyed and transmitted orally. Socrates's concern, therefore, was that the expansion of reading and writing technologies would completely destroy human memory.

To the same end, he worried that reading those concepts from that very same paper would also lead to memory degradation, as readers could skim through concepts quickly rather than have to listen at the pace of human listening. Socrates, in fact, wondered, "how could they possibly think that words that have been written down can do more than remind those who already know what the writing is about?" (Nehamas & Woodruff, 1997, p. 551). In Socrates's estimation, writing could never replace the kinds of critical dialogue that can happen in oral transmission. The ancient Romans largely agreed with Socrates and the Greeks, and in fact, "the ancients felt very strongly the relationship between what was spoken and what was written, and they assigned primacy to the spoken word; the written word was clearly secondary and was provided only to enable those who came later or were at a distance to recapture the actual speech, the sounds, the author's actual words" (Mathews, 1966, p. 12). Socrates's perspective, and that of other ancient Western intellectuals, was grounded on the idea of authenticity: that the moment of oral, spoken experience would more fully capture the primacy of the thinker's voice than writing ever could. In other ancient civilizations too, the moment of oral experience was also a sacred or holy one. Scribner and Cole (1981) studied the literacy practices of the Vai, a Mande-speaking people of northwestern Liberia, for whom memorizing verses of the Quran is a holy act (p. 129). Friesen (2017) also describes how reading religious texts in ancient Christian, Jewish, and Islamic traditions was considered the only means of engaging respectfully with holy doctrine (p. 38).

If we dig into the stories of ancient Greek and Roman education and communication, we see that even though oral communication may have been highly valued and lauded, it wasn't always the primary mode of communicating information. Beginning in Rome's late Republic (roughly the second and first centuries BCE), citizens of all classes actively learned to participate in communal life through reading, largely from parchment (Fischer, p. 69). In fact, as early as the first century BCE, Julius Caesar used valuable papyrus to create dispatches for his troops and folded them into pages, much like we would see in the form of a codex, or the form that we think of when we think of a book (Fischer, 2003, p. 82–83). Although these dispatched books were quite rare in Rome, over in Egypt, books and scrolls were more common because of extensive papyrus production. Although orality clearly gained cultural traction in the Western world, the variety and diversity of reading materials available in antiquity disrupts the common narratives that orality itself was the only means by which information was transmitted and remembered.

What remains debated about reading practices in the ancient world is how common it was to read silently in contrast to reading aloud, particularly when it comes to understanding how reading aloud or reading silently intersected with scholastic, secular pursuits. Scholars like G. L. Hendrickson (1929) and Josef Balogh (1927) argued that ancient readers were suspicious of silent reading, even for secular texts, because they were concerned that silent reading would lead to the elision of particular thoughts. Hendrickson, for example, cites the work of Syrian rhetorician Lucian and quotes him as expressing the following concern with reading silently:

> What do all your books profit you, who are too ignorant to appreciate their value and beauty? To be sure you look upon them with open eyes and even greedily, and some of them you read at a great pace, your eye outstripping your voice; but I do not consider that sufficient, unless you know the merits and defects of all that is written there, and understand what every sentence means (p. 192).

Lucian's concerns with reading silently are enveloped with the reader's ability to remember and understand the content of particular texts. In fact, Lucian argues that the speed achieved by silent reading is only manageable if the reader has already memorized, understood, and appreciated the text fully, thus suggesting that the change in reading modality could fundamentally impact understanding and appreciation of the text.

Lucian was not the only one skeptical of silent reading. St. Augustine's *Confessions* is one of the first recorded volumes where reading silently is explicitly noted as a surprising reading practice in the ancient world. In the *Confessions,* St. Augustine describes how his teacher, Ambrose, read silently, and remarks upon how amazing and odd the practice seemed:

> When Ambrose read, his eyes ran over the columns of writing and his heart searched out the meaning, but his voice and his tongue were at rest. Often when I was present—for he did not close his door to anyone and it was customary to come in unannounced—I have seen him reading silently, never in fact otherwise . . . I asked myself why he read in this way. Was it that he did not wish to be interrupted in those rare moments he found to refresh his mind and rest from the tumult of others' affairs? Or perhaps he was worried that he would have to explain obscurities in the text to some eager listener, or discuss other difficult problems? For he would thereby lose time and be prevented from reading as much as he had planned. But the preservation of his voice, which easily became hoarse, may well have been the true cause of his silent reading (Augustine, 1993, trans., 6.3.3).

This rather long and detailed description of Ambrose from St. Augustine suggests that St. Augustine was both curious and baffled by Ambrose's behavior. St. Augustine justifies Ambrose's actions in a variety of ways, from the practical considerations of Ambrose's prolific reading behaviors to the impact of his reading upon his listeners or students. It's clear that St. Augustine has significant respect for Ambrose's practice and recognizes its validity for Ambrose's course of vociferous study. However, St. Augustine's passage also seems to offer evidence for the fact that only certain kinds of readers could read silently, supporting what Lucian suggested too: that silent reading is only for the most disciplined of readers, not to be taken up by less serious thinkers.

Yet not everyone relies on Lucian's and St. Augustine's accounts to understand ancient attitudes toward memorization and reading. Classics scholar Bernard Knox (1962) argues that "ancient books were normally read aloud, but there is nothing to show that silent reading of books was anything extraordinary except the famous passage from Augustine's *Confessions*, and that is countered by the phrase of Cicero [a Roman rhetorician] which makes sense only if understood as a reference to silent reading of lyric poets" (p. 435). The "phrase of Cicero," that Knox refers to comes from a passage in Cicero's *Tusculan Disputations*, where Cicero describes how deaf readers may still be able to enjoy reading by engaging in silent reading practice (Knox, 1962, p. 427). Knox argues that this ability to refer to silent readings could have only been possible if silent reading were already a component of ancient life, even if reading aloud was more common.

If we think even more specifically of educational contexts that involved ancient reading performances and concerns with memorization, we may want to look to the situation of the lecture itself. According to Norm Friesen (2017), the lecture as a practice can be traced back to the High Middle Ages (1000–1500 CE) where capacities and resources for reading and writing, including access to books, was scarce. As Friesen describes, "the form and function of the lecture closely reflected these circumstances: its function was not one of disseminating or broadcasting to large groups of people. Instead, its raison d'être was preservation . . . Teaching and learning were similarly conceptualized as acts of preservation rather than as the creation of new knowledge or even the re-creation of what was already known" (p. 113). The performance of reading aloud within the lecture setting, then, was affected both by material constraints and social circumstances: books were scarce, but part of the work of becoming a scholar or learner in the medieval era was also taking rapid, word-for-word notes from the lecturer in order to pass on and preserve the knowledge of scholars that would not otherwise be able to enter into circulation. In other words, because the materials for remembering information were not available, practices like the lecture evolved in order to sustain the memory of the scholar's thinking.

Once the printing press was invented and the preservation impulse was less urgent, university lecturers adapted the lecture form, though they were still concerned with how well students would remember the information even if they had access to books beyond the recitation moment in the lecture. Indeed, even though students could simply refer to their books, recitation as a practice still remained rather commonplace and remains a common practice even today. Yet by the early modern era in universities, lectures became more of a gloss or a commentary upon the readings that students would have access to outside of the lecture space rather than simply word-for-word recitations from books (Friesen, 2017, p. 117).

In the late seventeenth and early eighteenth centuries, these educational practices gradually evolved as students in university education gained increased access to texts. Distinguished authors and thinkers of the noble classes, perhaps most famously John Locke, encouraged students to move beyond memorization even though memorization was one of the most popular educational practices at the time. Many students, in fact, engaged in repeated readings of whole books or stories as their primary methods of learning to read, an approach strongly advocated for by some of the century's leading pedagogues. In *Some Thoughts Concerning Education*, however, Locke warns that memorizing scores of Latin books will only "give [children] a disgust and aversion to their books, wherein they find nothing but useless trouble" (1712, paragraph 175). Locke does not completely dismiss the value of memorization; he encourages children to memorize particular phrases or sayings that may invite reflection, a skill that he believes allows them to "turn their thoughts inwards." To that end, many other famous public intellectuals still saw reading technology as a way to facilitate memorization skills. Thomas Fairfax, an English nobleman and the supposed author of a seventeenth-century pamphlet with educational advice called *Advice to a Young Lord*, encouraged young charges to "read seriously what ever is before you, and reduce and digest it to Practice and Observation, otherwise you'll have *Sysiphus* his labour, to be always revolving Sheets and Books at every new *Occurence*" (1691, p. 30). For Fairfax, memorization was an essential way to engage in active learning and avoid the Sisyphean task of rereading; he even suggested annotation in the margins of the books to allow the readers' memories to "speedily recur to the place it was committed to" (p. 30–32). In other words, Fairfax suggested a hybridized memorization and annotation practice to guarantee that ideas from readings were applied actively, moving within and beyond the material constraints available to seventeenth-century students.

These debates grew even more complicated in the nineteenth century when there was the next great boom in printing technology: the automated mass printing press. Automated printing presses churned out pages and bound them faster than any prior technology and made paperbound books (typically hardback) almost ubiquitously accessible and inexpensive. The nineteenth century also saw a tremendous change in schooling: child's labor was outlawed and all children had to spend their days in schools rather than on factory lines or farms. Although urban and rural children still had very different experiences with and avenues toward education, the concern about how children should use books and remember content from them became foremost again.

A typical school day in early nineteenth-century Britain mostly involved the rote recitation of select lines from scripture, philosophy, and maybe a little literature if they were lucky. According to Joseph Kay-Shuttleworth (1853), an economist who wrote about the social and economic conditions of the English poor, elementary and secondary school teachers occasionally tried to help students see the pleasures of reading; however, most teachers encouraged their students merely to read aloud, memorize, and recite lines of prose that meant virtually nothing to them. He criticized the teachers' approaches, noting that "except in one case, no endeavour was made to combine moral and religious training with intellectual instruction" (p. 383). After all, the goal of education was not to impart critical thinking; early British politicians saw mass education as a means of crime reduction. Therefore, a British child was considered literate when they were able to "recite from a tattered book . . . the extent to which he understood what he read was not inquired into" (Altick, 1998, p. 151). In other words, if a child could recite the words from the page even without understanding them, the child was literate enough to enter the workforce. Books and paper became utilitarian, equalizing vehicles for the emerging field of compulsory childhood education, and deep reading was of little concern to the average reader or educator.

By the turn of the twentieth century, when books were all but ubiquitous household items for people of all economic classes and genders, educational debates shifted again. The materiality of reading silently or reading aloud, reading on paper or engaging in recitation, was less important than understanding what might motivate children to learn and read in the first place. German empiricist Johann Herbart's perspective was influential to this end, as an emphasis on literature emerged (Adams, 2000, p. 312). In fact, "the purposes of reading were now held to be those of acquiring knowledge both for its own sake and its uses, of improving the intellectual powers, and of expanding one's personal capacity for personal and intellectual flexibility and fulfillment" (Adams, 2000, p. 311). Although form and content are challenging to divorce, the time at the end of the nineteenth and beginning of the twentieth century was a period when print was taken almost for granted. It was also a time when the logic of print itself became synonymous with the logic of being literate and of understanding linear text as a means of developing understanding of different kinds of content matter. As literacy scholar Deborah Brandt (1990) describes, "the nature of texts bequeaths meaning to the acts of writing and reading—not only in the sense of providing the means to arrive at meaning but in the sense of defining what it means to read and write. To be literate, in this view, is to be like a text" (p. 99). Although this understanding of literacy is, admittedly, limited, it is one that has allowed the printed book itself to become an invisible part of what it means to understand and remember concepts from texts themselves.

The concern with remembering information via reading technologies clearly evolved over the centuries, shifting as new reading technologies emerged and new kinds of readers accessed reading experiences. Remembering information has been a critical part of learning from different kinds of reading experiences, but readers have also worried about what kinds of materials they may have access to with changing reading technologies. Specifically, remembering texts is important, but it's perhaps all the more important to remember valuable information and to spend time remembering information from reputable, rather than untrustworthy, sources.

A Fear of Losing Authority: Will Reading Technologies Prevent Us from Understanding What Information Is Authoritative?

Our investment in remembering what we read and our subsequent worry that we might forget what we've read is grounded in the assumption that what we read inherently has value. To that end, a question that often emerges with the advent of new reading technologies is how we know whether the information we receive comes from a valid source. A question that every shift in reading technology has invited is not just *how* the work of reading happens, but how the information gathered and distributed in that reading technology is vetted by editors and publishers of that content. How do we decide which information gets distributed in our various reading technologies? Who makes those choices and how do those choices help us feel assured that we're reading authoritative work? Establishing a source's expertise is not a new issue: it is one that has been replicated in every major shift of reading technology over time, and it has impacted the willingness to read, adopt, and learn from works published within new reading technologies.

One way that authority was communicated in early book history was through assessing handwriting, specifically when that work was written by hand by a valued publisher or scribe. Many of our earliest reading technologies allowed writers to transmit and distribute the content by hand. Some scribes transcribed content directly from the authors or writers who dictated the content to them (though this primarily happened for original texts; much scribal activity involved copying biblical or legal texts). Regardless of whether the text was transcribed by the writer from the author or whether the scribe was copying from a previously composed written text, the human body was directly implicated in the process: from mouth to hand, the script of the scribe became emblematic of the authenticity and organic transmission of knowledge directly from the author's mind to the pages. The traces of orality were strong and readers knew that the content they received from a scribe's pages could be traced directly back to the author's person (and, therefore, the author's thoughts). Even in scribal culture, readers did not always know what to read and relied upon curators and instructors to guide them to particular texts. In fact, Seneca, an ancient Roman philosopher, advised readers in his second "Moral Letters to Lucilius" that, "You should always read the standard authors; and when you crave change, fall back upon those whom you read before" (trans. 1917, pp. 8–9). In other words, the design of documents from known scribes can be one way to judge written content, but remembering who you've read that you've valued in the past and relying upon your judgment of known authors is the best way to guarantee deep, sustained learning.

With the advent of the Gutenberg press, typesetters and publishers became the new gatekeepers for reliable information. Yet even as readers purchased what they understood to be machine-produced books, many still sought books designed to look as though they were hand produced. Historian Alberto Manguel describes, for example, how printing did not

> eradicate the taste for hand-written text. On the contrary, Gutenberg and his followers attempted to emulate the scribe's craft, and most incunabula have a manuscript appearance . . . It is interesting to note how often a technological development—such as Gutenberg's—promotes rather than eliminates that which it is supposed to supersede, making us aware of old-fashioned virtues we might otherwise have either overlooked or dismissed as of negligible importance (Manguel, 1996, p. 135).

The old-fashioned virtue at the heart of the move from scribal to mass publishing culture is a virtue that we will come to see is perhaps not so old-fashioned after all: that is, scribal culture privileged authenticity and authority above all else—values that, in contemporary reading cultures, we still value when selecting books of our own.

As text printed from large publishing houses became more widely consumed, consumers gradually understood that printed books developed a fixity of information and could be just as reliable as those that emerged from scribal culture. However, the proliferation of printed material made it harder than it had been in the past to distinguish which texts were reliable. Although most readers did not fully understand publishers' editorial processes, they could *see* in the pages of their hand-printed books that text was increasingly standardized from edition to edition. Elizabeth Eisenstein (1980) explains that the standardization and fixity of print in early modern England had several major consequences on readers; specifically, it paved "the way for the more deliberate purification and codification of all major European languages. Randomly patterned sixteenth-century type casting largely determined the subsequent elaboration of national mythologies on the part of certain separate groups within multilingual dynastic states" (p. 81–82). What this means is that the choices that printing presses made for publishing and typesetting books gave the perception that certain linguistic moves were completely fixed. The fixity of language in print itself also imbued print with the kind of trust that we might recognize today: if an idea is printed down and a particular word or idea is presented in a singular way, then that must be the definitive form of the idea intended by the author.

This fixity of form had many positive consequences for readers and for sustaining cultural knowledge at large. Walter Ong (1982) suggests that the fixity of print allowed modern readers to build their understanding of other peoples and places in ways that, by contrast, an oral society could not possibly fathom (p. 129). Contemporary readers may understand the feeling of connecting directly to an author or hearing someone else's voice through print so strongly precisely because print paved the way for authors to fix their ideas into stable, unchanging environments.

With that said, some book historians question whether the fixity or stability of print is the most accurate way to understand the history of the book itself (McKitterick, 2003;

Johns 1998). Adrian Johns (1998) argues that printed texts have never been stable even if we perceived them as such, making the case that "printed pages were not intrinsically trustworthy . . . The recognition of printed books as reliable thus depended substantially on prior representations of the Stationers' community as well ordered" (p. 624). As contemporary readers, we are inclined to trust a paperback book, released and distributed through an editor, because the act of paper printing imbues the text itself with some outside authority. We cannot say, then, that the *technology* of printing is what allowed people to develop fixed insights about language or the authors published, but rather it is the *social practices* that emerged from people reading mass-printed paperbacks that changed how people conceived of knowledge itself.

It is also important to note that early modern readers did not immediately rely on fixity of print to determine credibility of reading material. Early critics of print worried about the quality of books printed and complained about the errors made in print because of the speed at which they were printed. Historian Ann Blair (2010) clarifies that "the profit motive was perceived to threaten the quality of the final product, just as similar concerns are raised today about the projects to digitize books" (p. 47). Early modern readers understood that the market for printing books impacted what would get published and dispersed, just as contemporary readers understand that the contemporary profits collected through the circulation of online click-bait or inflammatory online articles may threaten the quality of writing in digital spaces.

The consumers perhaps most acutely concerned with the trustworthiness of texts were educators, as they saw youth as particularly impressionable audiences for potentially unreliable texts. Across the world, one of the largest publishing sectors that emerged as book production boomed was educational books. Even as the market for books diversified, educational books remained largely uniform, and hornbooks especially proved to be hugely popular, in large part because they standardized what educators saw as valuable to early childhood education: the ability to memorize individual letters and prayers. The *hornbook*, one of the earliest Western textbooks, was a thin paddle of wood covered with a transparent film to preserve the text beneath it, and every hornbook had roughly the same content: the alphabet, the first nine numerical digits, and the Lord's Prayer (Manguel, 1996, p. 139; Fischer, 2003, p. 235). Eventually, as compulsory childhood education became widespread worldwide, the hornbook faded into obsolescence and textbooks became popular. Most notably, Noah Webster's blue-back speller, first published in 1788, sold 80 million copies by 1888 (Green, 2001). According to Norm Friesen, Webster's speller brought in a didactic style that had once been more commonly reserved for religious books: the catechism (p. 103). A *catechism* tends to be a list of principles designed to inspire adherence to an authoritative resource. This pedagogical style, then, directly mitigated the potential effects of mass printing. By filtering and curating particular educational principles into a singular, authoritative space, the textbook replicated the top-down model of learning information from the authoritative lecturer who was reciting information at the front of a room.

Students in schoolhouses were not the only recipients of top-down, hierarchical learning in the Western world. Slaveowners, particularly in the United States, often saw it as a Christian imperative to teach slaves to read educational content. Throughout the eighteenth and nineteenth centuries, reading became a means of controlling slave populations, weaponizing religious piety and intellectualism (Monaghan 2005; Jackson 2010). Whereas some slaves found ways to leverage their reading as a liberating act, the legacy of memorizing verses from books is inextricably tied with the legacies of enslavement.

This legacy of educational books as a means of maintaining control extended into the nineteenth century with the McGuffey readers, the most popular textbooks in both England and in the United States. In contrast to Webster's spellers, the McGuffey reader curated a collection of fiction and nonfiction readings, often with a bent toward encouraging elementary and middle school students to practice moral virtue. McGuffey created readers for different age levels and grades, and the students were intended to progress through the collections over time (Vocke, 1991, p. 5). As a result, the McGuffey readers tended to create a national imaginary that largely privileged particular hegemonic perspectives of nationhood, a problematic positioning in terms of ignoring the marginalized voices that were part of the American experience (Reed, 2018, p. 399). In mitigating the concern with "unreliable" sources, historical textbooks like the McGuffey readers often perpetuated imperialist perspectives.

In the twentieth and twenty-first centuries, the McGuffey readers and the Webster spellers largely disappeared from public consciousness, but the textbook industry remains, and the education market's concerns with unreliable and nonauthoritative sources for student readers lingers perhaps even larger. Although major textbook manufacturers still dominate educational markets, they face major competition from digital resources, and most textbook publishers as of this book's writing have, in fact, shifted their operations primarily to online supplements for print resources. But where textbooks still often have an edge is precisely in response to the anxiety that has guided the conversation in this chapter: textbooks mitigate concerns with authority because they are vetted by people in the education business and designed to be read and constructed for educational purposes. Where we must remain careful is in understanding who gets to tell which kinds of standardized stories in print in the first place.

It is indisputable that in digital reading environments, we are able to encounter and explore a greater volume of texts than at any other moment in human history. And yet, the feeling of being overwhelmed by information, and of wondering what to do with the information at hand, is also not so unique. The accessibility of information in digital reading environments is, after all, not the first time that readers were faced with unprecedented access to a high volume of texts.

A Fear of Information Overload: Will Reading Technologies Overwhelm Us?

Erasmus, a prominent Renaissance philosopher, lamented how challenging it was to sift through all of the information available in the booming print industry after the invention of the Gutenberg press. Erasmus voiced frustration at the onslaught of new information and the inability to find a reprieve from the constant stream of books available to readers. In 1526, he considered:

> Is there anywhere on earth exempt from these swarms of new books? Even if, taken out one at a time, they offered something worth knowing, the very mass of them would be a

serious impediment to learning from satiety if nothing else, which can do far more damage where good things are concerned or simply from the fact that men's minds are easily glutted and hungry for something new, and so these distractions call them away from the reading of ancient authors (Blair, 2010, p. 55).

Although we might think primarily of the internet and computing eras when we think of the information age, concerns with managing how we need to learn what we need to learn from massive amounts of information has been with us alongside every major change in reading technology. When it comes to learning something new, we may struggle in a climate of information overload to determine where to focus our attention. How, in the past, have we mitigated the feeling of being overwhelmed that has arisen when we've accessed lots of new pieces of information? How have we kept track of what we've read and what we've learned from what we've read? In what ways have we demonstrated proficiency at sifting through and identifying the most pertinent or important readings for our pursuits?

Let's answer these questions by going back to those ancient times that Erasmus so longed for. As Erasmus would have known, for as long as alphabetic text has been composed, archivists have been tasked with storing, managing, and organizing that text. We know these archivists now as librarians, and, indeed, they are key figures in responding to feelings of information overload. They have historically helped readers manage, understand, and keep track of information. In ancient Mesopotamia, libraries stored all kinds of textual materials, from tablets to papyrus, though these records primarily contained administrative information, rather than literary or scholarly texts. The ancient Egyptians, however, were the first to take full advantage of the library's potential, not just for storing administrative records, but also for becoming epicenters of scholarly discovery. Much remains unknown about Egypt's Library of Alexandria, but historical records suggest that the library was built under the rule of Ptolemy I Soter sometime between 385 and 323 BCE. Although the exact number of scrolls stored and catalogued in the library is unknown, estimates are in the hundreds of thousands. It remains a mystery today how the Library of Alexandria was destroyed, but its legacy lived on in spaces that appropriated its curatorial and organizational techniques. Roman philosopher Pliny the Elder, for example, advocated for the textual note-taking methods that librarians at Alexandria practiced, including dividing text into numbered sections, creating in-text hierarchies and tables to organize information (Blair, 2010, p. 26).

Public libraries remained powerful cultural forces for organizing and storing information, though with the advent of the printing press, readers began to collect personal libraries as a way to organize and to discern information amidst a sea of knowledge. In the Renaissance period, middle-class merchants often collected books as a way to grow their library and understand their trades. Book ownership mitigated the feelings of information overload since access to books and experiences of reading could be limited to particular kinds of experiences and performances. As personal book ownership became more widespread, sixteenth-century inventors began to consider ways that readers could more easily manage the information from their vast collections. Perhaps most famously, Italian engineer Agostino Ramelli invented the bookwheel, a mechanical device that resembled a Ferris wheel where readers could place a heavy book on each segment of the wheel. The reader could then turn the wheel from a seated position to access a new book or easily flip between different books at different times. In *Le Diverse Et Artificiose Machine Del Capitano Agostino Ramelli*, Ramelli's book of inventions published in 1588, Ramelli said he purportedly invented the bookwheel as a way to help readers with gout, who were unable to move easily or lift heavy books, access and engage in multiple readings at once. That said, like many inventions created initially to accommodate people with disabilities, the device captured the interest of scholars eager to move between the vast numbers of texts available to them. Although the bookwheel was certainly not a common household item, it remains one of Ramelli's most notable inventions because of what it signified: an interest in holding and navigating multiple pieces of information at once in response to growing concerns about the ability of reading technologies to do so.

Even as readers found strategies for managing their feelings of information overload, the feeling that there remained too much information persisted. As print became even more available in the eighteenth century, institutions for learning became more interested in understanding how increasingly diverse student bodies could better access and understand the broad swaths of information. According to Chad Wellmon (2015), the eighteenth-century German institution model, often identified as the model upon which contemporary universities currently operate, was founded in response to "having been infested by a plague of books, circulating contagiously among the reading public" (p. 4). The German research institution's interest in guiding students through learning experiences grounded in disciplinary research emerged from an anxiety about readers becoming too lost in information and being unable to parse out relevant knowledge for scholarly application.

It should be noted that the concern with helping students manage overwhelming amounts of information was not uniquely confined to the eighteenth-century university. Once education became compulsory for children in the nineteenth-century Western world, the chief obligation for schools was to discipline and manage the swarms of children who needed to be in classroom spaces. Ideas were dangerous and classrooms were spaces to help students manage dangerous information and to cultivate obedience toward instructors and institutions of authority. Yet even with mandatory schooling, anxiety over people's attentional resources remained central in the late nineteenth century's cultural zeitgeist. Jonathan Crary (2001) suggests that a condition of modernity in the nineteenth century was grappling with information overload as a consequence of people's declining attentional capacity. Crary describes how nineteenth-century consumers saw themselves operating within "an endless sequence of new products, sources of stimulation, and streams of information" (2001, p. 13–14). Indeed, along with compulsory education, the nineteenth century also ushered in new informational inventions such as the camera for taking photographs and, by the end of the nineteenth century, stop-motion photographs. These new ways of accessing a full range of communicative expressions via mediated technologies stoked concerns reminiscent of those with feeling overwhelmed by print itself. For example, in 1895, social critic Max Nordau predicted that,

> the end of the twentieth century . . . will probably see a generation to whom it will not be injurious to read a dozen

square yards of newspapers daily, to be constantly called to
the telephone, to be thinking simultaneously of the five
continents of the world, to live half their time in a railway
carriage or in a flying machine and . . . know how to find its
ease in the midst of a city inhabited by millions (Crary,
2001, p. 30).

Nordau's prediction may sound eerily prescient: if we think
about our twenty-first-century condition where we can access "yards" of news and constantly be on the "telephone,"
we can see that Nordau was right about the contemporary
condition of accessing and juggling multiple streams of information at once. Although the rest of Nordau's argument
veers into a diatribe about his concerns with society's degen-
eration in response to the reams of information available,
the point remains that in the nineteenth century's moment
of shifting and expanding technological access to information, managing that information and finding equilibrium
within it has been foremost on people's minds.

What Nordau pointed to that may have particular reso-
nance with our contemporary concerns with information
overload is the attendant concern with *sensory* overload.
Just as Nordau cites readers' movements between newspaper, phone calls, and "flying machines," twenty-first-
century thinkers, including educators, have long expressed
concerns with the prevalence of images, video, and audio
text when reading in digital spaces. In an article on the
need to help students navigate digital environments, Alan
Rea and Doug White (1999) suggest that "as browsers and
HTML evolve with new versions, more options become
available . . . Web users need to learn how much is enough
and how much is too much. They must take into account
download time, audience, and purpose" (p. 433). In other

words, students navigating reading and writing tasks in digital spaces must take into full consideration their need to manage the experiences of multisensory overload that they may encounter. The need to manage information overload in the twenty-first century gives rise to a full industry of books and conversations to come that intersect with precisely what this book is attempting to do: grapple with strategies for adjusting to and being attentive of the material affordances and constraints of reading technology.

Putting It All Together: What Do We Have to Learn from the Past?

We've walked through the past and briefly covered the ways in which historical attitudes toward materials of and for reading have influenced reading practice both in and out of classrooms. When we bring the past to the forefront, we hear echoes of our own present and the way we now wrestle with the uncertainties of new media and modes for understanding and delivering information. While we navigate some new media ecologies with some unprecedented realities, we acknowledge that our moment is part of a larger timeline of moments in which others have wrestled with similar, although not identical, changes. Recognizing those struggles—and the attitudes toward them—may alleviate some of our own worries or give us new perspectives on how these worries may be implemented.

My hope is that you're struck by the ways in which different eras surface different binaries about what it means to be literate over time: Oral and written. Written and digital. Social and antisocial. Introspective and superficial. Deep and shallow. Sometimes, these binaries are appropriate. We know that the design and the materials of our media absolutely affect who is reading what and where in ways both good and bad. Changes in access to materials—and the accessibility of labor in producing those materials—invite new readers in and diversify reading practices.

Drawing these binaries essentially simplifies lived realities. As pervasive as these binaries are, the actual practice of blurring them is even more pervasive. We can say rather confidently that no one ever only engages in literate practice in one particular way, just as no one really ever learns in any one narrow way consistently. Let's remind ourselves of the ancient Greeks and Romans again: while lore has it that the Greeks' primary mode of reading was by listening to oral speech, increased historical evidence suggests that this mode may not have been primary at all, but rather was primary *under certain circumstances*. Our assumption about the oral mode as the primary mode emerges from the fact that many of the written artifacts from the ancient Greeks are printed on scrolls without spaces between the words, a form and format better suited for oral recitation than silent reading. The content of scrolls tended to be literary prose or newsworthy announcements—moments designed for performance and for social engagement. The content of more mundane documents, like letters or receipts, appeared less often on scrolls and more often on sheets of papyrus and other such documents.

Different intended purposes of the reading acts changed the materiality and the praxis of reading. It is easy to privilege the literary moment, as that is perhaps a moment of elevated reading—reading that accesses the heart of human matter. These moments should be cherished, but they're not the only moments, and recognizing other moments of reading practice—even when they don't involve literature or even very interesting texts at all—may widen our understanding of what's available to us as readers and learners. If we don't recognize this range of practices, we run the risk of narrowing our understanding of the various forms that reading can take and, in so doing, we may see reading as a monolithic category. Additionally, we run the risk of not being able to see other ways to engage with text and, in so doing, we fear the consequences of reading in any ways *but* the ways that we find acceptable. The impulse to exclude and delimit what counts as reading may be rooted to our affective engagements with books and the critical role that affect plays in our notions of reading's past, present, and future. Our histories of reading, shaped by a complex interplay of medium and social practice, must also be interpolated with our histories as readers.

CHAPTER 2

THE HELD BOOK:

HOW OUR FEELINGS FOR BOOKS IMPACT
HOW WE TEACH READING

In the preface to Anne Fadiman's ode to books, *Ex Libris* (2000), she laments the fact that those who write about books often treat them like "toasters," or consumer goods. This attitude, she argues, "neatly omits what I consider the heart of reading: not whether we wish to purchase a new book but how we maintain our connections with our old books, the ones we have lived with for years, the ones whose textures and colors and smells have become as familiar to us as our children's skin" (p. x). It's this last part that sticks with me: the idea that books can become so intimate, so close to us that we can know them as well as our children's skin. It doesn't get much closer than that.

Much of this intimacy is evoked by the affective connection between the materiality of the book itself and the experiences this materiality affords. Andrew Piper (2012) connects acts of reading from printed books with building close relationships with his children too, remembering, "As

I begin to read, the kids begin to lean into me. Our bodies assume positions of rest, the book our shared column of support . . . As we gradually sink into the floor, and each other, our minds are free to follow their own pathways, unlike the prescribed pathways of the web. We read and we drift" (22). Describing the book as a "column of support" suggests that the object of the book itself brings people together in a way impossible to replicate otherwise. By comparing the drifting sensation of reading the paper book together with (the incomparable experience of) surfing the web, Piper suggests that the feelings, sensations, and cognitive processes of reading are all intertwined.

Piper goes on to express that the value of a printed book emerges not just in the moment of reading itself, but in the moment of passing down books as heirlooms. He imagines that when he passes on his old books to his children, he will "be sharing with them a sense of time. Books are meaningful because as material objects they bear time within themselves. They convey a sense of time passing in a double sense—my having been there for some period of time and my no longer being there. Digital files, on the other hand, do not register in time in quite this way" (Piper, 2012, p. 107). The visual, tactical, and sensual wear of a book imbues it with the same kind of intimate and familial value that Fadiman notices. Just as children's skin ages and wrinkles with time, so too do the pages of books. A digital file, on the other hand? When it ages, there's not much to see— perhaps some extra pixelation, an error message, an outdated file extension, and then ultimately, nothing at all. (It should, of course, be noted that digital files do leave behind material traces, but ones that aren't immediately visible to the consumer. One need only see pictures of a server farm to know that this is true.) With digital files, then, we may not be able to see the signs of aging, of use, and of care—and we can't *feel* them either.

These intimate narratives about books and reading can impact how we perceive of books as cultural signifiers of intellectualism, refinement, and humanistic engagement. In educational settings, we may not always describe books as objects we bring to bed, pass on to family members, or sniff in bookstores, but we do talk about how we use books for learning, and surveys of undergraduate students suggest that many students themselves find comfort and pleasure in reading from printed books. In fact, the past twenty years of survey research on undergraduate preferences for reading materials suggest that more students express strong preferences for reading from print books than digital books for a combination of emotional and pragmatic reasons (Mizrachi, Salaz, Kurbanoglu, & Boustany, 2018; *Library Journal Research*, 2018; Baron, Calixte, & Havewala, 2017; Farinosi, Lim, & Roll, 2016; Hobbs & Klare, 2016; Corlett-Riviera & Hackman, 2014; Mangen et al., 2013; LaRose 2010).

The results of over two decades of survey research are surprisingly consistent. In one of the oldest studies of student reading preferences, librarian Cynthia Gregory (2008) found, in a survey of 106 college students at a small liberal arts college, that student responses about preferring print over electronic books expressed sentiments like "nothing compares to a print book" and "[I] like to have a book in hand/hold and take home" (p. 270), which in Gregory's words, "further indicate that our human love of the book as cuddle object remains quite strong in the digital age" (p. 270). Even calling a book a cuddle object in this analysis reinforces the notion that paper books signify emotional attachments to particular kinds of material reading experiences.

More recently, linguist Naomi Baron, psychologist Rachelle Calixte, and educational specialist Mazneen Havewala (2017) found very similar results from a broad international study. They surveyed 429 undergraduate students in the US, Japan, Germany, Slovakia, and India and found that students surveyed also often preferred print for academic reading as a result of emotional attachments or concerns with material constraints. For example, only 3.7% of respondents "identified something emotional or aesthetic as what they liked most about reading onscreen . . . Where positive emotional/aesthetic comments about reading onscreen did appear, they involved expressions of enjoyment (e.g., 'It is fun') or personal judgment (e.g., 'it's 'smart'/sophisticated/stylish')" (2017, p. 598). By contrast, participants commented that they enjoyed print, found it relaxing, and that it was "real reading." They also wrote about liking the smell of books (p. 601). These results consistently show how deeply attitudes toward print and screens alike impact willingness to take up reading in different spaces for different purposes.

In an even more recent and even larger study, librarians Diane Mizrachi et al. (2018) surveyed 10,293 college and university students, both at the undergraduate and graduate levels, from twenty-one countries worldwide from 2014 to 2016. With a clear goal to "assess the preferences and self-reported behaviors of readers engaged in learning from text," they found, as in earlier studies, that students communicated an overall preference for reading academic texts from print over digital materials (2018, p. 7, p. 11). They discovered that this preference for reading from print was tied directly to students' self-reported perceptions of improved abilities to retain and apply knowledge from print, concluding that "while factors other than learning performance clearly play a role in determining preference, this data suggests that readers have a sense of awareness about the impacts of format on their own learning and that this factor does contribute to format decisions and behavior" (Mizrachi et al., 2018, pp. 26–27).

By contrast, the *Library Journal Research*'s (2018) survey study of 306 student responses (gathered in partnership with EBSCO Information Services) demonstrates that a slightly greater number of students surveyed preferred using e-books for academic reading than print books, and many reported using an increasing number of e-books for academic reading (p. 35). In fact, over half of the respondents (52%) cited using more e-books over the past year, citing reasons like convenience, cost, and greater diversity of content (*Library Journal Research,* 2018, p. 27). The differences between the *Library Journal Research*'s and Mizrachi et al.'s conclusions suggest a diversity in how our students experience their reading but also show that access and perception of access are factors inherently aligned with preferences.

Personal preferences for reading, then, are formed not only by emotional or childhood attachments, but also by longer-term academic experiences. I agree ultimately with Mizrachi et al.'s suggestion that these findings provide us with numerous opportunities to "balance more carefully the competing concerns about formats, learning, costs and access and to look for ways of improving the usability and likeability of e-formats for tertiary learners" (2018, p. 27). There simply is much work remaining to make digital reading appealing for our students, even two decades into a moment when digital reading experiences continue to be accessible and affordable.

It is worth noting that faculty in universities also tend to express clear preferences for reading in print over reading in digital spaces. Librarians Kelsey Corlett-Riviera and Timothy Hackman (2014) found that faculty respondents to an institutional survey had strong feelings toward the benefits of reading in print, even as faculty and graduate students were among the most frequent respondents to use e-book repositories for research. They shared the response of one faculty member with a particularly strong attitude toward print reading: "The library, with its tangible books that you can hold in your hand, is our life-blood: indeed one might argue that without the material existence of those books, such academic areas as English will suffer dramatically reduced enrollments. The idea that our scholarship might be forced somehow to reorient itself wholly or mainly around e-books and PDFs is simply PARALYZING" (Corlett-Riviera & Hackman, 2014, p. 273). The contrast that this particular faculty testimony draws between tangible books and e-books suggests that these material entities confer entirely different values: the print book signifies a materially different kind of work than the e-book does, one that communicates the lifeblood of a particular discipline. Materiality, for this particular faculty member, is tied directly to the labor itself.

We can see that preferences for reading are tied to our emotional experiences of reading and how those experiences impact our willingness to do particular kinds of work. Although one could argue that engagement in material practices may shape feelings—rather than feelings shaping material practices—there is a clear iterative relationship between what we do and what we feel about what we do. We cannot untangle the conditions of our material lives from our feelings, and it can actually be quite tricky to parse out precisely what parts of our reading experiences are shaped by feelings.

It is likely that those of us who work in college environments love books more than the average reader. After all, many of us peddle our knowledge in the form of books or written articles. The manuscript itself is a symbol, especially for those on the tenure track, of making it in terms of contributing to a larger intellectual conversation. I recognize that my own emotions around books are shaped by the intellectual, vocational, and class context of which I am a part. When it comes to acts of reading, literacy scholar Bronwyn Williams (2018) notes that our identities can be enveloped in our practices, and vice versa. In fact, Williams suggests that, if we are to understand why people engage in particular reading and writing acts, we must consider examining a combination of social forces (including technology) and internal influences in order to figure out why people behave and think about reading in the ways that they do. In so doing, we can see that "our perceptions of what we can or cannot do are internal and embodied, even as they are engaged with the social context of the moment" (Williams, 2018, p. 9). What this means is that how we practice reading, both in terms of our material conditions and our cognitive strategies, is inherently inseparable from how we *feel* about reading. Composition scholar Cydney Alexis (2017) argues that "considering the demonstrated power of objects in the process of becoming possible selves, and people's reliance on object constellations to perform identities and trades, we should be asking deeper questions about how objects assist, even shape, writers in learning, negotiating, and maintaining their writing practices and writing identities" (p. 33). Alexis has investigated how mundane writing objects, like Moleskine notebooks, form writerly identities, and I would argue that we also need to investigate objects that shape reading practices and identities, particularly as they correlate to the performance of academic and readerly identity.

If we are to say that social, technological, and material forces affect literacy acts, broadly speaking, we must take a closer look at reading in particular and what role books play in shaping how students see themselves as readers. Understanding our students can, thereafter, help us understand how to shape our pedagogy and approaches to reading acts. Let's examine where emotional attitudes toward printed books have come from and how those attitudes might impact people's motivation to engage in acts of reading or identify as readers, particularly in educational contexts.

Where Do Emotional Attitudes toward Books Come From? Childhood Exposure and Our Feelings for Books

Psychologist Daniel Willingham (2017) posits that our willingness to identify as readers may emerge from a combination of cognitive, emotional, and behavioral assessments that we make over time. Although Willingham acknowledges that more research needs to be conducted on how attitudes toward reading form, he concludes that "your reading attitude is mostly emotional. It's based on whether reading seems rewarding, excites you, or interests you. It's not a reasoned judgment of its value, or an appraisal of your behavior"

(p. 138). He goes on to say that "one source—probably the primary source—of positive reading attitudes is positive reading experiences. This phenomenon is no more complicated than understanding why someone has a positive attitude toward eggplant. You taste it and like it" (Willingham, 2017, p. 138). In other words, engaging in repeated positive reading experiences and, thereafter, experiencing the positive emotions that can form positive associations to reading may help students be motivated to read insofar as they are constructing a readerly identity.

Positive associations toward reading and a readerly identity often form early in a reader's life. Childhood experiences with reading may, in fact, be critical to developing the motivation to read and a positive association with reading itself. Neuroscientist Maryanne Wolf (2016) has studied early childhood literacy development and she contends that early childhood experiences of reading "simultaneously expos[e] the children to emotional experiences and narratives they might never otherwise have. And for some children, such experiences are their personal vehicles that transport them away from wherever they are and give them reason to aspire and contribute what they know" (p. 62). When reading gives children a strong sense of understanding others' interiority, they develop greater capacity to empathize with others and feel motivated to understand how their lives connect with others' experiences.

Wolf contends that this ability to access others' interiority and aspire toward inspirational, deep thinking comes from the experience of reading from print books in particular. Because information on screens can often move quickly and in automated and animated ways, Wolf argues that when children read on-screen, they are receiving more information than from printed books. Therefore, they have less time to process that information. With diminished time and ability to process information on-screen, they may not be able to develop working memory of what they gain from books or what they're processing on-screen (Wolf, 2018, p. 122). Wolf then urges parents to continue developing children's early experiences of reading from books so that children can experience "the physical and temporal thereness of books before they encounter the always slightly removed, slightly ersatz screen. Many very young viewers all too quickly are literally and cognitively left to their own devices—to be continuously entertained by a very flat thing, which possesses neither the lap nor the voice of their most beloved persons reading and speaking just to them" (2018, p. 133). What Wolf encourages is aligned with what Willingham concludes: when children have positive experiences, via hearing books read by beloved people in their lives, they form positive associations with the material objects for reading that may shape their practices later on.

There is historical precedent for acknowledging the value of exposing children to physical, material reading experiences. Literary scholar Patricia Crain (2013) charted the history of children's books in the Western world and argues that our contemporary attitudes toward books as containers for virtue, imagination, and empathy can be traced directly back to how early children's book development kept the educational function of books at the core of book marketing. She explains that, with the explosion in the distribution and publication of children's literature in the late eighteenth and early nineteenth centuries, publishers often made design choices that invited children to claim ownership over the objects of the books themselves (Crain, 2013). For example, many mid-nineteenth-century books had places for children to write their names on a nameplate, a move that "declares ownership not only in the book at hand but in the constellation of experiences, and of rights and privileges, that the book represents and that are represented by the fact of reading and writing" (Crain, 2013, p. 160). The portability of a book, to be held in a loved one's lap as Wolf (2018) suggests, and the ability to write one's name and own a print book, as Crain (2013) describes, continues to re-inscribe the attachment that readers may form between material object, experience, ownership, and identity.

The design of the printed book itself has contributed to cultivating a culture of individual ownership around reading from print. Printed text, historically speaking, has codified language use and, as a result, we can say that book objects have what Lisa Gitelman (2014) refers to as "bibliographical identity." Given the fact that readers can trust that printed, hardbound books will look exactly the same and have the same information across chapters, page numbers, and even paragraphs, readers can say they "are 'on the same page' . . . Certainties like these help make modern texts self-evident, giving them that 'air of intrinsic reliability' that today frames print media" (Gitelman, 2014, p. 113). With this level of trust in print media established, the emotional connections, and the abilities to find solace in the fixity and permanence of books deepens even further.

Designated spaces for reading can also contribute to our feeling that print offers fixity, permanence, and authenticity. Libraries, bookstores, and coffee shops are all intimate, albeit public, spaces where books have been stored, accessed, debated, and discussed for centuries. According to Adrian Johns (1998), the seventeenth-century coffeeshop was a major site for accessing print books and newspapers. As a result, cafés became intimate places for people to gather, affiliated with the excitement and passion that reading often evoked. The café today remains a gathering place for many to access the materials and spaces of reading, but we also can't discount the cultural pleasure and power of the bookstore to this end. Literary historian James Collins (2010) argues that "the absence of physical boundaries has led to the creation of elaborate taste distinctions sanctioned by authorities who, to use Pierre Bourdieu's term, *consecrate* certain forms of consumer activity as cultural pleasures" (p. 32). Just as cafés once consecrated spaces for debate, discussion, and engagement, spaces like the contemporary bookstore and café also communicate intimate connections to reading experiences, driven by a pairing of consumerist and intellectual pleasure. Essayist David Ulin (2010), for example, describes the intense experience of walking into a bookstore and what it evoked for him:

> The sensation was animal. I would walk into a favorite bookstore, Spring Street Books in lower Manhattan, say, and just the sight, the smell, the breadth of all that writing, lining the walls and piled on the frontlist tables, would hit me in the bowels. All of a sudden, my stomach would roll and my sphincter would tighten, and I would feel an urgency that was physical and metaphysical, an expression of my body and my mind (p. 19).

Ulin's description of the way his body feels when entering the bookstore is so striking and evocative because it describes a subconscious, embodied reaction to the multisensory experience of being in a bookstore. This description suggests that Ulin cannot control how he feels about books because the books themselves trigger such an intense and internalized experience of pleasure and excitement. Not to mention that the bookstore itself is the ultimate third place, a place with a magnetic sense of place, that magnifies the intensity of emotion and feeling of community with the books themselves (Oldenburg, 1989). Book objects, then, become an object of lust, compelling to the point that "metaphysical urgency" drives the consumption of print (Ulin, 2010, p. 19). Jacqueline Rhodes (in Alexander, Micciche, & Rhodes, 2013) also describes reading from books with an echo of lustiness when she describes her awareness of "the material fact of the book: its weight, its heft, the thickness of pages yet to go, the smell of it" and experiences how she "lie[s] in bed in anticipation of my reading. Sometimes, I am seduced. Sometimes, I see a new text—or even an already re/read text—and think, in essence, *I'd like to tap that*" (p. 65). Books, in other words, invite anticipation, the giddiness of discovery that is enveloped with what gets uniquely evoked by the material. Affective engagements like this make compelling emotional cases for reading books not only as rarefied cultural objects, but as objects of intimacy.

It's clear that many elements of print culture, from early childhood experiences to the fixity of document design and public spaces for reading, can create positive, authoritative, and trustworthy associations with the objects of books themselves. Forming positive associations with print books is all to the good in terms of inspiring continued interest in reading activities and reading identification. To that end, all of this research may make us wonder: why bother reading from digital books at all? If we now know all of the tremendous emotional benefits of reading from print books, is there any point in trying to push ourselves and our students to read deeply in digital spaces at all? To answer these questions, let's look to understand current undergraduate students' attitudes and experiences with reading in academic environments.

Student Attitudes toward Reading on Paper: What the Research Tells Us

We know we're reading in digital spaces all the time, even as we simultaneously recognize the value of reading in print spaces, both in adolescent and in early childhood years. Yet how do our values for reading align with our lived experiences of reading?

According to 2016 survey data from the Pew Center for Internet and Research, 80% of adults between the ages of 18 and 29 report reading books in both print and e-book formats regularly, demonstrating that as more people of traditional college age own multiple digital devices for reading, they are also engaging in more flexible acts of reading (Perrin, 2016). To that end, librarians Katherine Hanz and Dawn McKinnon (2018) found that in a survey of undergraduate student library users that students reported using e-books more frequently for research purposes than for recreational purposes (p. 8), which suggests that there is a clear need to help students understand how to handle the different purposes and needs involved in reading in digital spaces. That is, even when students state a *preference* for reading in print, they may very well opt to read in digital spaces out of convenience, accessibility, and efficiency (Gierdowski, 2019b; Jaggars, 2014). So, even though students may not have deep, emotional connections to e-books, they are still turning to them and could benefit from the deliberate ability to understand what they might get from an e-book reading experience, beyond simply logistical ease of access.

Many students have already developed some sophisticated understanding of navigating across print and digital spaces. In interviews with high school students about their reading habits, reading scholar Daniel Keller (2014) found that "At home, most students use technologies that tend toward speed and brevity, yet they also read books and enjoy the slow, deep immersion offered by extended narratives. Online social interactions may be perceived as fleeting and shallow, yet the observations here reveal rhetorical choices that are sophisticated because of how they achieve continuous attention" (p. 75). In contrasting speedy technology with slow books, students are already beginning to recognize the affordances and limitations of what they can do in different spaces, especially when it comes to their home and recreational lives. Outside of school, however, this understanding could be more fully fostered so that students bring greater metacognitive awareness to the work that they do in and across schooling environments.

So, why should we ask students to read in digital environments given all that we know about how they feel about reading books? If student preferences and dispositions are clear, why should we try to advance practices that may run contrary to those preferences? The conclusion to Baron et al.'s (2017) intensive study may be a good starting point to this conversation, as they suggest that "we should devote serious research attention to the question of what kinds of texts or subject matters make most educational sense in which formats. As in so much of education, one size likely doesn't fit all" (p. 603). Context matters, in other words, for assessing and understanding these data points. In particular, Gierdowski's (2019a) research on learning environment preferences of community college students speaks to some of the tremendous differences between how students at two-year and four-year institutions may experience and orient themselves to their reading spaces. In a comparison of responses to Gierdowski's study of community college students' access to information technology and Galanek et al.'s 2018 study of students' access to information technology at four-year colleges, Gierdowski found that two-year and AA-degree-earning students were twice as likely to prefer learning in online environments than students at four-year colleges (Gierdowski, 2019a; Galanek et al., 2018, p. 14). Although community college students weren't asked about reading explicitly, the interest in learning online from students at two-year institutions suggests that personal preferences and preferences for learning may inherently be complicated by their lived learning experiences. It therefore behooves us to continue asking students about their preferences and experiences in our own local contexts, as the responses may either align or diverge accordingly.

When conducting my own research on undergraduate students' perceptions of reading across print and digital spaces, I noticed the contexts for students' lived experiences with reading and writing affecting their dispositions in a number of ways (Cohn, 2016a; Cohn, 2016b). For example, when I asked students to explain their preferences for reading and writing in digital spaces, I asked them to break down which kinds of academic writing tasks they preferred in those spaces. That's when students would really get down to the details: when it came to brainstorming ideas for a research paper or reading a piece of literature, paper was hands-down the winner. But when it came to drafting that research paper or reading a technical article for a class, students consistently preferred typing and reading on their laptops. It's not that students always preferred paper; it's that they preferred it for particular kinds of academic tasks, especially ones that required substantial personal investment or drawing upon personal inquiry. Pleasurable tasks too, like reading a novel or writing a personal journal entry, always seemed to lean toward the paper-based preference. Drafting the research paper or reading the technical article, on the other hand, were perceived as tasks better conducted on the computer because the computer space was more efficient for composing and for reading documents where students felt like they may need access to dictionaries or other resources to understand the piece.

In my research, it's not that students universally found paper to be the better conduit for understanding knowledge. It was that paper became intimate for them, and was the way that they felt they could find greater personal connection to their work. In the words of one interviewee, "you can't curl up on a big comfy couch with an iPad!" (Cohn, 2016a). This student burst out laughing thinking about how you might read on the couch with a digital device; she shares Fadiman's perspective from the beginning of this chapter, in other words, that paperbacks are intimate whereas screens are not. There is a certain irony to this point given that paperbacks are just as mass-produced as iPads at this point, but the persistent cultural attachments to print still have an impact on where and how students approach reading tasks in different contexts.

These preferences also speak to some tacit assumptions that students may have about what it means to read academically or for pleasure. Concerns with eye strain, physical comfort, and absorption or focus are legitimate and inextricable from understanding students' learning experiences. They may also be, largely, but importantly, not universally generalizable. One experience that may not be captured within these concerns is disability. Deborah Wolter (2018) worked with disabled elementary school students and noticed that many of them developed excuses for avoiding reading because traditional approaches to reading texts or accessing them from print materials did not engage them. When students struggled mightily with reading, they felt frustrated and upset and sometimes placed the blame for their struggles on to the books themselves. Wolter tells the story of a fifth-grader named Sam who

> would feign all kinds of allergic reactions when near books. He said they were dusty. They were moldy too. His eyes itched. His nose would run. His ears would plug up, and he could not hear. His tongue would swell up. He would show me every single little bump on his arms and hands and insist that I let him visit the school nurse or, at least, hand over the box of tissues (2018, p. 105).

Wolter found ways to encourage Sam to read outside of slogging through phonics or trying to get him to sit quietly with a print book in the corner of a classroom. She thought expansively about what reading could be, encouraging Sam to look up things he was curious about and explore across different texts without having to simply sit quietly. In other words, she didn't force Sam into reading from the dusty or moldy books that had become a metonym for his anxieties. Rather, she helped Sam see that reading for him could look different (while also recognizing that the books themselves were not at fault for his struggles). Although Sam did, in fact, have some learning disabilities that prevented him from reading as quickly as his peers, Wolter's ability to see that Sam's feelings for books differed from other students in part because he felt discouraged and allergic to books ultimately helped her develop some strategies to motivate Sam's eventual learning. In higher education too, we should recognize that replicating narratives around how we feel about books as being cozy and comforting may inadvertently lead to less inclusive learning experiences for some of our students.

Scholarship on affective experiences of reading and writing for school may also help instructors take on a more nuanced and inclusive understanding of what factors impact the feelings that students adopt for reading and writing in academic environments. Jacob Craig (2019) conducted a small qualitative study where he observed and interviewed students as they wrote in their preferred spaces and environments. He found that writing "practices have both a material and an affective history that influences and echoes throughout writers' evolving processes" and concluded that "even as materials, scenes, contexts, and situations change over the course of a writer's life, there is consistency in the affects writers seek out in support of their processes" (Craig, 2019). Through seeing how student writers often rely on materials to inspire particular practices (e.g., to generate focus, or to alleviate stress or academic pressure), Craig finds that we need to think more critically about how our associations with objects influences how we are or are not willing to do particular kinds of work, including the work of reading and writing.

In explicating how students take on different material practices for writing, Craig (2019) employs a critical concept from affect theorist Sarah Ahmed: *affect* is an evaluation of an object or place. What this suggests is that people's engagements with objects and places depends not just on how they feel about them, but on what attracts them to these objects or places and how that attraction causes them to evaluate or understand particular objects' or places' value. When that evaluation has occurred, people make judgments about the objects or places that shape their behaviors consistently from that point forward, creating what Ahmed (2014) refers to as a "stickiness" or "a form of relationality . . . in which the elements that are 'with' get bound together" (p. 90). In other words, once one feeling or idea gets stuck with a particular material object, it doesn't become unbound and it can shape engagement from that point forward.

When it comes to reading for academic purposes, the "withness" that many students and their instructors may experience is between print books *with* a feeling of focus or between print books *with* a feeling of comfort. This withness can then also help students and instructors alike form positive feelings for reading too: if we evaluate the quality of a reading feeling in line with a particular material condition (i.e., reading from paper), and we engage in that practice regularly, we may begin to feel fondness toward reading.

There are some trends to be attentive to in terms of the connections between performances and understandings of reading and academic reading acts. Our job now is to consider how we might harness those emotions to productive ends. That is, we can help our students develop the agency they may have in reading from print books, particularly if that's an experience that they have had more access to, and apply that agency to university contexts where they will need to read deeply across the variety of spaces that they may navigate.

The more confidence our students feel in new taskspaces, like digital spaces, the more emotionally invested they may feel in turn, especially when it comes to academic contexts where they may still be trying to understand the norms and behaviors in the new discourse communities that they could be navigating. As Susan Ambrose et al. (2010) find, "students can benefit from instruction that helps them to see important relationships and build more connections among the pieces of knowledge they are learning, thus leading them to develop more flexible and effective knowledge organizations" (p. 65). Developing a flexible grasp of how and when students navigate different academic taskspaces may also help them recognize that our connections to reading may even become *more* intimate if we develop a deeper understanding of how we make choices about where to read. Jonathan Alexander et al. (2013) contend that "reading's value and power is gained both by purposeful and guided choices as well as by accidents, associations, and sensory, felt pairings" (p. 46). We can help students develop strategies for navigating how they feel about reading in the various spaces they choose and the flexibility to move among those spaces. That way, they can recognize when they read with purpose and when they might read less purposefully. As a result, they may develop new pathways for learning successfully, weaving between the complex, variegated reasons and feelings for reading that they may experience.

We cannot change the intrinsic materiality of a digital space: it, by definition, always exists on a screen of some kind. For that matter, we cannot change the materiality of paper either. But what we can change is our orientation to those spaces and our approaches to them. We can alter the designs of these spaces. In digital spaces, for example, we have the power to adjust font types and sizes. We can embed hyperlinks and images. We can highlight and annotate. Similarly, on paper, we can adjust the design too: we can dog-ear pages and scribble in the margins. In other words, we can respond to what the materials offer us and play with the designs to our liking. Our students are, in fact, already providing some flexible models to this end, as they develop their own attitudes toward navigating reading, writing, and learning in the various spaces available to them.

....

Consequences: How Do Emotions Impact Our Willingness to Learn?

....

We know that emotional and affective connection to where we learn and how we learn can support sustained motivation. In *The Spark of Learning,* psychologist Sarah Rose Cavanagh (2016) argues that instructors should harness the power of emotion and direct it at learning, in large part because "emotion is already present in all experiences, perhaps even *particularly* so in cognition" (p. 24). Although thinking and feeling are often put at odds with each other; cognition and emotion are, in fact, completely intertwined, and the experience of feeling something deeply often gives a pretty big boost to problem solving. Cavanagh, in fact, suggests that instructors "should pay the most attention and effort to creating a positive climate in the classroom on days when your activities and topics require more creativity than focused attention to detail" (2016, p. 46). In other words, sustaining positive emotions in the classroom for particular kinds of cognitive interventions can help regulate engagement. Clearly, if we're not attentive to emotional conditions, we may lose sight of how to engage our students.

So, what does all of this mean for reading in deep and sustained ways in a digital age?

First, as instructors, we need to grapple with our own feelings for books. What associations do we have with our own academic taskspaces, from our material conditions of working to our practices? How do our own experiences influence what we teach and communicate to our students?

And how do our identities and privileges shape what we feel for and communicate about reading practice? As instructors, we may have lots of feelings about technology for learning. Taking stock of our own feelings is critical to understanding what messages or ideas we may communicate to our students in turn as we likely aspire to help our students understand and make sense of their own feelings for reading. We should aim not to impose our own feelings on our students. In some cases, our feelings about what kinds of reading are appropriate can be harmful and discriminatory (Gierdowski & Galanek, 2020). The more that everyone, instructors and students alike, can take a step back, examine their feelings, and think about how to leverage those emotions in the classroom, the more likely it is for a class to start a conversation about reading practices rather than ending that conversation.

Second, as we center students in their learning experiences, we have to take stock of their impressions of academic tasks as well. How do they associate particular material conditions with particular circumstances for learning? How do we help them cultivate new experiences and see how their college reading experiences may align with or diverge from experiences from their childhood or earlier educational interventions? And how do we help them see how regulating their emotions around learning and reading may align with their purposes for reading in the first place? When we help students answer these questions for themselves, they will likely make a variety of choices. They may wind up using mostly pen and paper to do their reading and writing work. They may wind up mostly using their laptops or smartphones to do that work too. What we have to combat is the judgment that our students' own choices and impressions for learning may be wrong. (And if you're wondering about the empirical evidence for using laptops or printed books to read academically, never fear; that discussion is coming in the next chapter.)

If we give our students both the agency to make the choices and the tools to empower them to make those choices in ways that may allow them to assess their reading, writing, and learning situations appropriately, we can move forward from instrumentalist arguments to critical ones. As Jonathan Alexander et al. (2013) suggest, we may find that we open up innovative and creative pedagogical approaches when we can "recognize and grapple with the emotional dimensions of reading and reading as a practice of often chaotic and associative inquiry" (p. 46). Indeed, understanding that reading is, in their words, "a complex jumble of feeling, thinking, choosing, happenstance, and embodiment" we may even be able to reinstate the playfulness of reading for our students, even if that reading isn't always just for entertainment or pleasure (Alexander et al., p. 46).

If we're not attentive to material conditions, we may lose sight of how to reach our students where they are. One way we can do that with reading on-screen is to help students think through what kinds of things they have enjoyed reading on-screen. We may ask them to consider what strategies they've used to get invested in things they might have read on-screen, from online fanfiction based on their favorite books and movies to discussion forum postings on news aggregate sites to listicle quizzes on entertainment sites. Although some of the strategies they might use to read in those spaces will not transfer to reading intellectually demanding scholarship, bringing their associations with digital reading out into the open will help them compare, contrast, and make connections. It may be equally as powerful to ask students to share negative emotional experiences of reading, either on-screen or in print. After all, many academic reading experiences induce stress, anxiety, confusion, and frustration. To what extent might these feelings also impact willingness to adopt reading behaviors and engagements in different material spaces? Beyond listening to and engaging with these negative experiences, instructors may also find it valuable and productive to help students conceive of strategies for working through negative emotions around reading in different spaces.

Understanding how emotions in one space may impact emotions in another can make students more aware of how they're feeling when they encounter reading in new spaces. The goal is not for students to decide they prefer or have greater attachment to e-books than to print books (or vice versa). Rather, the goal is to develop an awareness of emotions rather than to force one emotional perspective on reading over another.

The relationship between material objects and our physical selves is important to linger on as we consider not only how material objects make us adopt different attitudes toward reading, but also how material objects impact our cognitive abilities to engage with different sets of readings. That's what our next chapter covers: Can our brains adapt to reading on-screen? And if our brains can adapt, do we lose the ability to read deeply or engage in a sustained way with long and complicated texts? Even if we can find ourselves emotionally invested in reading on-screen, will the conditions of reading on-screen change how we read from a neurological perspective?

CHAPTER 3

THE BRAIN ON BOOKS:

WHAT THE NEUROSCIENCE OF READING CAN TELL US ABOUT READING ON SCREENS

It is a miracle of the human brain that you can read the words typed on the page before you right now. Just think about it: a small, central portion of your retina, called the *fovea*, processes the shapes on the page and then sends a signal to your brain, which interprets them and turns them into what you consider "words." Even though our eyes are only physically capable of reading twenty words in a visual space at a time, our brains can process the words quickly enough to make sense of much larger chunks of text from there. Regardless of what language we're reading in or how we learn to read in the first place, the same parts of the brain are always activated (Dehaene, 2009, p. 71). As it turns out, every human brain is conditioned to operate in the same way because of the uniquely complex interplay between visuals and semantic meaning-making.

That said, humans were never born to read. If we were, we would all instantly know how to read the second we popped out of the womb in the same way that our brains instantly know how to process acts like responding to our parents' voices. Reading must be taught because it's a social act. But our brains and bodies have been conditioned to respond to those social acts, and biologically speaking anyway, our bodies are capable of engaging in the activity that our social conditioning catalyzes. In fact, neuroscientist Stanislaus Dehaene (2009) explains that we cannot separate cultural uptake of reading knowledge from the brain science of reading at all. That's because of a phenomenon that he identified: the *neuronal recycling hypothesis*. Dehaene's theory is that our brains manage to recycle preexisting pathways for purposes that our brains were not hardwired to do (p. 7). When the brain recognizes that a certain activity may be similar to one that it has already formed a pathway to do, the brain will recycle that existing pathway. Dehaene gives the example of how our brain's visual system has enough plasticity to allow us to recognize and interpret words, letters, and sentences, even though the visual system is not *technically* designed to decode words (p. 7). In his words, "human brain architecture obeys strong genetic constraints, but some circuits have evolved to tolerate a fringe of variability" (p. 7). That means that the brain is not a blank slate for learning new things; there are limits. But the brain is *flexible* enough that it can recycle some processes, like vision, to engage in other processes, like reading.

Cultural interventions push the brain into the recycling process Dehaene describes. Maryanne Wolf (2018) clarifies that although reading may emerge from our brain's ability to recycle particular processes, oral communication is, in fact, hardwired (p. 17). Our hardwired language abilities can be recycled, so to speak, but to engage in reading, our brains need instruction to coax the recycling process into motion. In Wolf's words, "we must have an environment that helps us to develop and connect a complex assortment of basic and not-so-basic processes, so that every young brain can form its own brand-new reading circuit" (2018, p. 18). Wherever we read, whether that's on-screen or on the page, to create the kind of environment that encourages the brain's ability to read, we need to foster the reading process culturally. We can't expect our brains to do all of the heavy lifting for us, even if they often give us a pretty strong assist.

For those of us concerned with how the brain responds to reading acts, the neuronal recycling hypothesis makes one thing clear: our brains may not be using the exact same pathways for reading on-screen as they are for reading on paper, but they are already recycling those pathways anyway. Because our brains are already recycling so many of our hardwired cognitive processes (like oral language) to allow us to do what's been culturally instantiated (like reading), our brains have a flexible-enough capacity to adapt to what it might mean to read in a new environment. As Paul van den Broek and Panayiota Kendeou (2015) suggest, "multimedia processing may simply be an extension of existing processes—just as additional extensions will come to exist with future developments of information technologies" (p. 111). Basically, even if we might feel like our brains are slipping away from us when we spend hours seeking dopamine rushes on social media feeds or when we feel like we can't make our way through reading a long novel, that doesn't mean that our brains are broken.

Cognitive psychologist Daniel Willingham (2017) affirms that digital devices themselves can't erase all of the complex cognitive work that our brains are capable of doing when we read deeply. His reasoning is that

> cognitive systems (vision, attention, memory, problem solving) are too interdependent. If one system changed in a fundamental way—such as attention losing the ability to stay focused on one subject—that change would cascade through the entire cognitive system, affecting most or all aspects of thought. I suspect the brain is too conservative in its adaptability for that to happen, and if it had happened, I think the results would be much more obvious. The consequences wouldn't be limited to our interest in reading longer texts; reading comprehension would drop, as would problem-solving ability, math achievement, and a host of higher cognitive functions that depend on attention and working memory (p. 172).

What Willingham affirms here is that our ability to maintain higher-order thinking is not what's really at stake if we practice more of our reading in digital spaces. Rather, it is where we are motivated to pay attention and what practices we can establish in order to sustain that motivation. We may worry about what our brains without books might look like, but what matters is why we care about our brains on books in the first place.

In this chapter, we move away from binarizing narratives around whether screens make us stupid and printed books make us smart. Instead, we examine what kinds of cognitive strategies are available to us when we read in a variety of different environments. This chapter, in fact, aims to resist what rhetorician Daniel Keller (2014) identifies as a "deterministic" narrative around the relationship between reading and technology, that "increased media exposure (and that alone) will rewire brains differently from the 'normal' wiring, which assumes all media exposure besides books will rewire the brain in a similar direction/pattern" (p. 123). After all, as we established in Chapter 1, historically, we've seen ourselves trot out the same sets of concerns about how reading technologies will change the way we think and live for centuries. Why should we fall back on those same arguments and assume that reading off of anything that is not a paper book will rewire our brains for the worse? This chapter aims to explore the beauty and mystery of our brains on books to help us better understand what is at stake when we start to open up options for reading in a variety of media and spaces.

This chapter functions largely as a literature review of the cognitive impacts of reading to help establish what we know, what we don't know, and where we can go from here. This context also shapes the pedagogical chapters to come, as we consider how what we know about the reading brain might shape how we approach our teaching. If we are to adopt digital reading practices in our classrooms, we need to be able to help our students, our administrative stakeholders, and our peers understand *why* these choices are meaningful. We need to know how our brains work in order to justify the work that we do, because our brains, quite simply, are the engines of all of our thinking.

An Inside Look: What Does Digital Reading Look Like in the Brain?

In order to understand what digital reading looks like in our brains, we first need to take a step back and understand what any kind of reading process looks like in our brains (at least in some very basic terms). For a start, there is no single region of the brain where language activity happens. Rather, several different regions of the brain activate when we're engaged in a reading task or a listening task (though it should be noted that *seeing* words activates different parts of the brain than *hearing* words does). As David Rose and Bridget Dalton (2009) describe, the brain is a "distributed processor," where, broadly speaking, its distributed systems tend to accomplish three things while reading: one system recognizes patterns, another system generates patterns, and a third system determines which patterns are important to us (p. 77). If these three systems are not activated or engaged in readers (that is, if we don't help readers decode language, apply meaning to language, and identify value in language's meaning), that's when problems with reading can occur. Fortunately, there are many pathways to engage these three systems, and they might look different for different individuals. When we throw digital reading into the equation, these systems may activate differently.

So, how does the interaction of these distributed systems make way for deep reading in particular, the kind of reading we might worry about when we worry about digital reading in the first place? I use Maryanne Wolf's (2016) definition of deep reading here to explain that

> deep reading processes *underlie* our abilities to find, reflect, and potentially expand upon *what matters* when we read. They represent the full sum of the cognitive, perceptual, and affective processes that prepare readers to apprehend, grasp, and assimilate the essence of what is read—beyond decoded information, beyond basic comprehension, and sometimes beyond what the author writes or even intends (p. 112).

This definition captures what we want students to do in higher education learning environments: to fully contextualize and describe why a piece of text matters for what they're trying to learn and understand. Engaging in these kinds of deep reading processes, however, is even less natural than the act of simply decoding itself, and developing these abilities requires sustained guidance. Wolf (2018) explains that "it takes years for deep-reading processes to be formed, and as a society we need to be sure that we are vigilant about their development in our young from a very early age" (p. 38). We can't just expect deep reading to happen because it is possible for our brains to engage in deep reading; we have to be aware of what conditions make readers amenable to engaging in acts of deep reading in the first place.

Dozens of empirical studies have been conducted over the last 20 years that have aimed to measure how well reading comprehension and retention happens from paper-based and digital-based reading environments, and the results affirm the complexity around what makes deep reading possible. Many of these studies have primarily measured comprehension of concepts from text in timed or controlled settings. For example, Anne Mangen, Gérard Olivier, and Jean-Luc Valey (2019) conducted a controlled study where they asked young adult readers (without learning disabilities) to read a 28-page fictional, plot-driven story in a limited time setting as a way to determine whether the kinesthetic and material affordances of a printed book would impact the ability to retain meaning and reconstruct the narrative components of the plot. Although they were not necessarily testing deep reading skills, they were interested in assessing memory and comprehension.

To conduct this test, one of the groups read a short mystery story in a printed book form (i.e., a codex, or what you might think of when you think of a paperback book) and one of the other groups read the same story on an Amazon

Kindle e-reader device (p. 4). Of the selected fifty participants, only two regularly read on a Kindle for all of their
reading (including literary or pleasure reading), and these
two participants were put in the test group of users who
read the story from a Kindle device. In order to assess differences in comprehension between the paper book and the
Kindle device, Mangen et al. (2019) measured factual recall
of key plot moments, asked readers to identify where in the
text particular events occurred, and asked readers to reconstruct plots. They also correlated understandings of where
readers found events in the text and how able they were to
reconstruct particular plots.

On most of these measures, Mangen et al. (2019) found
that there was no significant difference between the Kindle
book and the printed book for comprehension (p. 7). The
researchers suggest that these results reveal that reading
particular genres or types of texts (i.e., linear, plot-driven
texts like the ones from literature that they tested) are similar across media because the cognitive processes around
accessing and engaging with these texts may be the same.
Because the texts were read on a Kindle device that was
not hooked up to the internet, the affordances that we may
think of as unique to digital environments, like hyperlinks,
were not part of the reading experience, which likely also
impacted the lack of significant difference in the results.
The researchers also suggest further research that explores
the affective dimensions of reading as well as the influence
of device ownership and comfort with device usage to complicate the findings (Mangen et al., 2019).

The complex interplay of material affordances, readers'
feelings toward particular texts, exposure to particular
texts, and time spent with particular texts have been
tested in other studies too. A group of researchers at the

University of Valencia (Delgado, Vargas, Ackerman, & Salmeron, 2018) conducted a meta-analysis of research on digital reading, collecting studies published between 2000 and 2017 that concern individual, silent reading of print text (i.e., text that does not take advantage of specific features of digital reading environments, like hyperlinks or web navigation). The researchers identified 54 studies that met their criteria, which included participants from a wide range of educational levels, spanning from elementary, middle, and high school to undergraduate students and graduates/professionals.

In this meta-analysis, Delgado et al. (2018) found that the outcomes of most studies showed that paper-based reading groups tended to demonstrate greater reading comprehension than digital-based reading groups, across different sample sizes and studies (p. 34). Their investigation found that some moderating factors had a significant effect on the studies' outcomes; for example, the advantage of paper-based reading for comprehension was significantly larger when a time limit for the reading task was imposed, whereas the advantage for paper-based reading was not as great when the reading was self-paced (Delgado et al., 2018, p. 34). The finding about pacing may have something to do with the expectations around the kind of reading that can happen within a time-limited task. Putting a time limit on a task may yield shallower or more superficial readings because the learner's expectations may be to absorb and then recall superficial facts quickly rather than to take the time to study or understand a concept deeply. This finding may also tell us something about the media students are conditioned to use to prepare for timed reading tasks.

One of the most important findings that Delgado et al. (2018) discovered was related to the increase in the screen inferiority effect over the past 18 years; that is, younger readers struggled more than older readers to comprehend information from the screen than on paper, and the intensity of the struggle increased in more recent studies than in earlier ones (p. 34). Even with the increased presence of digital devices in classrooms for younger students, the ability to comprehend or navigate through a digital text is not improved by mere exposure. We likely did not need any more reasons to debunk the myth that digital natives will just be able to figure out how to navigate digital environments, but here is yet another evidence-based reason not to subscribe to the idea that students who have grown up around digital devices will necessarily know how to use them for comprehension-based reading tasks. The ways that digital reading tasks are framed is crucial, and we're clearly not doing a good enough job at any educational level.

Reader expectations around how to navigate what to read also factors into the trend that favors print-based reading. Delgado et al. (2018) noticed that the genre of the text affected the severity of the screen's inferiority too. For studies that used only narrative texts, rather than informative texts, to assess comprehension, there was no marked difference in how the media impacted readers' comprehension (p. 35). However, for studies that asked readers to comprehend informational texts, the screen proved to be more consistently an inferior option (Delgado et al., 2018). This particular finding has multiple implications: first, readers engaging with informational texts may need to develop different reading skills for different purposes. The act of engaging in passive reading, where information is simply taken in without much processing, analysis, or annotation, only works successfully for certain kinds of texts, like narratives, for remembering information.

This finding corroborates decades of reading research that students' abilities to remember information depend largely on their ability to navigate that information and the infrastructures or environments of which that information is necessarily a part (Rodrigue 2017b; Howard, Serviss, & Rodrigue, 2010). A second implication of this finding is about the design of informational texts on-screen. Specifically, texts where users tend to access information may be designed to replicate the spatial and organizational logic of a printed text, even though we know from user research that a reader's patterns of scanning information online often differ vastly from how a user engages with a printed text (Nielsen, 2006; Pernice, 2017). Although we cannot ascribe retention problems entirely to design, we want to take into account that different kinds of materials require different strategies for reading, as Mangen et al. (2019) also identified in their research.

Strikingly, clear trends about the superiority of print for retention tasks have emerged over the past twenty years of reading comprehension research. A reasonable conclusion to reach from these findings is that particular habits, behaviors, and attitudes toward reading contribute to the greater challenge that many students experience when engaging in reading for information recovery in digital environments. So, as educators, what can we do with this information?

We can't necessarily blame our smartphones, our laptops, or any of our other digital devices for cognitive change; we have to look at the cognitive strategies we can develop through social practice in combination with our biological hardwiring. Does that mean that developers of digital technologies are off the hook in terms of designing extractive and addictive devices? Not at all. In fact, as consumers of digital devices, we should still work to resist the distractions built into the designs of technologies themselves where we can. But it does mean—and this should be reassuring!—that, from the perspective of brain science, we can control our reading destinies. And part of controlling that destiny might be naming the moves that are possible in digital reading processes.

An Outside Look: What Does Digital Reading Look Like in Practice?

In 1999, communications scholar James Sosnoski noticed that he increasingly read from screens, yet he found that his colleagues often preferred to read from printed-out copies. This observation prompted Sosnoski to reflect on theorizing the differences readers might experience when encountering text on-screen *and* understanding the pedagogical adaptations that may be necessary in response. He predicted that we would have "pocket computers" where reading would often be accessible and that, as educators, we needed a working pedagogical praxis to respond to this growing need (Sosnoski, 1999, p. 161–62). Sosnoski named several characteristics of hyperreading, from *filtering* through search engine results as a reading practice and *trespassing* on digital texts by copying, pasting, and remixing written content to *skimming* and *pecking* to locate keywords and concepts actively (p. 163). Sosnoski predicted the anxiety that we would lose the ability to read deeply in digital environments, and in response, suggested that he does not see hyperreading as a corrective or even a full-blown alternative that could replace print reading. Rather, he sees hyperreading as productively augmenting print reading as multiple possible practices, creating a world where reading might take much more diverse and multiple forms (Sosnoski, 1999).

Hyperreading is a more visible practice in digital spaces, expanding our conception of what is possible, but it is also a practice that is applicable to print reading, where we can just as easily move quickly in, across, and around the vast number of texts that we may be able to access. In fact, semiotician Gunther Kress (2003) suggested that any theory of reading in digital spaces should be attentive to the multiplicity of possible reading practices. He argued that many of the practices that Sosnoski outlined, like skimming, are examples of what he calls a *reading path*. He contends that reading a page that is simply text may invite readers to start at the top-left corner, read across to the right, and then return to the left one line down. However, he suggests that texts that may include other pieces of information, like images, subheaders, and perhaps even the inclusion of audio, would invite readers to move in other pathways (Kress, 2003). Kress contends that, aside from the cultural difference that may dictate whether alphabetic text is read in a different direction (if, for example, alphabetic characters are to be read from right to left rather than from left to right), the ways that we navigate and manipulate reading pathways should be an individual choice born out of different goals and purposes. Kress expresses that concern with skimming, scanning, and other nonlinear reading pathways is born out of a "challenge to social power"; he goes on to suggest that on-screen texts open up new ways of representing information that may be more inclusive of nondominant perspectives (p. 160). In other words, Kress sees digital reading as opening up new meaning-making possibilities and inviting in new voices.

In user experience research, researchers have engaged in eye-tracking studies to see where web readers' attention gets focused when reading on-screen. Jakob Nielsen (2006) of the Nielsen Norman Group, a research-based user experience group, found, through using eye-tracking technology, that many people tend to scan web pages and phone screens in an F-shaped pattern. This pattern suggests that users first read in a horizontal movement, usually across the upper part of the content area, and then they move further down the page for yet another horizontal movement. But at the end of the reading process, readers have tended to read more vertically, scanning for information more quickly. Nielsen's study suggested that the first two paragraphs are the ones most heavily read by web readers and that the inclusion of subheads, paragraphs, and bullet points may catch users' attention when they are engaging in the F-shaped scanning behavior on-screen.

Sixteen years later, another researcher from the Nielsen Norman Group, Kara Pernice (2017), revisited Nielsen's eye-tracking research and discovered, yet again, that the F-shaped pattern is alive and well both for readers on laptop screens and on mobile phones. Yet Pernice's study complicates Nielsen's original research, as she and her team found that readers engage in a variety of other scanning patterns when reading on-screen, including the *layer-cake pattern*, which "occurs when the eyes scan readings and subheadings and skip the normal text below," the *spotted pattern*, which "consists of skipping big chunks of text and scanning as if looking for something specific," and even the *commitment pattern*, where readers do, in fact, fixate on almost everything on the page (Pernice, 2017). Pernice concludes that web design still influences how readers engage in reading and encourages web designers and user experience specialists to adopt a number of strategies when developing text-heavy web pages, including using headings and visually grouping small amounts of related content together with different backgrounds or borders. However, Pernice complicates this conclusion by explaining how the variety of patterns her research team discovered in 2017 shows that users' scanning behaviors online are dictated not only by design, but by users' motivations and the goals they are trying to achieve via the page's content. Rather than relying on the F-shaped pattern for understanding how readers interpret web content, Pernice cautions writers and web designers to "optimize content and presentation" instead of "rely[ing] on the arbitrary words that people may fixate on when they scan in an F-shape" (Pernice, 2017). In other words, Pernice suggests that writers not worry too much about developing writing or design in a way that accommodates F-shape reading, but rather, that they design writing and web pages that are attuned to the goals and purposes of readers themselves.

As user experience designers have complicated hypotheses about hyperreading, educators remain concerned about what hyperreading patterns might mean for student learning. Even if these multiple pathways for reading exist, it can be challenging to decide when to employ these options or how to best leverage them for learning. With multiple choices for deploying reading options come multiple possible pedagogies, all of which must be chosen based on the larger learning goals and contexts. For example, Katherine Hayles (2010) grapples with the conversations on reading in digital spaces, from the neuroscientific evidence to anecdotes from educators, and reaches, in many ways, a similar conclusion to Sosnoski: we must think about how we help students toggle between close reading, hyperreading, and an understanding of machinic or algorithmic reading that impacts what appears in our search engines. Applied linguist Julio Alves (2013) also worries that students who engage in hyperreading may be compelled to engage in fast information-finding, whereas accessing printed books in the library's stacks encourages the more purposeful and slow pursuit of information while also offering students incidental knowledge that fuels acts of creativity and discovery. Hyperreading as a practice, then, needs to be named as one practice that may accomplish certain reading goals while hindering others. Daniel Keller (2014) argues for the value, in fact, of breaking down the binary between slow and fast reading that often predominates conversations about what digital reading practice looks like. He suggests that fast digital reading, like Sosnoski's hyperreading, is not a problematic approach, and what we can explore is how digital reading can be viewed more on a continuum where we understand that "for certain purposes and audiences, slower rhetorics work well; for others, faster rhetorics would be more appropriate" (p. 96). In other words, even if hyperreading may feel like a temptation for students who may otherwise not be inspired to read deeply, we can help students understand the rhetoricity of their choices, and why they might choose one kind of reading practice over another in different situations and circumstances.

Janine Morris (2016) also makes a call for breaking down the binary between print and digital reading, between hyperreading and slow reading because "it ignores the incredible overlap between the reading strategies we use to read both print and digital texts" (p. 126). Just as Keller suggests that instructors should help their students recognize when slower or faster rhetorics might be appropriate for reading different kinds of texts, Morris (2016) calls for instructors to help recognize the difference between the different kinds of texts that they encounter online. In other words, she argues that we should help students understand that reading a Tweet may call for a different way of reading than reading an online scholarly article (p. 127). Plus, Morris points out that hyperreading is not necessarily unique to digital environments; skimming and scanning documents quickly is possible in either printed or digital spaces, even as digital space may facilitate hyperreading practice (p. 128). When students note that this kind of practice can happen in a variety of spaces, their practices can get productively defamiliarized. That way, they have a broadened understanding of their options for reading both in print and in digital spaces. This might not necessarily change the results of the empirical findings; indeed, reading a narrative text on paper might still be the best way to get immersed in a really great story. However, what matters is being intentional in the choice—recognizing that our brains on books might adapt to our different circumstances when aligned with our particular goals and purposes.

Now that we understand a bit more about what digital reading looks like in the brain and in practice, we'll dig into the environmental and spatial conditions that make digital reading possible. After all, our bodies always affect what our brains process, remember, and retain. The more that we can understand how our bodies impact what our brains process, the easier it might be to understand the complexity of measuring the efficacy of reading in different environments.

Looking Inside and Outside: How Our Bodies and Brains Work Together to Help Us Learn

Cartesian logic posits that our bodies and our brains operate in separate domains from each other, meaning that what we do to and with our bodies has no effect on our intellectual capacity. Although Cartesian logic has long been debunked, many of the myths that Cartesian logic generated remain. I remember in graduate school that the advice I heard most often about writing was just to sit myself in a chair and stay there until ideas developed. Sound familiar to you too? Although there is something to be said for protecting mental time and energy when completing a project, the logic that stillness alone generates ideas was born out of a kind of modified Cartesian logic. How we use our bodies to generate intellectual thought is deeply personal; our experiences vary with our bodies' differences. It is just as fallacious to assume that sitting in a chair until ideas form will be helpful for everyone as it is to think that taking regular runs might be helpful for everyone. For most people, producing creative work or cultivating intellectual focus probably requires a variety of techniques within the ranges of stillness and activity (whatever that might look like for each individual reader and writer) precisely because the brain is not just an organ in our heads.

When we develop greater awareness of the diverse ways that our brains and bodies work together, we can work to avoid using language to describe reading that may malign certain behaviors as less valuable than others. As Deborah Wolter (2018) suggests, "Viewing people through a deficit lens leads to erroneous assumptions about their ability to learn language and literacy and unwittingly creates a vicious cycle of opportunity gaps, which in turn, creates achievement gaps in our schools and employment gaps in our workplaces" (p. 107). When it comes to reading across print and digital spaces, then, we risk falling into the same kinds of opportunity gaps that Wolter describes, thereby excluding reading behaviors, experiences, and bodies.

Up until this point, we have been discussing cognition from what we might call *standard cognitive science*, a domain that philosopher Lawrence Shapiro (2011) explains tends to cover perception, memory, attention, language, problem solving, and learning via standard methodological practices, like reaction-time experiments, recall tasks, and dishabituation paradigms (p. 2). Embodied cognition builds upon some of these methods to explore how concepts like perception, memory, and attention, for example, are linked to embodied action, which broadens the methodological approaches with which standard cognitive science engages (p. 52). Understanding what *embodiment* is gets us into even deeper philosophical territory, but in short, we might understand embodiment as the experience of having a body with sensorimotor capacities and using those sensorimotor capacities to engage in psychological and cultural contexts (Shapiro, p. 52). Diving into the field of embodied cognition and all the complex work that it does falls outside the scope of this particular book, but scholars are still grappling with the full implications of examining the complex interplay of circumstances that may impact how people think and learn.

What we do know is that our brains are constantly communicating with every other part of our bodies to dictate how we experience the world: materially, physically, and, intellectually. Learning scientist Guy Claxton (2011) describes how, contrary to popular belief, the brain is not dictating everything the body does, but rather, the body and brain work synergistically. He describes how the body is, in fact,

> like a medieval moot, a meeting that can reach a conclusion only by a process of respectful and attentive debate. A "moot point" is one to which there is no easy or obvious answer and which therefore has to be referred to the moot. Much of the work of the body does have routine solutions, so no brain-based conversation is needed. But—especially in complex social worlds—moot points continually arise, and for these the central conclave is essential (p. 81).

What Claxton's metaphor of the medieval moot illustrates is that all parts of our bodies work together continuously to regulate our experiences. Much of the misunderstanding about the connection between body and brain arises from some of the conditions that have, perhaps, made the concerns with digital reading so acute: that the experience of reading on-screen is so tied simply to visual stimulation that we may feel like the experience of reading is disembodied from holding a book in our hands, for example. Claxton also describes how touch is a critical component of how we make sense of the world and that anticipating what objects feel like allows us to generate "interwoven webs of expectation that link movement to sensation" (p. 58). The sensations of reading, the ways in which the tactile information of holding a book as object and feeling the weight and texture of pages, may, in fact, be linked to our anticipations of what engaging in reading as a cognitive process feels like. Once we divorce our expectations of those tactile sensations from the experience of reading, our bodies might expect something entirely different that may not fully prepare us for the cognitive task of reading.

Space itself impacts how we remember what we read and how we experience acts of reading. For example, researchers found that readers take longer to read sentences that describe greater spatial distance or a longer period of time. Willingham (2017) uses the example of reading a text about a soccer game to illustrate this complexity. Experts and novices alike would generally know that, in a text about a soccer game, the goal would be to track events to determine if the soccer team is going to win or lose since sports contests are about wins and losses. But a soccer expert probably has an even better idea of how to track these events than the novice and a clearer sense of what details might really matter to determine the team's success or loss. In Willingham's words: "Your situation model is colored by information outside of the text, namely other relevant knowledge from your memory. If that knowledge is missing, the situation model won't be the same" (p. 124). The body and brain, therefore, work together as in Claxton's moot court model, helping the reader process not only how they might imagine the physical experience of distance and space but also how their prior knowledge and experience with spaces might impact their orientation to and imagining of that space for themselves.

When it comes to remembering what you've written down too, the body and the brain also work together. Rhetorician Christina Haas (1996) studied how writers engaged with and remembered information from something they had written on a piece of paper in contrast to something they had written in a word processor. After observing the strategies that writers used to explain the structure of their texts, from pointing at their paper or screen to moving their materials to change their visual perspective on a text, she coined the term, *text sense* to describe the mental representation of the structure and meaning of a writer's own text. It is primarily propositional in content, but includes spatial and temporal aspects as well. Although text sense—as an internal construction—is distinct from the written textual artifact, it is tied intimately to that artifact. Text sense is constructed in tandem with the written text and seems to include both a spatial memory of the written text and an episodic memory of its construction (p. 118).

Haas (1996) found that writers had stronger text sense when they examined their writing on a sheet of paper because of the ways they could interact with the artifact of the papers themselves. Developing this stronger text sense also strengthened readers' working memories of the text, and Haas concludes that "it may be that these physical interactions provide a link—via bodily interactions—between the material tools and artifacts of text production and the mental processes and representations of writers" (1996, p. 133). Haas's research demonstrates that engagement in bodily interactions can help readers and writers make sense of one's body in tandem to one's practices as a way to develop working memory.

In fact, many writing and composition scholars have pointed out the ways in which writing practices are essentially corporeal and, therefore, embodied (Dolmage, 2014; Arola & Wysocki, 2012; Fleckenstein, 1999). Hannah Rule (2017) describes how she used a process of embodied simulation with her composition students to help students understand language through "visual, spatial, motor, affective, and other sensory modalities" (p. 21). Rule (2017) led students in guided visualization exercises, where students imagined how different sentences in passive and active voice revealed and created different visions or understandings of action based on the sentence construction. For example, Rule offered a sentence—"Jim builds his daughter a sand castle at the beach"—and asked students to try and imagine the scene at the beach (p. 30). She then prompted students to think about who received *action* in this sentence, and she and her students quickly had a discussion about the relationships at play in the full scene, rather than focusing on abstract grammatical concepts, like direct and indirect objects. Rule (2017) found that "once [embodied] simulation becomes the baseline for understanding the work of sentences, new ways emerge to understand and act upon familiar writing concepts" (p. 31). Although not all instructors who engage with reading may necessarily want to unpack and embody grammar in the way that Rule advocates, her exercise demonstrates the tremendous power in offering embodied visualizations of sentences and ideas from text to help students gain understanding and recognition of concepts that might otherwise be challenging to understand in a disembodied act of reading.

Because so much of our experience of the world is tied to how we move through it, touch it, smell it, see it, and hear it, we need to acknowledge that bringing digital reading into our cognitive practice may require understanding how that sensory experience of reading on-screen may shape our understanding and processing of the information. Readers and writers alike may need to find ways to manipulate and take advantage of how a screen can alter the material conditions of a text through moves like changing the appearance of a font (from its size, spacing, and type face, to color) or having one's work read through a text-to-speech application. In fact, many disabled readers rely upon digital technologies, like screen readers and color contrast modifiers, to help them engage in sustained ways with texts that enhance their embodied engagement to form deep reading pathways (Gierdowski & Galanek 2020). And as it turns out, everyone can benefit from using these same technologies for their own reading experiences. Although some components of text sense, like flipping pages or folding paper, may not be (and really shouldn't be) fully replicable on-screen, there may still be ways to develop active material engagement with digital reading. Digital reading practices have potential for capitalizing on the deeply intertwined body-brain relationship that is critical to processing complex ideas.

Regardless of how our bodies differ, most people experience interruptions and distractions within their embodied environments. How can our bodies and brains handle learning new information if we are trying to process lots of changes or ideas at once?

Losing Focus: Distractions and Multitasking

It might be weird to think about, but your brain is changing all the time. In fact, as you read this book, your brain is changing. Isn't that strange to imagine since we can't feel or see those changes? Remember that *neuroplasticity* is a tremendous property in human brains; it is what allows our brains to change pathways and shape faster than other animals' brains. Neuroplasticity is part of what makes humans so much more evolutionarily secure than other animals; we thrive because we have been able to adapt not just physically, but cognitively.

When it comes to learning, neuroplasticity should be good news since it is what allows us to learn and apply new intellectual concepts quickly and to a variety of circumstances. What potentially makes something like neuroplasticity scary for educators, however, is that what our brains positively respond to does not entirely feel under our control. Yes, we can adapt to learn new things quickly. Yes, we can be flexible in our approaches to others. But we can also be subject to the whims of a brain evolutionarily conditioned to respond quickly to novelty and external stimuli. Our neuroplastic brains are not brains conditioned to respond to quiet and focus; they are brains conditioned to respond to noise, to light, to movement.

The dopamine rush we experience, for example, when we see notifications pop up or new messages populating our inboxes is a hardwired response to novelty and change. We may very well recognize our own patterns and experiences with the endless stimulation of scrolling through a social media newsfeed, reading interesting stories, and staring at amusing photos with no end. We know that we can't always control all of the environmental conditions that affect our ability to learn, and we can often feel powerless over them.

Our neuroplastic brains, and their desire to change in response to dopamine-inducing stimuli, also get purposefully manipulated through the addictive design of new technologies. According to writers like Adam Alter (2018) and psychologist Natasha Schüll (2014), developers of new apps know the tricks to keep our brains hooked to the tools that we use. That's good marketing and business, of course. Even developers of educational technology tools use similar strategies to try and keep us hooked and engaged with their applications or software. The language learning app, Duolingo, for example, activates our desire for novelty through notifications and small prizes and awards that learners can receive as they work through the learning modules and sections.

Duolingo's approach is known as *gamification*, and it's but one strategy developers use to hook people into apps and keep them there. Sometimes, gamification, as in the case of Duolingo, can be used for good. Other times, it can be used to keep people invested in unhealthy experiences.

When it comes to engaging with addictive technologies, we know that it's not always our fault. Again, we are hardwired to enjoy exciting, novel experiences. But the question of how these "addictive" experiences can change our ability to learn is an important one for us to grapple with, especially in light of thinking about how our brains constantly change anyway, and to a variety of stimuli, not just the addictive kind. In truth, it's challenging even for the most sophisticated neuroscientists to name exactly what the long-term consequences are of the constant changes our brain experiences. Changes can happen so quickly and in such undetected ways that measuring their effects can be challenging.

Instead, we have to pay attention to the internal signals that we have available to us and remain mindful, to the extent that we can, of how certain environments, conditions, and circumstances make us feel and how they affect our own abilities to understand what's happening in the world around us. So, how do we help our students recognize when they might be getting sucked into addictive and unhealthy engagements with their technology and also help them develop enough awareness of these responses so they can prevent them from happening?

One way that we might help students combat these engagements is by understanding that, whenever they set out to engage in a task, whether it's an academic task or not, they are likely switching between a variety of cognitive engagements. And when they switch to different forms of cognitive engagement, they are conditioning themselves to respond and behave in particular kinds of ways. Educators Douglas Hartman and Paul Morsink (2015) explain that reading, whether it is on-screen or on paper, is yet another cognitive strategy, like solving a puzzle or calculating a mathematical operation, and the strategies we use for reading naturally mutate over time, depending upon the social and environmental conditions that may make way for reading to occur. In fact, reading strategies

> can and do coexist and thrive together, side by side in an eco-system of many practices, many epistemic beliefs, many conceptions of literacy, and many purposes for reading. Coexistence is often peaceful or even symbiotic; however, some practices may also be in "competition" with others. In the latter situation, some practices will become more widely adopted and used while others may die out . . . The reading practices that prevail are simply better adapted for success in a particular environment, under particular conditions, when used for particular historically situated purposes (Hartman and Morsink, p. 82).

What is helpful about Hartman and Morsink's observation here is that digital reading may just be an evolutionary extension of reading's evolution over time. Reading on paper and reading on screens can potentially *coexist* as cognitive reading strategies and may, in fact, be symbiotic in terms of how the approaches can support and inform each other. Wolf (2018) offers similar language for encouraging us to see digital reading as yet another cognitive strategy: we have to become bilateral users of digital and paper technology in order to sustain our ability to read, and read well, in a variety of spaces. So, part of avoiding the feeling that we are being addicted to our technologies or that we're being sucked into feelings outside of our control is recognizing when, how, and why we might shift between different forms of strategies and engagements.

But all of this talk of switching between different strategies and engagements may sound a little overwhelming to some readers. It also may evoke another cognitive process that we know we are wont to engage in when we read in digital spaces too: multitasking.

Multitasking has received a lot of attention in educational research because it is often cited as a reason why students should part ways from their digital devices when doing cognitively demanding tasks. *Multitasking* refers to switching between multiple, different tasks that are unrelated to each other. That might look like reading while playing a television program in the background or reading while responding to text messages at the same time. It may also take the form of reading while folding laundry or cooking dinner. The point is, multitasking refers to balancing two or more distinct tasks simultaneously. And we've known, for years, that multitasking means that no single task will ever get completed to full satisfaction or competence.

It is not news to say that multitasking is much easier to do when you are reading in the space of a digital device than reading a paperback book. After all, when you are reading a PDF in a software application or in a web browser, a notification can pop up in the upper-right corner of the screen that will then take you to your text messages, or to a social network, or to wherever else you receive notifications. When you are reading a document in the browser on your phone, you'll see text messages begin to stream in or a push notification from the *New York Times* app. There are a lot of tempting opportunities to veer away from the task at hand when switching between distinctly different tasks is at your fingerprints. Plus, if you are moving between different sets of written materials, from an in-depth article to a text message to a Tweet, your ability to understand any of those texts will come at a significant cost to your learning. As Paul van den Broek and Panayiota Kendeou (2015) put it, "Switching between documents comes with a cost to attentional resources and hence jeopardizes the comprehender's ability to attend to related information simultaneously and, thereby, to infer meaningful connections" (p. 108). In other words, you might be able to dive more deeply into a reading when you are following a citation trail and remaining present in the idea that a particular reading presents, but if you are trying to process one reading assignment while you are attempting to read a news article or a friend's status update, your memory, comprehension, and analysis of the text will inevitably falter.

It should come as no surprise that many empirical studies have measured that students' abilities to perform successfully on exams are compromised by multitasking, which may include text messaging, taking cell phone calls, responding to instant messages, or browsing social networks (Froese et al., 2012; Burak, 2012; Harman and Sato, 2011; Smith, Isaak, Senette, & Abadie, 2011; Kirschner and Karpinski, 2010; Levine, Waite, & Bowman, 2007). In a controlled study, researchers at the University of Southern Maine (Thornton, Faires, Robbins, & Rollins, 2014) found that students engaged in tasks that required increased attention and focus were slowed down even by the mere presence of a cell phone, even if they were not using it to distract themselves from the task at hand (p. 485). These kinds of results are initially quite alarming, as they suggest that the presence of materials themselves can inhibit students from engaging fully with the content of their learning.

Some multitasking studies have been contested, in large part because it is challenging to measure what distraction might look like in the controlled environments within which empirical studies tend to take place. For example, Eyal Ophir, Clifford Nass, and Anthony Wagner (2009) found that users who engaged in chronic media multitasking, or a constant switching between tasks on different media devices, tend to privilege exploratory information processing rather than the attentional control of a single task (p. 15585). However, when Wisnu Wiradhany and Mark Nieuwenstein (2017) replicated Ophir et al.'s study, only three of their seven tests replicated Ophir et al.'s findings (p. 2629). In fact, they did not find that chronic media multitaskers were any more vulnerable to distraction than those focused on a single task (p. 2629). Wiradhany and Nieuwenstein went on to conduct a meta-analysis of other existing literature on media multitasking and distractibility and found that the links were also relatively insignificant (p. 2639). This work does not necessarily mean that media multitasking *isn't* a problem for all students (it is), but that we should take the findings from controlled studies with an understanding of their contexts and limitations.

Other kinds of reading behaviors, like task switching and background multitasking conditions, may also be valuable for us to examine to develop a more nuanced understanding of the different forms that reading can take. For example, Lin Workaday, Tip Robertson, and Jennifer Lee (2009) found that expert and intermediate-level readers actually performed better on reading comprehension exams when there were background multitasking conditions, which included reading with a video playing in the background (p. 179). Although having a video playing in the background while a student is reading is fundamentally a different circumstance than multitasking proper, it is evidence that reading itself may not always look like silent concentration. To that end, Lin et. al (2009) contend that "it is possible that people perform better in an environment when they have more control and flexibility, and are more comfortable and confident. The media multitasking, therefore, becomes part of the individual comfort and control for learning and performance" (p. 182).

Researchers at Central Connecticut State University (Bowman, Levine, Waite, & Gendron, 2010) corroborated Lin et al.'s findings by exploring how a range of readers, from experts to novices, performed better on reading comprehension exams with varying levels of distraction during their reading process. They found that, although students took longer to read a text while they were being instant messaged, their performance on a test measuring comprehension of the reading did not suffer as a result (p. 932). What this suggests is not that engaging in instant messaging while reading is necessarily recommended, but that students can task switch without significantly impairing comprehension outcomes. Of course, as Bowman et al. (2010) caution, the lengthened time that students take to engage in the reading task while distracted suggests that significant costs to engaging in distractions while attempting to read remain. Multitasking itself remains a cognitively inferior approach, but students' agency over constructing their reading environment matters.

When students develop the agency to question, consider, and critique their means of learning, they tend to engage in deeper academic performances. In 2017, Maura Smale and Mariana Regaldo conducted surveys and interviews with students within the CUNY system and discovered that the students who earned the highest grades and felt the most connected to their academic work were also those who constructed holistic views of what Smale and Regaldo call their *academic taskscapes*. These academic taskscapes refer to choices around which devices students used to complete their schoolwork and when they used those devices. Smale and Regaldo concluded that "their holistic view of their taskscapes led them to make decisions about when and where to study that took into account the advantages and constraints of different locations and times" (p. 74). Encouraging students to develop the agency to make choices about where, when, and how they engage in academic work is critical to helping students foster metacognitive awareness of their learning.

In sum, we must be careful not to appropriate multitasking research to adopt a one-size-fits-all pedagogy toward our students' various reading practices. As Keller (2014) explains, "If we accept popular conceptions of attention and multitasking, instead of pursuing a more sophisticated understanding of the phenomenon, our perceptions of students' technology use may lead to ineffective pedagogy" (p. 103). Research on the reading brain has real, concrete implications for our students, and, at times, it may not be relevant to the work that we are trying to do.

It may seem simple to say that understanding the brain science of reading is as easy as understanding what helps people concentrate, retain knowledge, and analyze a text for the purposes of comprehension and engagement. However, the more that we unpack this statement, the more complicated we realize it is, as our ways of concentrating, retaining knowledge, analyzing, and comprehending texts may differ dramatically based on the social, environmental, and individual conditions that we find impact our brains. Our brains change and are impacted by the conditions around us, but not necessarily in the same ways. We cannot assume that one set of practices, one set of habits, or one set of styles will always help all people learn.

Consequences: What Does This Mean for Teaching and Learning?

I'd like to briefly acknowledge the very valid worries that we might have about the consequences of constant engagement with and access to digital reading as a cognitive strategy. After all, at this point in the chapter, you might be starting to wonder how we maintain our awareness of our environments and our shifting concerns with the affordances and limitations of those environments at all times. This awareness requires immense maturity and metacognitive development. Journalist Michael Harris (2014), in his book *The End of Absence*, describes how exhausting it is to become "responsible for the media diets of our children in a way that past generations never were. Since our children are privy to a superabundance of media, we now need to proactively engineer moments of absence for them. We cannot afford to count on accidental absence any more than we can count on accidental veggies at dinner" (39). Harris worries, then, that if adults do not manufacture moments of absence or disconnection from devices for children, they may not stumble into those moments quite as readily and may, instead, remain online, hooked to digital screens and devices without ever unplugging or accessing the range of options that both printed and digital reading make available to them.

The response to this concern brings us back to understanding that our brains and our bodies are connected. Yes, our brains absolutely are going to be altered when our necks are craned downward to stare at our phones all the time. Yes, our brains will absolutely be changed if we spend all of our waking hours curled over a keyboard at our desks. So, regulating reading habits is about drawing awareness to these activities. When we can help students to access and find themselves in different physical environments as often as possible, we can make space for the different kinds of intellectual experiences that reading across both printed and digital spaces may afford them.

Reminding students of reading's purpose and how our embodied experiences of reading may impact our purposes may also be a helpful practice. Broadly speaking, when we read, why are we reading? Who are we reading for? What work do we want reading to do for us? When we are able to answer these questions for ourselves, we can develop an even clearer sense of what tools—and their affordances and limitations—can do for us. Recognizing our purposes cannot always be the answer to curtailing feelings of being addicted to our technologies, but it can, at least, help us recognize why we're engaging in particular behaviors.

Equipped with our understanding of the attitudes, histories, and science that impact why and how we read, we can now consider how we bring these perspectives into our classroom. What does it look like to bring what we know into pedagogical spaces? That's what we explore in the second part of this book as we consider how to apply a digital reading framework to the ways that we engage our students in reading experiences.

PART 2

DIVE

EXPLORING THE DIGITAL READING

FRAMEWORK TO PROMOTE DEEP

READING PRACTICES

AN INTRODUCTION TO THE DIGITAL READING FRAMEWORK

CURATION, CONNECTION, CREATIVITY, CONTEXTUALIZATION, CONTEMPLATION

It's easy to draw a lot of binaries in our thinking about reading. We may be tempted to say that reading is good for us under certain conditions and bad for us under others. But what we've also seen in the chapters up until this point is that these binaries can just as easily be disrupted. We come by our assumptions about good and bad reading honestly. We may be drawing upon our own experiences or relying upon teacher lore to advance our understanding of what good reading should look like. Plus, assumptions tend to lie beneath the surface of our conscious lives. We often don't even think about why we do what we do or why we have particular preferences in our reading practices. We tend to do what we're used to doing, and it's easy to believe that everyone feels the same way. Yet in acting upon these assumptions about what good reading is or should be, we may dismiss reading practices that don't align with our own expectations or experiences.

When we say that reading can only happen in certain spaces at certain times, we're ignoring all of the students who can't read in those spaces at those times. These concerns bring the key tension of teaching reading directly to the fore: we know that reading well is important to understanding knowledge, but if we don't know exactly how to delimit what reading is, then what teaching reading well looks like can feel slippery and hard to delimit.

Although we defined what reading is in our opening chapter, it's worth revisiting the definition here within the context of teaching. As we move forward, we'll think about reading openly and inclusively as being the processing and acquiring of new knowledge, whether that's through visual or auditory modes or in digital or print spaces. As Maryanne Wolf puts it, "reading is ultimately about an encounter between a reader and another mind that leads to thinking beyond ourselves" (2016, p. 3). When we read actively, we consider not just our own positionalities, but we imagine ourselves applying what we're learning perhaps to ourselves, but also to places beyond us. To that end, when we conceive of teaching reading, we can focus on strategies that encourage students not just to absorb content, but to apply it, question it, and rethink it with the text's audience and purpose in mind.

I am not the first to name digital reading strategies as requiring unique approaches to engaging with text. Reading researchers have been tackling frameworks for reading in the digital age for quite some time. In developing a framework for digital reading in this book, I put several of these ideas in dialogue with each other so that we can fully unpack what teaching reading well across digital and print spaces and within many different disciplines may look like.

I've developed this framework with the guiding principle that the material constraints and affordances of our reading and writing technology must be central to how we conceptualize learning. We cannot escape the factors that dictate what kind of reading is possible to complete. We cannot ignore, for example, that when we read from printed books, the bindings and our ability to keep the pages flat (from curling up) may change what we're willing to read and how. We cannot ignore that when we read on screens, our eyes may strain from the blue light that projects outward. At the same time, we also cannot escape how the material factors of our reading experience shape our intellectual experience too. In a printed text, the experience of encountering written marginalia puts us in direct contact with past readers, whereas in a digital text, the experience of following a link (or even encountering digital comments or annotations) also launches us directly into a larger network of readers. Although the form of our reading does not necessarily stop us from reading anything, our material ability to access certain kinds of words, sentences, or phrases on particular pages necessarily changes our thinking and responses to that reading.

Acknowledging the material constraints and affordances of reading across print and digital spaces is, at its core, aligned with Universal Design for Learning (UDL). To accommodate the ways in which students may access learning in their classrooms or on the go, a goal of UDL can be, according to Thomas Tobin and Kristen Behling (2018), an opportunity "to reduce barriers to learning for everyone . . . we serve the broadest audience by situating UDL as a way to reach mobile learners through anytime, anywhere interactions" (p. 9). To that end, institutions have to consider how different students are able to enter into and participate in these growing choices for learning spaces.

Some instructors may have questions at this point about whose responsibility it is to give students choices about where and how they access their reading experiences, digital or not. Some educators argue that they can't necessarily anticipate all of the possible students that may enter their classroom spaces and, therefore, they cannot make multiple options for reading available to their students. To this end, I take up Anne-Marie Womack's (2017) argument that accommodation is "the process of teaching itself" (p. 494). Although a UDL framework is imperfect and risks flattening out disabled perspectives by assuming that any one universal set of pedagogies can work for everyone, Womack's case that UDL "begins closer to inclusivity than traditional design" is well taken and suggests that the more options we can give to our students, the more agency we can afford them, the more empowerment to learn we engender in them thereafter (p. 500). Inspiring this empowerment to reclaim their own learning through reading can, in turn, motivate students to read in the first place, wherever that reading may happen.

From here, I offer a brief overview of each part of the digital framework, wherein we explore some ways that pedagogical reading practice can be more attentive to the material conditions of reading and writing. I unpack these parts of the digital reading framework in the latter half of this opening chapter where I offer some mapping of the remaining chapters in Part 2.

The rest of the chapters in Part 2 take deeper dives into each portion of the framework, providing a greater understanding of how each strategy was developed and why each is effective. Each chapter in Part 2 includes examples that align with each of the strategies, too, so that you can test out a couple of these ideas in your own classes to see how they work. Not every strategy is right for each learning situation, but I'm hopeful that you'll find a thing or two here and there that may very well do the trick. You may also find that each portion of the framework may not have equal value to you, so I'd suggest starting with the overview here and then deciding how you want to proceed through the chapters ahead.

The five concepts within this framework capture five categories for engagement for readers to cultivate as they move between digital and nondigital spaces to do the work of deep, sustained, and engaged reading:

- **Curation** refers to readers' ability to collect resources, bring them together, and create new knowledge as a result. When readers are able to curate what that they are currently reading, they can make smart and mindful choices about which readings may help them understand and distinguish between different ideas. Because of the surplus of information available in search engines and online networks, the ability to curate may allow students to counteract the feeling of information overload they may experience as endemic to digital spaces. Curation is often more easily accomplishable in a digital environment than in print because digital texts can be easily copied and pasted to form new single texts. Even if text cannot be manipulated, copied, and pasted, links themselves can be aggregated in ways that allow readers to note cross-conversations in and among different texts. Curation can happen at multiple levels: students can engage in curation at the level of reading one text by culling out key concepts and creating their own *resource guides*, or interpretations, of particular readings. By encouraging students to engage in acts of curation, we help them recognize which pieces from readings are memorable, unique, and applicable for their learning.

- **Connection** refers to readers' ability to bridge what they are currently reading with prior knowledge or experiences. When readers are able to connect what they are reading with what they've read or experienced in the past, they can make deeper meaning of core content and manage to build a networked understanding of new concepts. By encouraging students to engage in acts of connection between, within, and across the readings they may encounter in digital spaces and in printed spaces, we help them understand the dialogic nature of reading itself and, in so doing, we help them capitalize upon the networks that can be formed through reading online. Digital spaces allow us to engage in connection because affordances like hyperlinking allow us materially to connect one full document to another full document (perhaps in the same way that the world's largest paperclip might). Similarly, opening multiple tabs in a browser or a PDF editor and launching multiple applications on multiple devices may allow us to move between texts to make connections.

- **Creativity** refers to a reader's ability to apply an idea from a reading and create something new as a result. When readers are able to create new knowledge based on something that they've read, they can build on what they've learned and become actively engaged in the reading process. The creation does not have to be anything big, extensive, or high-stakes: the creativity process can simply mean generating an independent thought or impression of the reading that differs from what is literally in the text, such as in an annotation. In digital spaces, readers can easily create derivative content based on digital texts. Because digital texts can be easily remixed, readers may be able to take portions of reading and move them to new places to create a response. Plus, images, videos, and even music can be integrated into text to build an understanding of reading grounded in conversation with multimedia. Beyond all of that, digital readers can quickly create diagrams, and even if they prefer to draw those diagrams by hand, those diagrams can then easily be scanned and transferred to a digital document so that the text and the image appear in one place. Although not all digital readers may want to engage in these kinds of practices, these options all exist in accessible ways to reach different readers where they are. By encouraging students to engage in acts of creativity, we help them understand that reading compels acts of writing and problem solving and that readings do not exist in a vacuum; rather, they are intended to inspire further creative thinking.

- **Contextualization** refers to readers' abilities to understand both the text's literal meaning and why the text was composed in a particular way. When readers are able to contextualize something that they've read, they consider both the content itself and the form that content takes. Readers who engage in contextualization have an awareness of the conditions and histories that shape the texts they've encountered. As more of our knowledge becomes algorithmically generated or produced by bad actors, we need to have a clearer understanding than ever of the contexts and situations for how knowledge is made and disseminated in digital environments. Without that ability to contextualize where information comes from and how information is designed and received, we may render invisible the environments that make particular kinds of writing possible. A key habit of mind for digital readers, therefore, may be to name exactly how their media impacts their messaging and what about the author's (or algorithm's) positionality and context might change what they are understanding in their texts and why.

- **Contemplation** refers both to readers' abilities to allocate attentional resources appropriately and to articulate a clear vision for why they are reading in the first place. Whatever we read (and wherever we read), we identify moments when we need to spend a greater amount of time on a single text rather than navigating or moving across multiple texts. The reasons for a single text requiring greater attentional focus vary (it may be due to text complexity, text density, or simply a text in a new discourse community or genre), but by engaging in contemplation, readers are able to discern when this attention is necessary and to practice expending that attention accordingly. Although engaging in metacognitive reflection is not unique to digital reading, it is important to identify contemplation as a strategy within our digital reading framework. Given the competing demands for attention within connected digital spaces, digital readers must develop insight into what kinds of spaces, materials, and practices are best for them to use to focus and engage with the digital text they are reading.

As educators, one of our major goals may be to help our students develop agency to make choices for their learning for themselves. Composition scholar Paul Corrigan (2013) puts it well when he expresses how he wants students to read both with depth and with distance: "We want students to distance themselves from the text in order to contextualize it, analyze it, and understand its difficulties. We also want students to be drawn into the text in order to be changed through the encounter" (p. 150). To engage in all of these processes at once, and to move across them with ease and flexibility, we may want to foster students' abilities to come to their own conclusions about what reading means for them and how to navigate the various reading situations that they are bound to encounter. After all, reading as a process is iterative; it requires that students comprehend what they've read, apply the new information they've learned, and then circle back to the reading again to see what else they may need to pick up to accomplish whatever their goals may be. As rhetorician Tanya Rodrigue (2017a) puts it: "Comprehension depends on a dialogical relationship between three sites of meaning: the meaning the reader brings to the text, the meaning embedded in the text, and the meaning the reader makes from interaction and engagement with the text. Meaning making and the triad of meaning interaction are fluid and recursive; new meaning is continuously made as the reader engages with the text" (p. 242). Reading comprehension, therefore, is not a one-and-done process; it is a challenge precisely because it demands continuously returning to the text.

It can be hard to make space to talk about reading in higher education, but if it has not yet been made clear, the stakes for doing this work are high, as they can influence how our students orient to and access learning core information critical to deepening their understanding of particular subject areas. I often tell my students as they're doing research for the first time to take what's useful and leave the rest. I offer you the same invitation as you make your way through the following chapters; read selectively for what strikes you as appropriate for how reading functions in your particular class or other context.

CHAPTER 4

· · · · · · · · · · · · · · · · ·

CURATION

When I was in college, one of my favorite things to make for a friend was a mix CD. I spent hours poring over all of the possible songs that I could burn on to a fresh, new disc. From considering the proper order of the songs to writing what to include in the liner notes for each one, I thought deeply about the role that each song would play to create the full listening experience. A typical progression might have the playlist open with something fast and peppy to catch the listener's attention, then move to songs that were a bit more pensive, usually ending with something meditative, but deeply moving. I would often even give my mix CDs names ("The Rock Out Mix," "Freshman Year Mix"). I wasn't the only one who loved making a good mix CD; my friends and I often exchanged them, and I still own many of these discs that I play in my car's audio system. Each time I listen to one, I'm always transported back to a very specific moment in my life; the CD serves as an auditory time capsule, a way to remember how my friends and I understood the world and the art within it.

I can't imagine any college students exchange mix CDs anymore (I can't even remember the last time I've even seen a disc drive in a laptop!), but creating playlists still remains a popular art online. On streaming music services in particular, songs and albums can be instantly accessed and played, and then reordered and saved according to a user's preferences. Although listening to music online may encourage listeners to seek out a song or two rather than a full album, many listeners have reclaimed the art of constructing and finding good playlists. Some music streaming services offer databases of searchable playlists where listeners can filter options by their moods ("Joyful," "Melancholy," "Peaceful") or by engaging in a particular activity ("Party!" "Workout," "Road Trip"). Some of these playlists may be generated by algorithms to align with particular user preferences, but as long as people love and care about music, I hope the act of creating playlists that perfectly match our moods, feelings, and moments will remain.

I haven't made a mix CD for anyone in a long time, which is a shame, really, because making one was, above all, quite fun. And the primary fun of making the playlist had a lot to do with the category of engagement that we're going to discuss in this chapter: curation. Deciding which songs to use, what order to put them in, and how to frame and justify the ordering is a creative act that requires both understanding a lot about the songs themselves and having a clear sense of the story that those songs may tell. There is no wrong way to make a mix CD, but therein lies the challenge: it can be pretty daunting to create a mix CD precisely because there are so many songs in the world to choose from. How do you possibly know which songs to choose at a given time for a particular experience? And how do the possible regroupings of songs and playlists change your audiences' reception of the CD?

Curation, by definition, is the ability to gather, bring together, organize, and analyze multiple, disparate things. When a user has curated these disparate things, they create one unified grouping or *narrative*. In the context of reading, a reader who identifies multiple ideas from a reading, brings them together, and creates new knowledge as a result is a *content curator*. When readers are able to curate the ideas that they are currently reading, they can make purposeful choices about which readings may help them understand and distinguish between different ideas. In other words, a successful reading curator can bring together multiple streams of thought to come to a unified conclusion about what the text means to them.

Let's think about another curatorial context to complicate what curation looks like even a bit further. When we think of curation, we may think of the professional curators who work in museums and art galleries. Their job is to create exhibits for visitors to experience a particular time period, artistic movement, or individual artist's work. A friend of mine works as a curatorial assistant at the Getty Villa Museum in Los Angeles, and when she gave me a tour of the galleries, I remember feeling very impressed with how she described the curators' decisions, from the placement of ancient Grecian urns to gargantuan bronze statues. At the time, the museum was not organized chronologically, but by theme (e.g., a gallery about women's lives in ancient Greece, a gallery about food and drink, a gallery about war, etc.). Organizing the galleries thematically, she said, proved to be a challenge for a museum about ancient history, in large part because the curators had to do some significant work to switch between the various contexts and events within which the objects and art existed. The curatorial choices at the Getty Villa not only affected what pieces of art were on display, but also how those pieces of art were organized and what text was included to describe each piece of art so that a gallery visitor could be properly oriented to the experience.

I'm drawing on examples from music and art because they concretely illustrate what curation is, but anyone who decides what and how to read is acting as a curator in some capacity. As instructors, when we put together a course syllabus and develop a reading list, curation is probably one of the main skills we practice. Because of our extensive knowledge and our backgrounds in particular disciplinary conversations, it can be easy for all of us to go a little overboard on our assigned readings; we tend to think that the hundreds of books we've read in our own scholarly lifetimes are critical for everyone to have read. But the truth is that most students will not need to read as much as we have needed to read to develop understanding. So, we wind up pruning back that collection, *curating* which pieces and which readings will be most essential for our students to understand the core concepts or theories in our particular courses. In other words, we're constructing our own educational galleries: pairing and matching our materials to create the perfect learning exhibit.

As we help our students understand that, when they read, they are making choices about what they're valuing, it is important to acknowledge that acts of curation are never neutral. Curatorial acts inherently reflect an individual's biases, perceptions, and orientations to particular topics, and the risk of curation is that we may wind up reinforcing the exclusion of marginalized voices from particular fields of inquiry. To that same end, when we invite students to engage in curation, we may also want to help them think critically about what they're choosing and what stories their curation of resources may be telling about their understanding of a particular topic. That might mean helping them interrogate the positionality of the sources they've found, recognize the methods of research conducted within the sources, and identify the time period of the sources they've discovered. This process puts our values and choices into critical check.

Curation has become a popular topic for writers on the web because so much of the activity that online browsers engage in is an act of curation. Bookmarking sites like Pinterest invite users to "pin" an assortment of online articles, from recipes and exercise routines to home décor suggestions and life hacks. When users pin these articles, they can then create curated collections of these pins so that articles of related topics can all be grouped together. Even more simply, saving articles from the web, either by bookmarking the page in a browser or by using an application or browser extension for saving articles, is a curatorial act in which users are selecting and sorting particular pieces. Even for users who simply use email and do not browse the web often, most email clients allow users to sort their messages into different folders or categories. This, too, is an act of curation.

Why is curation a particularly important reading strategy in a digital environment? Students reading in online spaces encounter streams of information from multiple spaces at any given time. From Google searches to the university library database to content from their social media streams, there is often an overwhelming number of things to read online, even when it's just for fun. Students may not even know where to begin in terms of saving and organizing all of these different pieces of information. Even as students read and concentrate on one particular source, they may encounter another link or idea relevant to their line of thinking. The student may then want to collect that related article and see if it makes sense to put the two readings into conversation with each other. At this point, they can create a curated collection of readings through organized bookmarking or for generating a references section for a school project. So, how do we help students foster ethical and creative curatorial practices as readers?

Scholarly Connections

Curating our understandings of texts is a long-established practice, though it has gained increased attention in a technological moment when it is easier to bundle understandings of texts together than before. Although reading acts like choosing to move beyond the current text midway through your reading experience in order to follow a citation trail or to reconceive a bundle of ideas you encountered may seem like a fractured, disconnected, or distracted reading experience, following up on particular, related thoughts is an essential reading and research practice. In *How Learning Works*, Susan Ambrose et al. (2010) suggest that the ways students organize the knowledge they've learned in a course can tell an instructor a lot about how they're learning and retaining that knowledge (p. 44). When instructors can support students in organizing information in their course and seeing interconnections across course readings, Ambrose et al. argue that students will "develop more flexible and effective knowledge organizations" even beyond the course itself (p. 65). Curating ideas can foster deeper curiosity and more active engagement in a topic than can simply digging deeply into one particular reading or idea.

Instructors have used a variety of technologies and approaches to help their students understand how to curate across different texts and to curate understandings of what they're finding from within texts too. In the humanities in particular, a lot of educators have devised activities to help students develop a focused understanding of how they would paraphrase, summarize, and reorganize particular texts. For example, Nancy Chick, Holly Hassel, and Aeron Haynie (2009) ask students to engage in an activity in which they draw out the themes in a set of poems and then map out where those themes emerge from overhead transparencies (p. 405). Chick et al. noticed that when the students were asked to compare their thematic mapping with those of other students in the class, their notions of the poems' meanings became more complicated; this in turn deepened their insight and their awareness of which themes were most important (p. 409). Chick et al. went on to ask students not only to make choices about what they found meaningful in a poem but also to learn to understand how others interpreted and curated meaning. By engaging in this activity via overhead transparencies on a projector, Chick et al. made the act of curation available to a limited public; keeping the curatorial act within the classroom space makes engaging in curation safe, if not fully archivable beyond the face-to-face classroom moment.

In addition to such close reading activities, other higher education instructors have designed content curation activities that ask students to conduct research and examine multiple sources as part of their research process. Paul Mihailidis and James Cohen (2013) teach communications courses in which they explain that "curation, as a critical media literacy skill in a digital and participatory context, can work on a micro-level to teach about bias, manipulation, frames, and agendas through student-driven storytelling; and also on a macro-level to teach about how information creation, distribution and reception help empower healthy civic engagement in participatory democracy" (p. 6). To teach these aspects of content curation, they used a now-defunct online source aggregation tool, called Storify, to help students generate curated information narratives. Within the Storify interface, students could aggregate Tweets, Facebook posts, and online articles to create linear stories about particular current events or topics. Through creating posts in Storify, students responded to reflective questions like these:

When is a story complete online?

What does authority mean in storytelling?

How are mainstream media reports different from peer-to-peer reports?

Can social media be effective in helping to tell a story?

How many different voices are needed for a story to be deemed complete?

How do social media enhance a story? What do they take away? (p. 10).

Questions like these not only help students recognize how a source communicates its ideas (that is, they develop a *rhetorical* understanding of source material) but also help students to understand how a variety of sources and perspectives can help us develop a complete understanding of an idea or a story.

In contexts in which both close reading and research are practiced, some educators have developed frameworks to help students understand the complexity of curation. Ryan Tracy's (2015) *curation framework* encourages curators to name the function of the sources they've curated. For example, a reader may curate a collection of sources to add value to a particular conversation or to extend awareness of a particular thought. A collection may also be used to attract someone new to a conversation or to show a particular audience how a certain concept or topic works. One way to use a curation framework like Tracy's may involve helping students think about who they're curating for and how the act of curation itself may impact an audience's perception of a particular topic, idea, or concept. Similarly, Mark Deschaine and Sue Sharma (2015) argue that there are five Cs that both instructors and students need to cultivate to become effective digital content curators:

- Circulation
- Conceptualization
- Critiquing
- Categorization
- Collection

Deschaine and Sharma say that this framework allows faculty to "be aware and become actively engaged in critical readings in their field of study and of the world" (p. 22). These researchers speak to the multistep processes that curation requires, emphasizing how the acts of collecting and deciding which resources to use are just as important as actually reading and synthesizing those sources. Sharma and Deschaine (2016) later apply this framework to teaching adolescent and adult literacy in particular, contending that "the larger audience that the Internet and Web 2.0 tools provide potentially increases and enhances the impact of assembled materials across all communities of learners" (p. 72). To accomplish these goals, they suggest that instructors consult with instructional designers about curation tools and experiment with open source resources (p. 77).

These frameworks may give rise to a variety of curatorial strategies unique to working in digital environments and accessing digital curation tools. For example, Laura Micciche (2014) explains that all reading is like using Pinterest, a platform where users create boards of pinned content related to similar themes and ideas (p. 50). Jason McIntosh

(2019) lists three different approaches to using digital content curation tools in a first-year composition course that he teaches: clipping, tagging, and annotating (p. 178). *Clipping* refers to the moment when you find something from the web and save a portion of it as a clip rather than the whole piece; *tagging* is adding a user-defined label or short phrase to something; and *annotating* is adding longer notes to a text. McIntosh has created activities for his students in which he invites students to use a particular Microsoft application (current as of 2019) called OneNote. In OneNote, students can create digital notebooks where they can save clips of particular articles, tag the clips they've stored, and annotate those clips and sources (p. 184). Although this particular application is not the only option for fostering these particular curatorial habits, McIntosh uses the example of this software to illustrate the kinds of curatorial capabilities he wishes to foster within college readers.

The K–12 space has also seen a lot of innovative teaching around content curation, particularly as K–12 educators have responded to charges to improve and develop digital literacy initiatives. The K–12 education blogosphere has been particularly receptive to sharing ideas about how to leverage browser-based bookmarking tools to help teach students curatorial skills. For example, Steven Anderson (2015) sees curation as a three-part process in which students gather, organize, and share resources online. Troy Hicks (2011) calls content curation a paradigm shift in digital reading, and, like Anderson, suggests the usage of bookmarking tools to help students keep track of sources. In fact, Jeremy Hyler and Troy Hicks (2014) suggest teaching students research skills at the K–12 level and cite source curation as a way to help students understand the basics of the research process before they get to college. Renee Hobbs

(2011) similarly advises K–12 instructors to use an introduction to the research process as a means of developing digital literacy. She describes a curatorial activity, called an *evidence chart*, where students are required to find ten information sources and list them from most credible to least credible using library and online sources. There is a lot of complexity to source evaluation as a process in and of itself, of course, which requires tapping into our fourth category of engagement, contextualization. We'll return to information literacy and developing an understanding of sources in that chapter (Chapter 7).

Identifying what's important in a reading, creating collections of various texts from across the web, and considering how and whether readings are in conversation with each other for particular audiences and purposes are all well-developed components of engaging in curation as a reading process. What are some other ways that we might engage and activate curatorial thinking as part of the digital reading framework? Let's explore a few example class activities.

CLASS ACTIVITIES

Curation activities wind up happening at about two stages of a term: at the moment when students have completed multiple reading assignments and can compare and put those reading assignments into conversation and when (or if) students conduct their own independent research. A third possible moment may occur when students are wrapping up the term and need to synthesize what they've learned as part of a final assessment. Curation activities can happen in both low-stakes and high-stakes contexts and can be adapted to a variety of texts and genres across different disciplines. The overarching goal of these activities is to help students curate collections of ideas—either within a single reading or across multiple readings—so they will have constructed their own individualized impressions of how concepts from readings are in conversation with each other or how those concepts connect to what the students previously learned in the course.

ACTIVITY #1: PIN THAT CONCEPT

ACTIVITY OVERVIEW

Students create a digital pin board where they first identify what their tags or categories are for breaking down key concepts in a reading. Then, they categorize key quotes from a single reading into these different tags. By the end of the activity, students should have a well-mapped collection of different ideas that may help guide them through a curated version of the reading.

ACTIVITY GOALS

- Isolate key terms/concepts to help curate different impressions of and approaches to the reading.
- Prioritize key ideas and understand what isolating those ideas reveals about the bigger-picture understanding of the reading.

BEFORE THE ACTIVITY

It helps to introduce the activity by showing students an example of what a pinboard looks like. Such a board can take several forms: you can show students pictures of analog pinboards, corkboards, or tackboards, which tend to be used in office or personal environments for creating assemblages of different materials. You can also show students a digital version of a pinboard by pointing them to websites where users can curate collections of resources. One example (current as of this writing) is the social network Pinterest, where users categorize different links they find online into distinct categories, like Recipes, Exercise, or Decorating. Another example (current as of this writing) is a bookmarking tool called Pocket, where users can add topical tags to organize articles that they find across the web. There may be other alternative spaces by the time that you're reading this book, but basically any example of a site (or analog tool) that allows readers to categorize and collect different types of texts and categorize them offers an example of what pinboarding can look like. You can find more examples of pinboarding-like tools in the appendix if you're still looking for other examples in digital environments.

You can introduce these examples of pinboards in either an asynchronous online environment (as part of a reading or a video that introduces the activity) or in a fully synchronous face-to-face learning environment.

ACTIVITY STEPS

1. Organize students into small groups or invite students to work individually. If the goal is for the class to come up with a shared resource, a small-group format makes the most sense. However, if the goal of the activity is for individual students to map and outline their own reading assignments, then assigning this activity as one for individuals likely makes more sense and can be done outside of class or virtually.

2. Give students access to a space where they can create collections of articles or texts to replicate what was

demonstrated for them in the prior step: the ability to categorize and cluster disparate pieces of information together. See the appendix for suggestions for pinboarding tools (current as of the publication of this text). An appropriate tool should allow students to see, in a single space, what their pin categories are and how many items exist in that category. If you do not have access to a lot of third-party, online tools, you can easily conduct this activity in an Excel spreadsheet or you can even use a paper chart, but the digital capability allows students to map and link their connections directly so that they can see how the information can be sorted online.

3. Direct each student to come up with a minimum number of tags for their pinned articles/texts individually. For example, students reading an article from the field of education might identify content tags like *student agency*, *structural inequity*, or *assessment*. Some students may struggle to generate these tags, especially before they've started the reading, so provide some tag ideas to help students in advance, depending on what you ask them to collect or categorize. In the education class, you could, for example, point to the abstract and see what kinds of key themes or ideas emerge. If there is no abstract to consult, you can also ask students to identify key themes in the class discussions or lectures prior to the reading and see what themes or ideas might be reflected in the reading itself. Another option is to scaffold the activity of developing the tags to become collaborative by inviting groups of students to brainstorm a few key words that they might use to describe some central ideas from the article they're

pinning. They can then use those central ideas from the brainstorming to develop an initial list of tags. It may help to limit the task and give students a set number of tags so that they do not feel overwhelmed. The goal here should be to get them thinking about how they can curate the large collection of information that they will encounter in their reading.

4. Once students have developed their tags, invite them to select particular quotes or citations in the reading that align with the tags that they've selected. Ask them to sort those quotes, citations, and so on into the categories to which those quotes belong.

5. When the students have completed that task, they should have a robust pinboard that collates their various findings into their curated categories. Optionally, you can invite students to reflect on what they learned from the activity through a written or oral statement. It can be helpful for students to synthesize what they learned or gained from a particular experience at the end of the activity. But the act of creating the pinboard alone and then having the resource of the categorized moments of the readings in respective pins may be enough for them.

ACTIVITY #2: CREATE A READING STORY

ACTIVITY OVERVIEW

Students create a story of their reading experience by selecting five or six moments from their time reading that stood out to them in some way, whether that was because they were confused, interested in, or even bored by portions of the reading. Students create this story by taking pictures (or screenshots) of an individual moment in the reading that elicited some reaction from them. On the picture (or screenshot), they add a caption in an image editing tool, and that caption can include texts, emojis, or other images to overlay the readings. They then weave those pictures together into one document to create their story of their reading experience for that day. The story then helps them to reengage with the text on another occasion and to have a stronger and more concentrated memory of what that reading experience means for them.

ACTIVITY GOALS

- Reflect upon and identify moments of reaction in a particular reading.
- Distinguish between different moments in the reading and isolate those moments for retention and memory.
- Offer creative and generative responses to the content in the reading.

BEFORE THE ACTIVITY

This assignment is easiest for students to complete outside of class, so if you are teaching in a face-to-face class environment, introduce the assignment in class to start with and then ask the students to complete the activity outside of class. If you are teaching this activity in a hybridized class environment, it is useful to introduce it face-to-face, but perhaps it is not altogether necessary; you can easily write and distribute assignments online. Similarly, in a fully

online class environment, you can introduce the activity
in a synchronous webinar, but you can also explain it in a
video or in an asynchronous module of written content (with
perhaps some accompanying images and screenshots or a
walkthrough video with visual examples).

ACTIVITY STEPS

1. Invite students to pick out a set number of moments
    during a reading (the number is up to you and based
    on the length and complexity of the reading assign-
    ment). For each of these set moments, ask them to
    first take a picture or a screenshot of the page they're
    reading and then add a caption to that page or screen-
    shot with their reaction to that moment in the read-
    ing. Are they intrigued? Confused? Surprised? Upset,
    perhaps? Curious? They can either add a text caption
    to illustrate that emotion or embed an emoji (or two
    or three) to illustrate how they're feeling. Encourage
    them to capture the moment and use the space of an
    image to illustrate in all of the ways that they can
    what their reaction is to reading a particular line,
    paragraph, or cluster of paragraphs on that partic-
    ular page. In other words, you are inviting students
    to think of the pages of a reading in units. If you're
    asking your students to do this activity for a fully
    online text (like an online newspaper or magazine
    article) where there aren't traditional pages or page
    breaks to divide up the content, you can invite them
    to take screenshots of particular moments or para-
    graphs in the reading. This way they are still think-
    ing of breaking down the length of the reading into
    discrete units, but the unit may not necessarily be a

page's worth of content. For the purposes of accessibility, offer students the option of recording audio reactions to accompany each moment they choose or just completing a plain-text caption (rather than using emoji or images).

2. Once students have collected their set number of reactions to the reading that they've completed, ask them to string those moments together into a linear story. This means putting all of the individual pictures together into one shared document or space (like a discussion forum, for example). Once the students have put their stories together, they should submit a brief paragraph (250–500 words is typically an adequate length) describing what they see as the ending to their reading story. What did they take away from the reading? What piece or pieces of information did they highlight in their story that they anticipate applying in another context of your class? This brief paragraph can also allow them to narrate the story, so to speak; how do they sum up the various reactions they encountered with their reading along the way? What do they make of/take away from curating these reactions in one space?

3. Invite students to post their stories in a shared classroom space, especially if all of the students are creating stories about the same shared reading. A place for sharing these stories might be in a course learning management system's discussion forum, a shared wiki, or a private class website or blog. You can also assign a follow-up activity in which students compare their attitudes across their different stories and how those attitudes influence their willingness to read and their interest in reading a particular piece.

ACTIVITY #3: WHERE IN THE WORLD DOES THIS IDEA GO? CREATING A KEY CONCEPTS MAP

ACTIVITY OVERVIEW

Students working with multiple sets of readings create a map of how the different readings are related to each other. They are responsible for clustering and mapping the readings into groupings that help them see which ideas are in conversation or have related threads to each other. Once they have their clusters sorted out, they name those clusters, identifying the key commonalities that bring them together.

ACTIVITY GOALS

- Identify similarities across disparate sets of readings and ideas.
- Look for patterns across huge swaths of information to determine shared points of connection.

BEFORE THE ACTIVITY

You can facilitate this activity either for individuals or for small groups depending on which collection of readings you'd like students to map. The primary restriction to this activity is that it needs to be conducted for multiple sets of readings; the idea is to get the students to see connections across different distinct ideas rather than having them dig deeply into one particular reading or context. This activity can be facilitated in or out of class depending on the timing and the modality of your class.

You should also decide whether you want students to find connections between readings you assign or between readings they chose to find independently for a research project. The students' orientation to the assignment is likely to differ depending on whether the readings are from an assigned single course context or are ones they're perusing as part of an independent research project.

ACTIVITY STEPS

1. Explain to your students that you will be charting shared conversations across different sets of readings. You can explore what conversations or overlapping ideas you want them to identify as a group or you can allow them to interpret the concept of a conversation for themselves to see what arises (either outcome leads to interesting discussions and still allows them to accomplish the goals of the activity!). For example, in an English literature class, you can invite students to identify the themes of any literary texts they have read. Then, you can ask students to write down these themes as possible nodes for conversation that might emerge in nonfictional and theoretical texts that they have also been reading to help them analyze those literary or fictional texts.

2. Invite students to create a map of the different readings that you assign or that they choose to connect. They can create the map on paper drawing different circles or columns to illustrate the different readings that they're clustering together. They can also use digital mind-mapping software, which has the benefit of allowing students to archive and keep track of the conversational clusters they're organizing. (See the appendix for examples of digital mind-mapping tools current as of this book's writing and publication.) The

benefits of having students map on paper is that it is a technical low barrier to entry and students are able to start and end the activity with relative speed. The benefits of having students map online is that they can maintain a record of the conversation and they have an unlimited canvas to generate the ideas that they may be brainstorming. For fully online classes, you can either ask students to submit and upload pictures of drawn mind maps or use a digital mind-mapping tool.

3. By the end of the activity, students should have a completed map of the shared connections that they've noticed. An optional follow-up to the activity includes some conversation about what students learned from creating their maps. How did finding the connections between the texts allow them to see ideas that they perhaps had not noticed in the readings before?

KEY TAKEAWAYS

- Curation allows students to manage multiple streams of information at a time.
- Practicing curation must involve some ethical interrogation of why certain texts are included as part of a reading practice.
- Curatorial practice reveals students' differing learning pathways through content.

CHAPTER 5

. . . .

CONNECTION

I've moved among a lot of small apartments in my life. Each time I move, I wind up with a task that I absolutely loathe: assembling some new piece of furniture (bathroom cabinets, bed frames, coffee tables, you name it) to fit into the space I've just inhabited. Most of these new items comes from IKEA, a chain furniture retailer famously known for its particleboard, assemble-it-yourself furniture. IKEA furniture is supposed to be easy to assemble, and small, paper booklets illustrate how each piece of furniture should come together with all of the pieces, screws, and nuts.

I've always struggled mightily to understand how to read these instruction booklets. At first, I thought the problem was that I couldn't connect the visualization on the paper to the physical supplies I had. I would look at a drawing in the booklet and think, "Wait, is that round thing illustrated in frame 1 the same thing as the round plastic screw? Or maybe it's the metal nut?" Sometimes, the connection is obvious; at other times, it takes a lot of trial and error. Beyond my struggles to comprehend the basic assembly of the furniture, I also often struggle with knowing just what the final product is supposed to look like exactly, and one wrong move can make the whole piece of furniture just look . . . off. Every piece, in other words, has to be assembled just right in order for the whole to make sense. Otherwise, I spend time doing a lot of unscrewing and prying off tiny screws, praying, in the process, that the holes in the particle-board do not become too warped from my innumerable hammering and screwing errors.

Can IKEA do anything to make its instructions clearer? Well, I'm (clearly) no furniture assembly expert, but I think that my IKEA assembly woes have a lot to do with the second digital reading practice in our framework: *connection*. When I assemble IKEA furniture, I'm constantly guessing at how one piece of the furniture connects to creating the whole piece. I have a sense of where I need to go, but as I'm assembling, I can easily lose track of what I'm trying to build. Similarly, if I'm absorbed in reading an article or a book chapter, disconnected from a particular context, class, or idea, I can easily lose sight of how it's connected to larger sets of issues, frameworks, conversations, or contexts.

In digital environments especially, connection can be a challenge both at the level of the individual text and across multiple texts. When you access a text on an e-reader, it may not be obvious how long a text is, and the internal headings for the text may not be easily scannable. Without quickly flipping through the length of the text itself, seeing how it is organized and what's to come, it may be challenging to get a sense of where the text is going or how it builds from beginning to end. Certainly, readers can scroll through a full text or swipe the digital pages to get a feel for its larger body, but that interaction may not be as accessible as it is in a bound stack of papers or a book.

Further, across multiple texts, finding connection may feel as elusive as putting together the IKEA furniture with its disparate pieces, especially if these texts are accessed, read, collected, or even annotated within multiple interfaces—from a browser window to a separate software application to an app on a smartphone. These differences in interface design of multiple texts online may make it hard to understand how the ideas are connected therein. That's not to say that interface design differences in printed documents can't also make finding connections a challenge, but the lack of what Christina Haas (1996) refers to as *text sense*, or the physical markers of differences in pages, may make seeing or understanding the theoretical and conceptual connections between different readings a greater challenge.

Connection is a strategy for building successful, engaged, thoughtful, and sustained digital reading because, in any reading spaces, readers should aim to bridge what they are reading on the page with their own prior knowledge or experience. Readers who don't practice connection may struggle in the same way that I do with assembling IKEA furniture: to further the analogy, they may be able to understand some parts of building the piece of furniture, but unless they really understand the bigger picture—what the final piece of furniture looks like—they can struggle. Indeed, just as when I'm assembling IKEA furniture and forget to put a particular screw in a particular space, a student may skip a particular reading or omit pieces of the reading if they don't see how it necessarily fits into the bigger picture for their learning goals.

Of course, there is one big difference between assembling IKEA furniture and reading: when it comes to building a piece of furniture at IKEA, there is really only one way to build the item. One wrong move, and the whole piece is off. When it comes to reading, however, there is not just one single way to connect one idea to another. In fact, multiple configurations may be "right" and offer different ways for illuminating the conversations therein. The connections still matter within and across readings; even if we can consider multiple configurations, a series of connections still needs to happen. With reading, unless we understand the context of the information we are learning and are able to connect that context to other things we know about that particular topic or idea, we may find ourselves navigating only through disconnected pieces of particleboard. So, what does it take to foster connections between and among readings?

....

Scholarly Connections

....

Before we can expect students to make connections between what they're reading and the larger scholarly or topical conversation, we first need to make our own intentions for why we've assigned a particular reading assignment clear. Composition scholar Michael Bunn (2013) argues that when instructors both explain why they've assigned a particular reading and articulate how a reading assignment will help students build upon prior concepts or work toward a new project, then instructors can help "generate motivation on the part of students to complete assigned reading and can help them to understand that reading and writing are connected activities" (p. 512). Although not all instructors assigning reading are having their students produce writing as the end product, when students see that reading is an activity that can lead to further action on their part later, it can motivate them to read more deeply and be more engaged in the reading. Indeed, when students understand that their reading can do more than just help them perform well on a test or a quiz—for example, they can also transfer that knowledge to a project, a lab report, an article, or whatever else is produced in their discipline or profession—they can pursue reading with greater intentionality and enthusiasm.

Part of helping students see how reading is connected to larger disciplinary or professional activities is helping them understand that reading, as an activity, is not just about gathering information, but is also about constructing new meaning. As Christina Haas and Linda Flower (1988) describe, "A text is understood not only as content and information, but also as the result of someone's intentions, as part of a larger discourse world, and as having real effects on real readers" (p. 170). In Haas and Flower's study comparing the reading habits and choices of first-year readers with experienced (i.e., graduate student) readers, they found that "while experienced readers may understand that both reading and writing are context-rich, situational, constructive acts, many students see reading and writing as merely information exchange: knowledge telling when they write, and 'knowledge-getting' when they read" (p. 182). The assumption that reading operates this way remains common today and is advanced by the training that many students receive in primary and secondary education around close textual reading as an isolated activity. Although developing close reading skills is beneficial to students, the pivot to seeing reading as a rhetorical act, or an act embedded in social contexts and situations, is an essential move to seeing reading as inherently a process of forming connections across theories and applications of knowledge.

Hyperlinks, a unique feature within digital reading environments, have tremendous value for making reading as an act of connection even more visible. Research spanning more than a decade consistently demonstrates that even when undergraduate students simply anticipate that following a hyperlink will help them advance a personal interest, expand upon their existing knowledge of a content area, and/or improve their prior knowledge, their comprehension of the text improves without exacerbating the cognitive load of the reading task (Hamdan, Mohamad, & Shaharuddin, 2017; Amadieu, Tricot, & Mariné, 2009; Madrid, Van Oostendorp, & Melguizo, 2009; Salmerón, Kintsch, & Cañas, 2006). Yet some studies of undergraduate student reading behaviors have shown that many undergraduates don't always recognize the relevance of following hyperlinks, even when the hyperlinks could advance their knowledge or deepen their understanding of a text in meaningful ways (Wineburg & McGrew, 2019; Azmuddin, Nor, & Hamat, 2017; Rodrigue, 2017b; Protopsaltis, 2008). Helping students understand *when* following a hyperlink is valuable to their learning is a form of engaging in connection as a digital reading strategy. Although hyperlinks might not always be relevant to a student's learning goals, they are a tool endemic to digital reading environments that could consistently help students form connections and bridge knowledge across new subject domains.

One method commonly discussed in the literature for helping students recognize reading as a process of forming connections across theories and applications is active note-taking. James Lang (2016) argues that reading comprehension can be particularly fostered through active note-taking, as it can "help [students] forge rich, interconnected networks of knowledge—ones that enable each existing piece of information in our content area to connect with lots of other information, concepts, and ideas" (p. 96). Lang cites a study by Cornelius and Owen-DeSchryver (2008) in which students who actively filled in partially completed lecture notes—and patched together content based on what they heard in lecture and read outside of lecture—performed more strongly on exams than students who received full lecture notes in advance (Cornelius & Owen-DeSchryver, 2008, p. 11). This evidence from the scholarship of teaching and learning suggests that when students are actively engaged in conceiving of what they know before and after the reading—and in how that ties into the larger context and purpose of the course itself—they demonstrate greater understanding of what reading really accomplishes: connecting a thinker to the larger world of ideas.

It may not necessarily seem like it's a college educator's "job" to teach students reading skills that enable connection, like note-taking, but many students may not acquire these skills in any other places or have access to academic skill development in this way. In a multiyear study in which undergraduates at a large, public research institution were interviewed about their college reading experiences, Tara Lockhart and Mary Soliday (2016) found that many students reported reading practices as a critical component of their ability to enter into academic discourse communities in their upper-level courses (p. 24). Lockhart and Soliday conclude that "helping teachers to understand, from students' points of view, how reading strengthens their self-awareness, flexibility, and self-efficacy, as well as their perceptions of learning integration and how to capitalize on prior learning, is an important precursor and corollary to successful curriculum development and implementation" (p. 35). Although Lockhart and Soliday primarily studied how reading and writing were incorporated into writing-specific courses, curriculum that centers reading, even outside the writing class, has a similar impact in helping students understand reading as a process in which ideas are actively engaged to projects and knowledge formation within a particular discourse community or profession. Paying attention to and pointing out how reading operates in digital environments may be all the more important to this end, even if the intervention is simply a small moment of pointing out or making visible a way of thinking that instructors may have internalized or taken for granted.

Beyond these strategies, helping students form connections across different readings may also require an even more sophisticated understanding of the contexts within which academic reading take place. Meghan Sweeney (2018) argues that if we view reading "as a process of enculturation within disciplinary communities of practice" rather than as "a skill to be mastered," students will have a stronger sense of reading as grounded in the conventions of an academic discipline, profession, or community (p. 77). Sweeney makes the case that if we help students understand who the audiences are for reading practices, we can help them make better connections between their own reading experiences and the content that they are learning as part of a particular reading activity or assignment. Sweeney, in fact, suggests that audience awareness should be considered a threshold concept for college reading. A *threshold concept*, a term coined by Jan Meyer and Ray Land (2006), refers to a concept that transforms the way a learner understands "a previously inaccessible way of thinking about something" (p. 3). Understanding audience awareness as a threshold concept for college reading usefully centers connection as part of our digital reading framework. In order for students to see how one reading fits into a larger conversation, they also need to understand who the audiences and what the contexts are for the readings with which they're engaging.

One way to do that may be through some hands-on reading activities. Donna Qualley (2019) designed an activity for an upper-division undergraduate course on literacy development where students created dynamic, multimedia maps of how they saw connections across their readings. Using a multimedia presentation-building tool, called Prezi, Qualley's students "put information that struck them as interesting or important anywhere on their Prezi screens, either as they were reading or soon after they finished. Their content might include concepts, definitions, explanations, examples, memorable points, personal connections, questions, or other commentary . . . With each reading, students frequently found themselves reorganizing earlier information as they encountered the new content, often adding ideas they had neglected or overlooked the first time or deleting stuff that seemed less useful or critical to them in hindsight" (pp. 21–22). Qualley discovered that when students completed this activity, they often actively rethought their understandings of the course readings, forming new connections and questions that allowed them to build opportunities for inquiry.

When we can help students develop an awareness of audience as part of their reading process, we can also help them clarify what effective reading practices might look like. Ellen Carillo (2019) acknowledges that knowing what active reading processes look like is a huge challenge for novice readers, and she suggests that we show students models of effective reading practices. She clarifies that "strong models of reading might include texts that have been annotated with comments that help contextualize the subject, make connections between that text and another text, define key terms, ask questions, notice gaps, fill in gaps, and recognize how the text is working rhetorically" (p. 151). She recognizes that these models may be hard to find and identifies sources such as the *Washington Post* and *Annotated Books Online* to help students recognize what different models of audience-situated, rhetorical, and active reading can look like (p. 152).

Helping students understand the purpose of their reading assignments, situating reading in the context of class conversations and key terms, and pivoting students' understanding of reading from information gathering to information-applying are all well-developed components of forming effective college readers. What might fostering these reading habits look like in the classroom? Let's explore a few example class activities.

CLASS ACTIVITIES

Cultivating connection across texts can take the form of both low-stakes and high-stakes activities and/or assessments throughout the term. The activities detailed here may work across a variety of disciplinary contexts, so they can be adapted to a variety of texts. The overarching goal of these activities is to help students make connections across the texts they may be encountering in your class, as well as to texts that may be part of the larger disciplinary conversation in the field that you're teaching. Each of these activities aims to help students build confidence in making connections so that each text they read is connected to a conversation that goes beyond the text and that helps the students understand the context of what they're reading.

ACTIVITY #1: KEYWORD SCAVENGER HUNT

ACTIVITY OVERVIEW

Students hunt for keywords that you preselect in a particular text. Once students identify the contexts for these keywords, they engage in a process of connecting the contexts of these keywords with other themes they encountered earlier in the term. By the end of the activity, students have a table where they've compared passages from the text with a log of course themes.

ACTIVITY GOALS

*   Locate key terms in context of a reading and connect those key terms with other class conversations.
*   Develop awareness of how local moments in a text can connect to global concepts and themes in a course.

BEFORE THE ACTIVITY

Before you begin, develop a list of keywords that you would like your students to identify in a particular text that students have already read. These keywords can be key terms or concepts from your field that are reflected in the reading, or they can be phrases that are particularly central for your students to know to understand a particular theory or concept. The curation of the keywords is up to you, but the goal here is to give your students words that allow them to locate passages that they can connect to prior themes they've encountered during your class.

As part of your introduction to the activity, give your students the collection of keywords. You do not want to belabor the activity itself but offer brief context for why you selected those keywords, making your own curation and selection process transparent to your students so they can understand how *you* break down readings. For example, you might share with your students how the keywords you've selected are examples of particular concepts that are central to other practitioners in your field, or that the keywords you've selected all emerge out of lecture content you've shared, or that they are key concepts that emerged from discussion section conversations that you all have had in the past.

ACTIVITY STEPS

1. Students hunt for the keywords in the digital text that you provided when you introduced the activity. They can mark the keywords using a digital highlighter function in a PDF editor, color-coding the keywords with different colored highlighters to offer them a visual map of where the keywords are appearing across the text. Offer students an alternative to color-coding, particularly students who might be fully or partially color-blind. For example, students can also select a particular shape to use as a key for the particular keywords (e.g., they may use the pencil tool in a PDF editor to draw a circle, a triangle, or a square to denote the different keyword moments they're identifying across the reading). Yet another option for making this activity accessible is to invite students to create a log or a table in an Excel spreadsheet in which they can keep track of the page numbers and passages where the keywords appear. This way, everyone has a systematic way of tracking the passages they're noting.

2. Once students complete the scavenger hunt, invite them to reflect on the connections they made between the local passages they identified and the core concepts in the class so far (especially if they took their own notes in an initial read of the text). Some guiding questions for forming these connections might include these:

   - In what ways did the passages you noticed for Keyword 1 overlap? What are the commonalities across these various passages?
   - Were any pairs of keywords connected? If so, how? What passages advanced similar ideas, concepts, or themes?
   - Select one passage connected to a keyword of your choice. How did this passage advance, change, or confirm your understanding of that particular keyword?

   This discussion may take form in multiple modalities. If you are teaching a fully face-to-face class, you may have students get into small groups to work through these guiding questions and then regroup in a large-group discussion. These questions can also be facilitated as part of a large-group discussion. If you are teaching a hybrid (i.e., partially online) class, these questions can be discussed during the *synchronous* portion of the course, whether that's face-to-face or over webinar software (i.e., a streaming video conference). If you are teaching a fully online course, these questions could be answered over a discussion forum (if you are facilitating the class asynchronously) or during a synchronous webinar.

3. Once students have reflected on the connections,

ask them to map those connections more systematically. If you are teaching a fully face-to-face class, this mapping exercise may be better conducted as a homework assignment to connect what happened during the class session with what the students do at home. If you are teaching a hybrid or online course, this may also be part of the asynchronous portion of the class session, as students may complete this connection phase at different paces. If you choose this route, ask each student to create a three-column table in a word processor or a spreadsheet: the first column includes the keyword(s) they hunted for, the second column includes passages the keyword appears in or links to such passages, and the third column names course themes or prior connections in the course (see Table 1 for an example). The first column is easy to produce. The second column can be produced either by copying and pasting portions of the passages in the PDF or by creating direct hyperlinks to the PDF so that students can jump directly to the passages they found as a reference point (creating yet another map of ideas directly from the reading). The third column is for students themselves to conceive; this is the last step for them in terms of connecting what they learned during the discussion.

4. An optional final step for this activity is to invite students to compare their tables. What common passages did students identify? Did students find the same key themes across their charts? What do the similarities and differences tell the group about the understandings of the text?

Students can share their tables in a few different ways. They can upload their digital tables to a shared cloud-based folder (e.g., Google Team Drive, Dropbox, Box, or a shared file system in a course learning management system) so that students can look at and compare each other's work. Another option for a hybrid or fully online class is to engage in a synchronous webinar during which students share their screens and walk each other through the tables they've composed. Another option for sharing the charts may be to ask students to upload their tables as attachments to a

Table 1. Keyword Scavenger Hunt Activity Example

Keyword	Passages	Course Themes
Note-taking	"These outcomes reflect the note-taking literature, which has generally reported that note-taking has its largest influence on performance through its storage function" (Morehead, Dunlosky, & Rawson, 2019, p. 773).	Memory, Materiality
	"Course policies overwhelmingly reinforced the idea that learning happens in print and face-to-face while digital technologies are only useful for accessing readings, note-taking, and communicating with the instructor outside of class, thus narrowly imagining what academic work entails" (Craig and Davis, 2019, p. 79).	
	"Tamara also preferred to annotate her readings on paper, revealing that 'it's a lot easier to jot down notes on the side.'" (Smale, 2020, p. 3).	
Cognition	"The shared margins may also afford student improvement in reading com-prehension, general critical thinking skills, and metacognition" (Sprouse, p. 43).	Memory

discussion forum in a learning management system. In a face-to-face, hybrid, or online class, students can then access the discussion forum to open and view the files, using the threaded reply feature in the discussion forum to give each other feedback on their ideas.

ACTIVITY #2: HIGHLIGHT AND LINK
....

ACTIVITY OVERVIEW
....

Students work within a digital annotation tool (either a PDF editor or a social digital annotation tool) to highlight a specific number of sentences. Each highlighted sentence needs to be accompanied by a link that the student associates with the highlighted passage: the link can be another academic article, a Wikipedia entry, a popular news article, a video, a meme, an image, or a gif. By the end of this activity, students are able to connect interesting moments they're noticing in their reading with other interesting ideas they've picked up outside of the class context.

ACTIVITY GOALS
....

- Identify and isolate key passages of interest and curiosity for further exploration.
- Link isolated passages to past contexts or associations to build connections across in-class and out-of-class learning.

BEFORE THE ACTIVITY
....

Pick a reading that you think may be challenging for your students to connect to contexts outside of your class. For example, in the writing classes I teach, I often do this activity with an article that leans more heavily on an abstract theory. I find that a theory reading, or a reading that deals with an abstract concept, is most generative because it invites students to think creatively about connections to their knowledge outside of my particular class environment. Plus, theory articles are always challenging to get into, so finding a concrete foothold in an abstract idea can help students make their way through the reading with greater ease and motivation.

ACTIVITY STEPS

1. Invite your students to highlight a few sentences in the reading you've selected for them. As the instructor, it is up to you to select the number of highlighted sentences that you want your students to identify; you may choose that number based on the length of the reading, but a general rule of thumb for an annotation assignment like this one is not to exceed more than one highlighted passage every two pages. The goal is to get students to focus on a particularly salient passage or idea (rather than a scattershot collection of too many diffuse passages/ideas), so the fewer highlights on the whole, the more effective the exercise is likely to be. In your prompt to students, encourage them to highlight passages that (a) invite them to ask a question, (b) pique their curiosity, (c) remind them of something else they learned in a different class or context, or (d) change their understanding of a concept.
2. Ask your students to include a hyperlink to one piece of outside content per highlighted section. For

example, if a student has highlighted one sentence, they have to include a hyperlink to an article, Wikipedia entry, popular news article, meme, image, video, or gif that allows them to connect the content of the reading to the text, image, or video that they already encountered prior to this reading. Along with the link, the student should offer a brief (I suggest one to two sentences) explanation of why they made their particular connection between the highlighted passage and the linked article/image/video they've chosen.

This hyperlink could be embedded in a digital annotation space in two ways. If your students are using a desktop-enabled PDF editor, they can use the sticky note function to copy and paste a link there. The students can then send the marked-up PDF back to you. A more collaborative version of this exercise invites students to include their highlights and links in a social digital annotation platform, where students can see what their peers have highlighted and linked in the same document. As of this book's writing, several social digital annotation platforms exist that have this functionality; see the appendix for a list of these tools.

3. Invite students to reflect on the experience of creating the connections between their highlights and their links. If you are teaching a face-to-face class, this conversation may happen during a class session. In a hybrid or fully online class, this conversation can happen over a discussion forum or during a synchronous chat session. This reflection can also be in the form of a privately submitted written document upload, especially if, in the reflection prompt, you

invite students to expose some vulnerable insights about their experience. The goal with this final step is to help students articulate what they got out of the experience of making the connection. This might also be a space for students to share that they did not understand the value of the connection; if this is the case, this can be an opportunity for an instructor-led conversation with the students about common reading challenges and ways to surmount them in an especially challenging text.

ACTIVITY #3: READING SIDEWAYS: RESEARCHING IN-TEXT CONCEPTS OUTSIDE THE TEXT

ACTIVITY OVERVIEW

Students pick either a person, place, or event mentioned in the text and research that *one* person, place, or term online. They identify an online resource that they think best helps a reader understand the context for that person, place, or event, and link that item into the reading. By the end of the activity, students see that a digital reading process involves making connections *beyond* the text to understand the reading's full context.

ACTIVITY GOALS

- Develop comfort with leaving a text in order to deepen understanding of the text.
- Practice information literacy by researching and understanding the context for information within a reading.

- Develop a site of inquiry into the reading via an unknown or new concept.
- Connect the main ideas of the reading with other people, places, or events beyond the reading.

BEFORE THE ACTIVITY

Invite students to identify a person, place, or event listed in the reading that they do not recognize or that they would like to learn more about. If you are teaching a fictional text, you may want to focus students on identifying a particular character or place mentioned in the novel that students can learn more about outside of the text (for example, if the person or place is derived from something nonfictional or is of historical significance).

ACTIVITY STEPS

1. Once each student has picked a person, place, or event from the reading, ask students to read *sideways* by moving outside of the reading platform that they're using (whether that's paper, a PDF reader, or some other kind of digital reading device) and into a web browser. Invite students to search for the person, place, or event online and identify an article (this could be a Wikipedia entry or some other longform expository or encyclopedic piece of writing) that helps the student learn more about the particular person, place, or event identified in the text.

2. Students then add the link to a PDF of the reading *or* to a shared collaborative working space. Such a space can include a discussion forum in a learning management system, a shared collaborative document (like

a Google Doc), or a wiki entry (a shared page that all students can edit).

3. Look at all of the sources that students find. Ask students to cluster into small groups. For example, small groups can be organized by students who researched people, students who researched places, and students who researched events. Alternatively, small groups can be formed by overlapping, content-based topics. Once groups are formed, students should compare what they found and respond to the following prompts:

   a. How did going sideways from the text affect your ability to concentrate on and understand the reading?
   b. How did the information you found from moving sideways change your understanding of a key concept in the reading?
   c. In what ways will you move sideways in the future? For this class? For other classes?

4. Engage the class in a closing reflection. Use the reflection as an opportunity to discuss how students chose the links for their chosen person, place, or event. For example, as the facilitator, ask the group questions like, "What made you decide to identify the links you chose?" and "How does seeing your peers' links alongside your links change or affirm what you're learning about this person or place?" Use the conversation as an opportunity to discuss search results and how those various search results affect their perceptions of and orientations to the reading. The variety of sources that students find suggest myriad entry points into a text, revealing the variety

of connections that can be made in and across sets of readings while also opening up opportunities for future research inquiry and investigation.

KEY TAKEAWAYS

....

- Connection invites students to see how a current reading experience builds upon their prior knowledge.
- When we can guide students to help them see how particular concepts or key terms may be identified in a single reading or as part of a shared conversation across multiple readings, we are engaging in acts of connection.
- Engaging in connection fosters curiosity in students to promote inquiry-based thinking.

CHAPTER 6

. . . .

CREATIVITY

When I was learning to sew for the first time while attending a women's retreat, my emotions vacillated between excitement, fear, frustration, and humility. I was excited to learn a new skill among friends and develop the resourcefulness to make a rather banal, but nonetheless essential, item of clothing to add to my dresser. Yet I took for granted how challenging it would be to create something new for the first time and to learn a skill for which I had underestimated the complexity. One of my friends, a master seamstress, brought all of the supplies (fabric, thread, sewing machines) for a small group of us to learn to make a simple pair of cotton underwear using a fairly straightforward pattern. Yes, you read that right: underwear was my first sewing project. For some, the project was a new challenge, while for others, it was a way to build upon prior skills. My friend gave us the precise measurements for a range of waistband sizes and even brought models of the final product so we could have a clear idea of what we were creating as we moved from cutting cloth to threading our fabric through the sewing machines.

The whole experience was low-stakes; we were just there to enjoy learning a new craft and to become self-sufficient seamstresses. And yet, I struggled mightily with the task. I couldn't quite figure out how to align the fabric with the needle in the sewing machine. I kept getting confused about where the back of the underwear was supposed to go in relationship to the front (a rather essential thing to understand to make wearable underwear, as it turns out!). In other words, even when all of the information and instruction was handed to me, I still struggled to make the end product we had decided to produce.

I wish I could say that I persevered and stuck through the challenge, but in all honesty, after hours of failed attempts, I gave up. Although I (falsely) assured my seamstress friend that I would return to the task, I had no real expectation that I would finish anything myself. To my surprise, she finished the task for me later that day. Quietly, she handed me the final product a few hours later; the underwear was a little crooked from my failed sewing attempts, but nonetheless, complete. I was touched and a little embarrassed that she finished the task for me. But I could also appreciate the kindness in her gesture and the encouragement that she implicitly gave to me. Even in my defeated moment, she helped me finish something to take home from the experience, a reminder that I had tried and could try again.

I'm always grateful when I get the opportunity to try a new craft now and then precisely because it reminds me of what the creation process feels like. When I can remind myself of what it's like to do something that requires a very different way of thinking than what I normally do (i.e., sit at a computer, read stuff, write stuff), I can put myself back in the position of being a student. Learning to create something new is not easy. It requires tremendous guidance, framing, and practice. A saving grace to the experience of sewing for the first time was that I could rely upon a pattern. Because I was a first-timer, I know I would have been lost without that framing. Plus, when you're new to sewing, you'll find that you get a lot of chances to redo your work. Mess up a seam? You can always take it out and try again. In other words, the stakes for failure in this situation were relatively low, and I could keep trying to sew for as long as my patience and energy allowed. If I were to develop greater expertise, I would probably not only make fewer mistakes, but I could also, perhaps, begin veering away from the patterns. And maybe, with even more practice, I could have finished the project entirely on my own.

When we think about becoming academic readers, we may be able to use sewing as a kind of metaphor. Specifically, if people are not used to creating new knowledge from things they have read, they may need some guiding questions, models, and ideas (just as a beginning sewer might need a pattern) to see what this process may look like. As they develop more practice responding to reading, they may be able to develop their own strategies and approaches (just as an advanced sewer may be able to deviate from patterns more regularly).

In this category for engagement in our digital reading framework, *creativity*, we can conceive of reading as a method of actively building new knowledge. Although we tend to think of reading as a primarily passive activity, one where we absorb knowledge and just let it sink in and enter our consciousness, the process of reading goes beyond simply letting ideas, stories, and facts wash over you. It's about taking those ideas, stories, and facts, and creating your own knowledge from and connections to them. When it comes to reading, we may not always see the benefit of creating something immediately after we read. Students might have various expectations of reading. Many may not think there is anything to do after reading; they may wonder why the act of reading itself isn't enough. Others may find that simply making it through a reading feels like a victory in and of itself; adding on other creative acts to the process may feel like a cognitive hurdle. And perhaps for others still, reading may simply feel more pleasurable when it simply involves kicking back and appreciating what's on the page—in other words, reading primarily for entertainment purposes.

Especially when it comes to digital reading, the act of creativity becomes more important because it is tempting to stay passive in our reading practice by simply falling down the rabbit hole of continuously recommended, algorithmically generated links that can make the reading experience feel like an endless exercise in wandering. It is hard to resist these algorithms, pause, and try to process what we just experienced instead of riding the wave of collecting endless new ideas without fully making sense of them. Even when we read off of static documents, like PDFs or word-processed documents, it may not always be clear how to engage in active annotation processes, like writing marginalia. In this case, the barrier to entry can seem high, though knowing how to leave marginalia on a static document is primarily a matter of learning how to navigate a new interface. What acts of creativity can do, then, is to help us take a step back from the passive process of getting lost in a tunnel of readings or getting stuck in a static interface and try to pause and think about what we're inspired to write, build, or consider after we've read.

I recognize that the word *creativity* may initially have something of a grandiose connotation. We may even think of an evil genius like Dr. Frankenstein cackling, "my creation!" as a lightning bolt thunders through the sky and his monster comes to life. But in this case, engaging in creativity can be much lower stakes. Responding to readings and producing something creative alongside them are not things that have to become major projects. Rather it can simply be a process that inspires new ways of thinking and learning in the reader.

Creativity, therefore, invites readers to say something, make something, or build something in response to what they just read. The more we can get ourselves to move into spaces where we feel a need to respond and in which we feel empowered to say or do something, the more we may feel moved to build and develop our own knowledge in the first place. If we can help students recognize that a part of learning to read deeply is digging into the messiness of new ideas, then we'll have accomplished some vital work toward stoking student curiosity and engagement.

Scholarly Connections

Scholar-practitioners in teaching and learning have approached acts of creativity in response to reading in a variety of ways. David Bartholomae, Anthony Petrosky, and Stacey Waite (2017) open the most recent edition of their reader and textbook *Ways of Reading* with the statement that "one of the difficult things about reading is that the pages before you will begin to speak only when the authors are silent and you begin to speak in their place, sometimes for them—doing their work, continuing their projects—and sometimes for yourself, following your own agenda" (p. 1). With these words, they frame the task of academic reading as being precisely about speaking in response to a reading, creating new knowledge rather than waiting passively to understand a text's meaning.

A common way of taking on precisely what Bartholomae et al. suggest is through annotation, or the process of responding to a reading with independent notes. More precisely, annotation refers primarily to the act of adding marginal or summary comments on a particular reading. As Remi Kalir and Antero Garcia (2020) suggest, annotation can share five common purposes: "to provide information, to share commentary, to spark conversation, to express power, and to aid learning." Yet annotation does not just have to happen with text on a page. Kalir and Garcia establish that annotation as an act can be multimodal, insofar as notes can take the form not just of words or sentences, but also of symbols, images, or even animated moving GIFs.

Annotation has a long history, and can be dated all the way back to the late seventeenth century. As cited in Elspeth Jajdelska's (2007) research on the legacy of silent reading, an educator named Thomas Fairfax suggested that his pupil, a young lord, should always annotate what he reads, advising him to

> Trust not to your Memory but put all remarkable and notable things that shall in your reading occur to you, *sub salva Custodia* of Pen and Ink, but so alter the property by your own *Scholia* and Annotations on it, that your memory may speedily recur to the place it was committed to (pp. 30–32).

Without using annotation as a memory aid, Fairfax warned that his pupil may wind up duplicating his labors, a warning that may be pretty relatable to students and scholars today! What Fairfax perhaps couldn't anticipate either are the ways in which annotation can foster the work of creating new ideas both individually and as part of a larger group in a process called *social annotation*. Individual annotation has been possible for as long as individuals have owned print books and marked them up in the margins (the term *marginalia* was, in fact, coined by Samuel Taylor Coleridge in 1819). And, of course, annotation has always been social insofar as annotations written in the margins can be stumbled across by anyone who finds a book on the shelf or out in the open. With the current ease of sharing information, including via text and online, social annotation has become all the more visible; annotations are being shared in digital platforms or spaces where readers can see comments that others have left in a dynamic, online space. Amanda Licastro (2019), an instructor who practices social annotation in her undergraduate writing courses, encourages educators to consider: "What type of annotations do we value as educators and how can we teach students to practice these habits effectively? Furthermore, how can we use annotation to promote critical reading skills that will facilitate learning and transfer to future reading situations?" (p. 88). She suggests that social annotation in particular can decenter the instructor in the annotation process and help students see their annotations as part of a larger dialogue beyond the classroom space.

Ample empirical research has been conducted to explore the impacts of annotation on learning (Miller Lukoff, King, & Mazur, 2018; Yeh, Hung, & Chiang, 2016; Reid, 2014; Sun and Gao, 2014; Gao, 2013; Kulkarni and Chi, 2013; Pargman, Hedin, & Hrastinski, 2013; Novak, Razzouk, & Johnson, 2012; Archibald, 2010; Johnson Archibald, & Tenenbaum, 2010; Nokeleinan, Miettinen, Kurhila, Floréen, & Tirri, 2003) across a variety of disciplines. For example, Johnson et al. (2010) and Hwang, Wang, & Sharples (2007) both explored students' comparisons between individual annotation experiences and social annotation experiences in two different course contexts (Johnson et al. surveyed 254 students in a first-year English composition course while Hwang et al. surveyed 70 students in an online and in a face-to-face multimedia applications course). In both of these studies, Johnson et al. (2010) and Hwang et al. (2007) found that students both preferred and tended to perform better on reading comprehension tasks when they engaged in social, as opposed to individual, annotation. As Janine Morris (2019) reflects, "When annotations are shared, students who are unfamiliar with annotation as a practice might learn new strategies from instructors or other students to apply to future readings. Students could then reflect on the differences between their reading processes and those of their classmates and be encouraged to try out new strategies going forward" (p. 117). In other words, social annotation provides rich opportunities for students to build upon the knowledge they might otherwise have developed or considered only on their own.

Results of empirical studies on annotation must be tempered with the acknowledgment that annotation is a skill that needs to be scaffolded and taught to be fully understood and applied. Carol Porter-O'Donnell (2004) describes how, in her English class, she guides students through a group activity where they use a bank of symbols to annotate a short story together. This bank of symbols helps students to identify places in the reading where, for example, key characters appear or settings are described. In the margins, students are instructed to summarize what's happening, make predictions, formulate opinions, make connections, ask questions, analyze the author's craft, write reflections, or look for patterns in the story (Porter-O'Donnell, p. 83). When she gave students these clear directions, Porter-O'Donnell found that students developed a deeper understanding of the readings they completed (p. 86). Although Porter-O'Donnell's activity focuses on giving students a key for annotation that they can use for reading and writing in print, the concept of guiding students to what they may want to look for in a reading is a critical component to helping students create new knowledge via annotation.

Models of effective active reading behaviors can be another way to encourage annotation practice or, more broadly speaking, to help students see a connection between reading and writing as methods of learning. In a survey of instructors who teach reading and writing, Michael Bunn (2013) found that many implement an assignment where instructors assign model texts to help students identify strategies for their own writing. In other words, the reading can function as a way to learn about the craft of writing itself (Bunn, 2013, p. 507). Students feel more motivated to read if they see that reading can serve dual purposes: it can help them learn new content and also expose them to clearer and effective ways of writing. This may seem like a technique primarily useful for reading in writing courses, but this model may be a powerful way to teach students about how to write in particular academic genres, like scientific articles, conference proceedings, or even graphical abstracts.

Acts of creativity can also capture some of the imaginative and affective responses to reading. In fact, Paul Corrigan (2012) suggests using painting as a way to help students engage in their reading process. Corrigan requests that his students bring paints and paper to class and asks them to paint in response to a short passage of their choice from an assigned text. He offers the students clear rationale for the activity before the painting begins, helping them see that the act of creating a painting in response to a reading may help students remember and process the text in a way that they might not otherwise find accessible with words. Although Corrigan conducts this activity in a literature class, it can just as easily be used in response to other texts the instructor wants the students to engage with beyond just information gathering or content understanding. And if we wanted to convert this kind of activity to a digital reading environment, we can replace the act of painting with having students create a visual online or with a stylus on a tablet or smartphone. Visual outlines can be easily created in mind-mapping applications, which are easily accessible and usable (see the appendix for examples of mind-mapping applications current as of this book's writing).

We can see that having students annotate readings, emulate readings based off of model texts, and create visualizations of reading are perhaps some of the most common ways we can help students engage in acts of creation before, alongside, and after reading. The beauty and challenge of engaging in such creative acts is that we and our students can move beyond these strategies in whatever ways make sense, as the goal of creativity as a reading strategy is simply to see what we can build beyond the text itself. So, what are some other strategies and approaches that we can use to encourage students to create new knowledge beyond the space of their reading? Let's explore a few example class activities.

CLASS ACTIVITIES

We can engage students in creativity throughout the term, with both smaller, low-stakes activities and higher stakes assessments. These particular activities are not designed to be culminating, summative projects, but we can certainly use them to scaffold capstone assignments or projects. In fact, you can scale all of these activities up or down in terms of what students produce depending on how you introduce the activities and how the activities fit into the larger course progression. In these activities, students have the opportunity to build or design something explicitly outside the text itself and/or to revisit ideas from within a text in a new way. These activities are meant to be generative starting points for helping students see that new ideas can be created and developed from what they encounter in their readings.

ACTIVITY #1: VISUALIZE THAT! READING INFOGRAPHIC

ACTIVITY OVERVIEW

Students create a visualization of a section or two of a particular reading that the you select. The students' task is to remediate the text-based reading content and turn that content into a visualization that may help their classmates (and them) understand the content in a different modality.

ACTIVITY GOALS

- Translate ideas from a text-based form into a visual form.
- Develop strategies for rethinking the communication of content learned from a reading.
- Showcase the diversity of perspectives and interpretations of a reading that are possible within a class community.

BEFORE THE ACTIVITY

Provide your students with a section (or two) of a reading that you think is particularly important to their understanding of the reading. Alternatively, you can ask students to choose a particular section of the reading that they thought was particularly relevant and/or useful for their understanding of the reading task.

This assignment can be facilitated in small groups, but it may be most effective as an individual task for each student to take on. Each student's own ability to interpret the reading via visual tools helps them gain an understanding of the reading in their own terms.

Students can use a number of already available tools and technologies to create digital visualizations/infographics; these range from slideware creation platforms to other third-party, browser-based infographic design tools (to see some suggestions for tools that are current as of the writing and the publication of this book, see the appendix). That said, students can just as easily draw visualizations by hand with pencils or pens and paper. Regardless of whether you're teaching a fully online or face-to-face course, you may want to give students choices about whether they'd prefer to draw their visualization by hand or on-screen. Students who create hand-drawn visualizations may need additional instructions for scanning, sharing, and/or uploading their work to a digital space so that it can be viewed on-screen alongside digitally made creations.

ACTIVITY STEPS

1. Ask students to create an *infographic* or *visualization* of the reading or section of a reading they chose; encourage them to remediate a block of text into a visually compelling form that may incorporate

symbols, shapes, and images. An alternative way to facilitate this activity may involve asking them to use a spreadsheet to chunk out disparate ideas from the section, which also allows students to dig in and think differently about the form and key ideas of a text (especially if creating a visualization within an infographic-creation tool or on a sheet of paper is not possible for some students). As another alternative, students can produce a short (a few minutes in length) audio-recorded mini-podcast about their impressions and understanding of a particular reading section.

2. When students have completed their visualizations, invite them to share their work in a designated class space where they can see each other's end products. A space like a discussion forum in a learning management system works well, as does a shared documents folder that provides space for sharing files.

3. An optional way to end this activity involves students explaining to each other the logic behind their visualizations or why they made particular choices in visualizing their course content. For a face-to-face class, a gallery walk might be an option—where students either tack hand-drawn visualizations on a wall, print their visualizations out and post them around the room, or display them on their laptop (or smartphone) screens for people to look at around the room. If students produced a mini-podcast or an audio recording, they can contribute to the gallery by playing a portion of their podcast or audio clip and explaining their choices.

ACTIVITY #2: READING TOGETHER: A GROUP ANNOTATION ACTIVITY

....

ACTIVITY OVERVIEW

....

All of the students in a class read one article together. Depending on the size of the class, students add their annotations to the text either in one space or in separate spaces after dividing into smaller groups. The students' task, using a digital annotation tool, is to add questions, comments, and/or reflections to the shared document. They can choose whether to leave their annotation in the form of text, an image, or a link to an outside resource. By the end of the activity, the text showcases the class's variety of voices and perspectives on the assigned reading, thereby making the shared dialogue around the reading visible to the class community.

ACTIVITY GOALS

....

- Develop shared community dialogue around a particular reading assignment.
- Understand the variety of strategies and approaches toward annotation as a reading practice.
- Showcase the diversity of perspectives and interpretations of a reading possible within a class community.
- Spark questions and inspire future inquiry through social annotation practice.

BEFORE THE ACTIVITY

....

Pick a text that you want all of your students to read. This may be a foundational or core reading for the course that unpacks some central theories or concepts for your discipline. Alternatively, this can be a reading that you think will inspire conversation in some way, perhaps because the reading frames questions for the readers to consider or because the topic typically invites discussion or has been a subject of past discussion.

Before you have students dive into the work of annotating a text together in one space, it is useful to establish what social annotation is and what value it provides and how to engage in respectful discourse in a social space.

To start, show students an example of what social annotation is, perhaps by showing them an example of marginalia from a used book, written by multiple people, or an example of multiple participants contributing to a shared reading on an online social annotation platform (see the appendix for examples of social annotation platforms). Ask students what experiences they've had, if any, with annotating texts on their own or annotating texts as part of a group. Then ask students to volunteer, either through an in-person discussion or through written responses, what they understand to be the role of or value in annotating publicly.

After students understand what social annotation is and what the value such an annotation practice has, offer some guidelines for etiquette and for creating an inclusive space for conversation in the marginalia. This means offering some model language for writing annotations and/or for responding to peers so that students have a sense of what the practice looks like. Alternatively, solicit a bank of ideas from students on ways to express an idea politely and respectfully.

Regardless of whether you're teaching in a face-to-face or fully online environment, make sure to identify a space for students to engage in social annotation so that the experience is as consistent and as shared as possible.

ACTIVITY STEPS

1. Ask students to complete a certain number of notes
    within the shared annotation platform. This likely
    (almost always) means that most students complete
    their required number of annotations and offer noth-
    ing further. Yet the value of assigning a set number
    of annotations is to guarantee that each student gets
    to participate equally, which is a valuable goal worth
    centering. Consider offering students a list of guid-
    ing questions to get them thinking about what they
    might want to put into their annotations. Example
    prompts may include:

    -   Which parts of the reading were the most inter-
        esting to you? Write an annotation based on the
        parts that stood out the most.
    -   Which section of the reading did you have a ques-
        tion about or not understand? Note the section
        either with a pointed question or simply a state-
        ment (e.g., "I'm not sure what this section means
        exactly.")
    -   Which part of the reading surprised you? Where
        did you learn something new? Why did it sur-
        prise you?
    -   Which part of the reading connected with some-
        thing you learned in class or earlier in the term?
        How did that section reinforce or advance what
        you had learned in class?

2. When students have completed their assigned anno-
    tations, ask them to read through their peers' anno-
    tations and make a list of the trends they noticed.

What kinds of comments did their classmates leave? What patterns did the students notice across their peers' comments? Was the class drawn to annotating similar or different sections? What do the overlapping annotations say about the class's understanding of or interest in the reading? What do the differences tell us about the class community's understanding of or interest in the reading?

3. This activity can end at step #2 in an open-ended discussion in which students process what they learned from seeing each other's annotations in a shared space. Another way to extend the assignment is to have students take the time to respond to a set number of comments from their peers, creating some dialogue between the initial annotations marked on the reading and more threaded responses marked thereafter. Some students may already be compelled to leave responses to their peers' readings in the first round of the activity, but others may be more reluctant to do so. Instituting a requirement may inspire dialogue to happen in a more sustained fashion.

ACTIVITY #3: CREATING A READING MAP VIA COLOR-CODING IN AN INDIVIDUAL ANNOTATION

ACTIVITY OVERVIEW

Using a color-coding scheme, students annotate a text in order to create a visual map of particular moves that a text is making. By giving students a color-coding scheme or key, you can help students identify what to look for when they are annotating a reading and offer them a way to create a guide that will help them review the reading later.

ACTIVITY GOALS

- Identify trends or concepts within a particular reading via a visual annotation method.
- Practice using an annotation schema that can transfer to other kinds of reading tasks.
- Compare individual annotation practices with a peer; consider how different readers may use the same coding schema in different ways, thus showing the range of interpretations available, even with a shared schema.

BEFORE THE ACTIVITY

Pick a text that you want all of your students to read. A shared text is important for this activity because each student will eventually share their annotation work with a peer, and they may have an easier time appreciating and understanding differences of interpretation if they've all read the same core text. This activity can be facilitated either in class or out of class, depending on how much you want students to engage with each other in real time. Depending on how long and complex the reading is, you may want to ask students to take space between the task of color-coding and the act of sharing their color-coding work.

ACTIVITY STEPS

1. Ask your students to use different colored highlighters in a reading annotation or PDF editing tool

according to a color scheme that you've predetermined. Here's an example: when I facilitate this activity, I give students a color code to follow. Their goal is to identify and highlight the different components of a particular type of reading they're exploring—in this case, a research proposal.

a. Introduction: yellow
b. Preliminary Literature Review: blue
c. Problem Statement/Research Question: green
d. Genre/Audience Statement: purple
e. Project Objectives: red
f. Methods: orange
g. Conclusion: pink

In this activity, I tend to pick colors that I know are accessible, even to students who may struggle to distinguish between different colors. However, as an instructor, it's important to be flexible with this activity. Letting students know that they may pick different colors than the ones you've assigned if they need to is a great workaround. The goals are mostly to get students finding, identifying, and marking the sections of a text that you'd like them to notice and having students look for the same patterns across the texts that they're reading.

For some students (especially those who may be blind or color-blind), color-coding is not a particularly meaningful way to create a reading map. As an alternative, students can also create a spreadsheet with columns labeled with the same categories as the color labels. By copying and pasting portions of the readings into the columns with the key codes you've identified, students can still learn the concept of mapping effectively.

2. After students have finished color-coding or sorting their documents, ask them to pair up and share their coding. This can happen in a face-to-face class environment, or highlighted documents can be uploaded and shared in a discussion forum space in a learning management system where the materials can be visible to other students in the class community. If students are paired up in class, they may engage in a conversation in which they justify their choices and see where their color-coding is similar or different. If this activity is happening asynchronously and in a discussion forum, invite students to write a brief reflection along with posting their annotations; in the reflection, students should explain how they decided to color-code particular sections in particular ways. Student respondents to these initial postings may want to comment on what they saw as the similarities and differences between their annotations and their peer's annotation.

3. After students finish sharing responses, invite a large-group discussion on the differences they noted. What might the differences indicate about their understanding of the text? This discussion can be a moment in which the instructor unpacks some conceptually difficult challenges or when students may be able to comment on the challenges they encountered when identifying various consequential moments in the text.

KEY TAKEAWAYS

....

- Creativity encourages students to build or create something beyond or in response to a reading.
- Acts of creativity do not have to be big to be effective; in fact, small interventions to create something new based on the task can be more effectively paired with reading assignments.
- Creativity can take many forms and the goal is ultimately to allow students to reframe what they're reading in line with their own understanding and experience of the reading itself.

CHAPTER 7

. . . .

CONTEXTUALIZATION

Rarely have I felt so out of my element as when I went to a car dealership. Although I am a frequent and capable driver, I still felt completely unprepared when I arrived at the dealership to buy a car. As a car salesperson shuffled me through the showroom and the lot, pointing out the features that he thought I would find important ("And look, this car has eight cupholders!"), I still felt overwhelmed by the technical details, the terminology, and all that I knew I did not know about what would help me make a satisfying car purchase. So, I went home and did the one thing I know how to do pretty well: research.

Yet the process for researching a new car still felt utterly baffling. I hopped online and kept desperately modifying search terms to try and find answers ("best small car," "affordable reliable small cars," etc.). I soon realized that it wasn't the search terms that were the problem: it was my inability to assess the contexts and publications of the advice articles I found. Should I trust the car ranking lists from the *U.S. News & World Report*, a brand I recognized from their rankings of colleges and universities? Or should I instead turn to devoted car magazines, like *Car and Driver*? Or maybe I should find, instead, columnists at major newspapers who write about developments in the automotive industry? I wound up reading information from all of these sources and found that their advice on what to look for in a car and what to value really differed depending on the publication itself, on who the author was (if I could find an author the article had been attributed to in the first place), and when the article was written.

Reading through the advice on what kinds of cars to buy and what to value became largely an exercise in *context decoding*: what were each of these car publications trying to tell me about buying a car and how did the values in these publications align with my own? Even when I couldn't always understand the technical specifics mentioned in some of the articles (there are a lot of acronyms in the car world that took lots of additional searching to understand), I could glean what different publications valued and how those values would drive the arguments and information presented thereafter. Some publications, for example, were clearly aimed at car buyers who wanted the flashiest, fanciest vehicles available. Other publications seemed more focused on helping buyers save some cash when purchasing their car. Others still were basically just advertisements disguised to look like editorials. I found myself becoming all too aware that sifting through basic search engine results was, perhaps, inadequate; soon I was skimming the websites for car-related publications themselves, seeing what I could find beyond the pages of generic search results.

Given my own lack of expertise and experience in understanding a car's inner workings (or the automobile industry at large), I knew that whatever research I did would probably be less informed than that of an expert. But I also knew that I had some skill in recognizing and identifying the positionality of the sources I found, and I was eventually able to amalgamate the perspectives that I deemed valuable to come to a conclusion for my purchase (combined with my own test driving experience, of course). But the experience of doing research about cars showed me one critical thing: context matters. The context for a reading—where you've found it, who wrote it, and where has it been disseminated and accessed—inevitably shapes your perspective and interpretation of what you've just read.

Part of developing a critical reading practice is understanding why a reading has been published in a particular publication, at a particular time, and by a particular author. A reader who engages in contextualization understands the positionality of a reading and how that positionality impacts the information available. Understanding a reading's context is also known as reading *rhetorically*. When we read rhetorically, we focus not just on the text itself, but on how and why the text is arranged in a particular way, and on how the author's perspective contributes to the text's construction. When we read rhetorically, we understand that a text is designed for a particular audience and with a particular purpose in mind. Knowing this context reveals the essential ways in which a text is positioned as part of a larger conversation or dialogue.

Paperback and hardback books famously give readers clues about where the book comes from and how it is connected to a piece of literary culture. A savvy reader, for example, can recognize the publisher of a book and learn something about the publishing conversation that the book is a part of. Printed books also often contain information about other books that the author has published or even a brief biography of the author herself, all signs that might help the reader understand how that book is connected to a larger context. In the case of many online texts, however, the reader may encounter a text in a completely decontextualized fashion: a reader might come across a floating PDF inside a learning management system or perhaps a blog post that they pick up from a Google search and read without fully investigating what other articles appear on the blog or who the author of the blog is. It's possible that even in print spaces, readers never really had a deep understanding of how the text they read is contextualized by larger cultures or histories. But in a digital environment, the reader may need to more thoroughly investigate the text they encounter than they would in print. Online, readers may need to do more research about the text to understand where the text comes from and why that matters to them or the larger context of professional or academic conversations.

The ability to understand, question, and critique the environments in which we encounter text is, therefore, all the more important in a digital age. Practicing *contextualization* as a digital reading strategy may involve amalgamating lots of disparate pieces of information about a text in order to appreciate its content fully. When I engaged my own students in practicing contextualization, they sometimes asked whether they "really" need to investigate all of the information in and around a source. Admittedly, engaging in contextualization can take some additional time and labor on the part of readers, especially since they may even need to return to engaging in contextualization multiple times over the course of a reading to remind themselves of their purposes and contexts for reading. But once readers begin to pay attention to where texts come from, how they are written, and why they are written, contextualizing becomes faster with time, and doing so and discovering even more about the information they are reading shapes the reading process even more centrally. Our students soon see that every decision a writer makes is shaped not just by the information immediately in front of them, but by who is crafting that information and where they disseminating it.

When I figured out which car I wanted to purchase, I felt like a more empowered consumer (even though I recognized how much more I really could have learned about cars). The example of contextualizing when getting ready to buy a car is a relatively safe one. Intellectually speaking, however, the stakes of engaging in contextualization as a critical component of a digital reading practice are really quite high. If we read text at face value and don't understand the full context of the text, we risk losing sight of how arguments in the digital age are shaped by *people*. When we lose sight of the people behind the arguments, we run the risk of dehumanizing texts and textual production. Texts, after all, emerge alongside the media and environments of their time. The more that we recognize how media distribution, circulation, and authorship are intertwined, the more thoughtful we can all be about how we understand and contextualize the texts that we encounter.

Scholarly Connections

In higher education, engaging in contextualization may not happen often because reading is commonly understood as a pathway to mastering or *uptaking* content-level knowledge (Smale, 2020; Lamb and Parrott, 2019; Myatt, 2019; Athreya & Mouza, 2017; Wolf, 2016; Carillo, 2017; Bunn, 2013; Chick et al., 2009). Christina Haas and Linda Flower (1988) acknowledge the difficulty in pivoting away from reading as a "knowledge-getting" model to understanding reading as a more complex dialogue between writers; they suggest that instructors pivot their mindset from seeing themselves as individuals who teach texts to individuals who teach readers (p. 169). When instructors can become co-readers with their students, Haas and Flower argue, instructors "can both model a sophisticated reading process and help students draw out the rich possibilities of texts and readers, rather than trying to insure that all students interpret texts in a single, 'correct' way—and in the same way" (p. 169). Although there may be cases when it is important for an instructor to help students develop basic comprehension of a text's main ideas, it is critical for the instructor to help students recognize that reading cannot be practiced in one, monolithic way; the approaches students take hinge upon their purposes for reading in the first place.

One major reason that students read is to conduct research for a class. Practices for conducting research, however, have changed significantly over the past couple of decades because of the ways that search engines, social networks, and other online databases have altered the ways that people access and understand information that they find online. According to research from the American Press Institute (2015), half of the users surveyed from the millennial generation tend to look first to search engines for diving deeply into a topic. Although some of our current undergraduate students are now considered to be younger (or older) than millennials, we may be able to safely extrapolate that these search trends still apply to our own students.

In fact, Project Information Literacy, a nonprofit research institute that conducts scholarly research on how high school and college students engage in finding and assessing current events and news online, surveyed over five thousand college students on how they access and understand the news (Head, DeFrain, Fister, & MacMillan, 2019). In this survey, students reported accessing news both for personal and academic purposes from a variety of aggregated search tools, including search engines, social media, and library databases (Head et al., 2019). It is worth noting that many students reported using social media more for personal research than for academic research, but search engine use still predominates the research work-flow. A quote from a student interviewed as a follow-up to the survey captures a typical workflow the researchers encountered: "When I just want an update on the world, I go to a news site and scroll around. When I'm fulfilling an academic assignment, I specifically search the news site or Google the topic. One is general, the other is very targeted to my academic needs" (Head et al., 2019). What this response suggests is that students are aware that news sites and search engines have different purposes, but students still have room to grow toward understanding the nuances behind the results that may appear within different search engines or when they use different sets of key search terms.

Search engines allow us to see a variety of results, pruned from an algorithm that may or may not be aligned with our particular interests. Although search engines may more efficiently help us find pieces of information, they do not automatically help us understand the importance of particular texts in particular environments and, more perniciously, they may reinforce cultural or societal biases. For example, Safiya Noble's *Algorithms of Oppression* (2018) is an essential read to understand how search engine results on topics about Black culture and women tend to reinforce White supremacist and patriarchal thought in disturbing ways. Although we may be largely habituated to turn to major search engines, like Google, for research results, the truth is that search engines designed by corporations for making the web a profitable space were not necessarily intended to be spaces for academic research or inquiry. I'm not suggesting that search engines are not valuable tools for reading, research, and discovery; on the contrary, we live in a golden age of information availability with tremendous access to new ideas and opportunities for inquiry. However, when we trust major, free, corporate search engines, we put faith in an algorithm that may not be designed for our intentional reading purposes. Practicing contextualization as a digital reading strategy, therefore, requires understanding how the algorithms of our search engines and social media feeds may shape the kind of content we encounter and the situations in which we encounter that information.

The Association of College and Research Libraries (ACRL, 2017) constructed a framework for information literacy for higher education that centers six core concepts for developing more mindful reading practices: authority is constructed and contextual, information creation is a process, information possesses value, research emerges from inquiry, scholarship is part of a conversation, searching involves strategic exploration (p. 8). These six core concepts center students' development of critical self-reflection as part of the research process while also establishing that an understanding of information is largely shaped by critical contexts.

Frameworks like the one developed by the ACRL can be supplemented by hands-on techniques and strategies. In a study of expert online readers' strategies (including a mix of 45 undergraduate students, PhD students in history, and professional fact-checkers), Sam Wineburg and Sarah McGrew (2019) noted that one of the most successful strategies for understanding a website's context and identifying biased information was *lateral reading*. Lateral reading refers to a practice where readers open up a separate internet browser tab or window to a search engine and look up the writer, source of publication, or organization associated with a publication on a website. Wineburg and McGrew (2019) noted that "when reading laterally, fact checkers paid little attention to features of a website like its appearance or contents. Instead, they quickly leapt off the landing page to open new tabs. Fact checkers, in short, learned most about a site by leaving it" (p. 31). This strategy is noteworthy because, as Wineburg and McGrew (2019) point out, it takes advantage of the understanding that it may be misleading to read a website closely to learn about its context. Instead, when readers read outside of the source, they are allowed to contextualize where the website or web source exists within a larger web ecosystem of digital information circulation.

In an e-book for student readers, Mike Caulfield (2017) developed a heuristic for students to follow as they evaluate sources that they encounter that invites them to use four moves: check for the author's previous work; go *upstream*, or check the source's origin, to see where the current text is published; read a text laterally by finding the source of the text itself (i.e., where it is published) and see what other people have to say about the text; and *circle back* by returning to the text itself and finding other search terms or pieces of information in it to follow through and follow up on. Caulfield, then, offers an actionable plan that builds upon the work of the expert fact-checkers from Wineburg and McGrew's study. Renee Hobbs (2018) similarly offers students some guiding questions to consider as they are evaluating a text for the first time, including "How does this message portray people and events? What points of view and values are activated?" and "How does the message reach people, and what form does it take?" These kinds of questions and heuristics invite students to consider critical questions at the core of cultivating contemplation: What is the purpose for this text and who is the audience? Julie Coiro (2015) also includes students' abilities to name an agenda in a digital reading. Specifically, she encourages a reading heuristic where readers can identify what the author wants the reader to do with the information in the reading. "Perceiving agendas rather than just assembling texts," in Coiro's words, activates greater critical thinking (p. 55).

Other scholars advocate for students to be able to justify how and why they've decided to use sources they've vetted to construct arguments or to arrive at particular conclusions in their learning. Alice Horning (2019), for example, developed an inquiry project where she asks students to take note "of how their sources contributed to the points they wanted to make, and how they related to other source materials that they had reviewed for their projects" (p. 46). Although doing this task may have meant that students slowed down to process the material they were learning, doing so also allowed them to develop a keen understanding of what a research-based citation trail is and how the writing of one text may have informed another.

Developing students' awareness of where and how texts are published may also foster in them greater awareness of how they might approach their own reading and understanding of texts for academic purposes. Johanne Diaz (2012), for example, advocates for helping students closely read digital archives in which academic and historical texts can often be found within university libraries. Diaz describes how

> the examination of primary texts in digital archives challenges students to reconsider what a book is and how it functions as a series of editorial choices; it encourages them

to make persuasive claims about the differences in the appearance of an early modern lyric when it is situated in different contexts; it enhances their ability to work independently and derive pleasure from the serendipity of the archive; and perhaps most important, it can actually get undergraduates—and teachers—to work toward a clearer and more effective definition of close reading (p. 425).

Diaz's exercise offers students an understanding of contextualizing reading on multiple levels: her activity helps students understand how accessing work within a digital archive complicates the text itself, how digital text circulation impacts reading practices, and how they can engage with books that may not be natively online, but that currently exist and are accessible in online spaces.

A huge part of conversations about how to read in digital spaces involves identifying what kinds of texts exist online and how texts get circulated and distributed in various online spaces. Tanya Rodrigue (2017a) makes the case that in order for students to adapt to reading in digital spaces, they need to understand the genre conventions for the kinds of readings that they encounter online. Rodrigue defines genre in four ways: "(1) genres are multimodal, (2) genres invite recurring reading practices . . . , (3) genres invite engagement with other genres . . . , and (4) genres are rhetorical. . . . Genre awareness, I claim, has strong potential to help students formulate a customized digital reading plan that invites the kind of comprehension needed for strong engagement with digital texts" (p. 236). These understandings of genre require students to contemplate where the reading they access online comes from and how its particular role and context online shape how the text is presented or what moves are made within the text itself.

By naming and understanding these moves, students are better equipped not only to comprehend the basic content of what they're reading, but also to name the kind of intellectual work that the text is accomplishing and how that intellectual work influences the larger meaning-making conversation of which the text is (or is not) a part.

Carolyne King (2019) similarly encourages educators to invite their students to turn to the material forms of texts to develop a critical understanding of how their engagement with these texts may be part of how they contextualize and make meaning from these texts. King designed a series of activities in which students "translate" a print-based academic text into the style, or more specifically, the genre, of a Buzzfeed article (i.e., a list with moving GIFs and images) or a Huffington Post article (i.e., a blog post) as a way of demonstrating how the design and contexts for encountering information may change and shape students' understanding of that information. In other versions of the activity, King invites students to consider how a print-based text might have be composed differently if the author had known that the text would be read on a mobile device rather than on a laptop or on a sheet of paper (p. 111). These kinds of activities, King posits, "ultimately offer purposeful strategies for helping students to recognize and theorize reading as an embodied and material activity" (p. 111–12). Knowing that reading is grounded in material experiences, as tied to particular genre moves, reminds students that the media they use in their encounters with texts might shape their understanding of the texts themselves (and, resultingly, their contexts).

For students to engage with these online genres, however, other scholars suggest that the students take a step back to consider the current educational contexts in which they are reading online and how their attitudes toward online spaces may impact what they're willing to read and why. Ellen Carillo (2019) explains that, in the early twenty-first century, students and educators are in the middle of a perfect storm about reading because of "a set of educational standards that encourage the reverence of texts and ignore the value of the reader to the reading process, the widespread use of the Internet and related technologies that promote passivity, and a political administration that releases fake news, denounces real news as fake, and provides what it calls alternative facts" (p. 137). In response, Carillo (2019) suggests that instructors adopt reflective strategies that might "help students understand that they do not randomly arrive at interpretations but that interpretations are inflected by a range of factors. Teachers might also focus on the range of different readings and interpretations (rather than coaxing students toward one) that students have developed" (p. 149). Carillo's textbook for students, *A Writer's Guide to Mindful Reading* (2017), directs these suggestions toward a student audience, encouraging students to try on a range of reading strategies that might help them develop a clearer sense of who they are as readers and how their identities as readers inflect their work as writers and, perhaps more broadly, learners.

Understanding the time, place, and purpose for the reading itself can be a complex process. Yet encouraging engagement with contextualization may foster deeper and more critical appreciation of texts, as recognizing the positionality and subjectivity of readings themselves may also clarify the purposes for encountering and reading those texts. What are some ways that we might foster these complex acts of engagement around contextualization? Let's explore a few class activities.

CLASS ACTIVITIES

Contextualization is most likely to happen at the point when new readings are introduced into a class or when students are undertaking independent research or source investigation. To that end, these kinds of activities may be best facilitated either at the beginning or middle point of a term so that students have the available skills they need to assess the readings they're encountering and to determine how these readings might shape any culminating examinations, projects, or assignments they're given thereafter. As with most of the activities in this book, these contextualization activities can be scaled up or down depending on where they appear in your course, but unlike the other activities, these particular activities may require some special disciplinary framing, especially if students are investigating or understanding the context for foundational articles in a field in which the students are novices. As you read these activities, then, you may want to consider how or whether you need to usher students into the context for what they're exploring. Doing so helps students develop burgeoning expertise in the academic or professional field in which you've identified or they're discovering readings.

ACTIVITY #1: ZOOM IN, ZOOM OUT: READING FOR DETAIL AND READING FOR THE BIG PICTURE

ACTIVITY OVERVIEW

Students toggle between reading a passage at a detailed level and at a big picture level, noticing the differences in what they learn from the text when they read in those two different ways. By the end of the activity, students should be able to recognize when close reading strategies and when big picture reading strategies are appropriate for future reading tasks.

ACTIVITY GOALS

- Develop awareness of different ways of encountering, understanding, and analyzing texts.
- Identify the strengths and limitations of close reading strategies and big picture reading strategies.

BEFORE THE ACTIVITY

You can facilitate this activity either as an in-class activity for a fully face-to-face class or as an out-of-class activity either for a fully face-to-face class or a partially/fully on-line class. The activity goals may be best accomplished when students participate in the reading activity at the individual level, though a social component is still useful for students who may want to compare their experiences.

ACTIVITY STEPS

1. Assign the students a passage to read. Because students are engaging in some close reading work, a shorter passage may be better so that the task remains manageable as a low-stakes activity. The nature and the length of the passage should be up to you, however.
2. Introduce the two different ways that you'd like students to read the same passage: close reading and big picture reading. You may need to give a mini-lecture

to explain that *close reading* means interrogating what is happening at the sentence level whereas *big picture reading* means contextualizing the content in the reading within a larger inquiry-based framework. Invite students to ask questions about these two strategies. A productive component of the conversation may include asking students to share when, where, and whether they have engaged in these strategies in other class contexts. For example, it is likely that many students encountered close reading in an English literature class, either in high school or in college, as this is a common technique in literary study. Many students may have encountered big picture reading in more of their social sciences or science classes where the content is more important than the language of the reading or the way that certain sentences are framed. As the instructor, you want to establish that both of these strategies have their merits in different disciplines. As an example, you might explain how close reading a science paper may help students better understand the methodology and the positionality of the scientific researchers and how they frame the conversation. As another example, you might explain how big picture reading an article about history may help students comprehend the main concepts or ideas that they need to understand a historical movement or context.

3. If you are facilitating this activity in class, give students a set amount of time to deploy one of the two strategies (either close reading or big picture reading). Allow students to participate in these reading strategies in whatever way they choose, whether

that's through in-text annotation and silent reading or by reading the passage aloud. The only deliverable that students should produce by the end of the allotted time is a couple of written sentences that summarize what they learned from the reading. What are the top three takeaway points that they gleaned from the reading after they employed the first strategy?

4. Next, pivot to the second reading strategy. Again, invite students to annotate or read the passage in any way that they so choose, but ask for the same deliverable: What are the top three takeaway points they gleaned from the reading after they employed the second strategy?

5. Invite the students to compare and contrast the two reading strategies. How do their takeaways on the reading differ when they do a close reading instead of a big picture reading? Are they similar? Different? In what ways?

6. Close the activity by asking students to reflect on their experience and to think ahead to how they might transfer the work that they did in this activity to future reading assignments in other class contexts. When might they use close reading in the future? When might they use big picture reading? How will they decide when to use one of these two strategies? What will influence their ability to decide which of these two strategies is potentially the best choice for understanding the content that they're learning in another class (or even a professional) context?

ACTIVITY #2: THE JOURNALISTIC INVESTIGATION: GATHERING THE WHO, WHAT, WHERE, WHEN, WHY

ACTIVITY OVERVIEW

Students treat their understanding of a reading as though they are journalists, investigating the background and context of the reading they are doing for the class. They take the results of their investigation and consider how this background knowledge of the source informs their reading of the source's content.

ACTIVITY GOALS

- Develop an understanding of a reading's author and positionality and understand how no source ever emerges from a neutral or completely objective space.
- Contextualize and frame content after coming to understand a reading's background and context.
- Articulate why understanding the background of a particular reading matters.

BEFORE THE ACTIVITY

This activity can be conducted either for one particular reading or for a variety of assigned readings. The point here is to have students think twice about the contexts for their assigned readings; the exercise's goals can be accomplished whether all of the students investigate the same source or whether different students investigate different sources. You can also facilitate this exercise either *before* the students complete the reading or *after* the students complete the reading. The sequencing may change the nature of the reflective work that this activity includes (starting at step #4), but the ability to accomplish the activity's goals is possible whether the activity is conducted before or after the source has been read.

ACTIVITY STEPS

1. Instruct students that they are operating as special investigators or journalists to further explore their readings. Explain that when many investigators or journalists are trying to get the scoop on a particular story, they need to gather the who, what, where, when, and why (aka the Five Ws) for any sources that contribute to their understanding of a story. Students are taking on the same task by investigating (a) who wrote the reading, (b) what the reading is (very briefly) about, (c) where the reading was composed (e.g., Was it published in a "born-digital" environment, like a blog or website, or was it published in a printed book? What is the original source of publication?), (d) when the reading was written, and (e) why (as far as they can tell) the reading was written in the first place.
2. Students can identify the Five Ws for the reading during in-class time if the class meets face-to-face, or, just as easily, as a homework assignment or as an asynchronous assignment (i.e., not everyone has to complete the activity at the same time). The activity may actually be more effective for students if they have ample time to do a full background check (if you will) into the source that you've assigned them;

that way, they have the space to fully understand the nature of the publication that the reading you selected comes from and have an opportunity to get to know the author of the source and the author's position on the subject. Plus, for readings students have found online, it may be especially important to give students time to figure out where the article or blog they read was originally published, especially if they found it from a news aggregator site (like Google News), a forum (like Reddit), a bookmarking site (like Pocket or Diigo), or a social media feed.

3. After students have identified the Five Ws for the reading, invite them to engage in either reflection or discussion about the value of identifying these. In a written form, a verbal discussion, or some combination thereof, invite students to consider how gathering the Five Ws for the source impacts their understanding of the source content.

   a. If students read the source *before* they gathered the Five Ws, ask them to consider how their understanding of the reading's content changed once they gathered the Five W information.

   b. If students read the source *after* they gathered the Five Ws, ask them to consider whether learning about the reading's background and context alters or shapes their understanding of the source content in any particular way. Did their understanding of the main themes or ideas of the source change at all after gathering the additional contextual information? Why or why not?

ACTIVITY #3: FOLLOW THE CITATION TRAIL: UNDERSTANDING HOW WRITERS BUILD UPON EACH OTHER'S RESEARCH

ACTIVITY OVERVIEW

When students recognize how texts often build upon past ideas, they can better understand the context of an author's particular ideas within a course reading. In this activity, students start with one assigned reading and then each uses an online search engine tool to find an article or reading that cites this foundational text. Each student then continues to use the search engine tool to see who has cited the second source they discovered. Once each student has discovered a citation trail of three or four sources that link back to the foundational text, students will regroup with each other and collectively put together the trails of sources each has found, showing the number of possible research conversations and contexts in which the foundational text can be used.

ACTIVITY GOALS

- Understand what a *citation trail* is and how authors cite each other to advance key ideas.
- Build a deeper understanding of context: both at the level of time and place of publication, and at the level of acknowledging that research and text emerge from an intellectual conversation.
- Collaborate with peers to build a shared knowledge repository about a core course reading.

BEFORE THE ACTIVITY

Pick one key reading for which you'd like your students to understand the full scholarly context. Aim to choose a text that is foundational to your course, one that you'd like your students to build off of in subsequent discussions or course projects. This activity works most successfully if students have already read this key reading so that they are already familiar with the basic content and core ideas of the reading. Therefore, it may be best to facilitate this activity at the early to midway point of the term after students have a basic grasp of the key ideas but still need to deepen those insights.

It is easiest for students to conduct this activity if the key reading you select has been archived digitally and/or is already in a digital format. That said, this reading does not necessarily have to be one that they've accessed digitally, as long as it's possible for them to find it in a digital search database in which the original text has been cited.

ACTIVITY STEPS

1. Ask students to find the foundational text for themselves in a library search engine database or a search engine like Google Scholar. Within this search engine, the students type in the metadata for the foundational text (i.e., title, author, date) and then conduct a search to see who has cited the original piece. Ask each student to select one article that interests them from the list of cited sources.

   Note: In a tool like Google Scholar, students can select the Cited By link at the bottom of the entry; in library databases, the option to see who has cited which pieces may appear in a different way in the interface. I encourage you to consult a librarian at your institution if you're not sure how to conduct this kind of search within your school's available databases or search engines.

2. Each student now has a source that has, in some way, cited the foundational text. Ask each student to skim the new source that they've found and identify where the foundational text is cited. In a shared collaborative work space (e.g., on a whiteboard, in a collaborative document, in a wiki, on a sheet of paper), ask each student to note the new source that they've found and to write a sentence or two about what their new source has to say about the foundational text. You may want to pause the activity at this point to discuss the following questions:

    -   How did the source you found either change or affirm what you knew from reading the foundational text?
    -   What new information have you learned about the foundational text based on the sources you've found that cite the foundational text (if any)?
    -   In what ways does the collection of sources the class has found help us understand the foundational text? How do these sources build upon or complicate what's in the foundational text?
    -   What would you say the key themes of the foundational text are based on the collection of new sources that we've gathered?

You can end the activity at this step, keeping it focused on the goal of providing students with a fuller and deepened understanding of the current scholarly context for the foundational text. Or you can continue the activity if you want the students to see an even longer citational trail for the foundational text, particularly if the foundational text cites a variety of complicated ideas that need to be discovered through additional citations.

3. To continue, ask the students to follow the citation trail one more time by taking the metadata from the new source they've found and entering that information into the search engine once more. They then repeat what they did in step 2, seeing who has cited the first source they've found to identify a second source.

4. In the second source, students should identify where the author has cited the first source they found. Then, in the collaborative document (where students linked the first sources they found to the foundational text), students can contribute another column or table with information about how their second source builds off of the first and, consequently, how (or whether) conversation with the foundational text has remained.

5. Once this information has been gathered, you can pause again to facilitate a discussion with the following questions:

   a. In what ways does the second source build off of the first source? Does the second source build off of the foundational text at all or is the second source now too far removed?

   b. How does seeing your own citation trail and the citation trails of your peers help you to understand core concepts from the foundational text?

c. What would you describe as the context for the foundational text now that you've seen what other scholars have to say about it and how such scholars have used the foundational text to build their own ideas?

KEY TAKEAWAYS

- Contextualization allows students to take stock of the environment in which they access and engage with readings.
- Practicing contextualization invites exploration outside of the source itself, and allows students to understand who is behind the composition, circulation, publication, and distribution of the text itself.
- To engage in contextualization is to be attentive to the intersections between the content of the reading and the environment for reading.

CHAPTER 8

....

CONTEMPLATION

Meditation and yoga have become increasingly popular practices, especially on college campuses. At Stanford University, a whole building, called the Windhover Contemplative Center, is dedicated to contemplative and meditative practice for anyone who works at the university. The Windhover is a wood-paneled building with floor-to-ceiling windows, at which visitors can pull out a yoga mat from a collective area and find serenity amid the bustling college environment. Granted, it is more common to find someone taking a nap inside the Windhover than meditating in a disciplined way, but the campus commitment to the concept of the Windhover remains rather clear: the university believes its students, faculty, and staff need a space in which to take time out of the day to breathe.

Effective meditative practice is challenging because it's not just zoning out and finding "space." Rather, it involves a deliberate quieting of the mind, a purposeful attention to breath and the body, and an awareness of how the body and mind converge. Becoming a master at meditation takes years, lifetimes even, to accomplish, and some practitioners attend week- and month-long retreats to become truly disciplined contemplators. Developing enough awareness to stay present and reach a higher plane of consciousness is serious work.

Engaging in *contemplation* requires a similarly serious effort to that involved in meditation. As readers, we have to know when it's important to stay within a single text and just stick with it, even when it's hard. There are moments when we must spend time mulling over a sentence, untangling its complexities, and returning to the same idea over and over again to make sense of it all. Regardless of media or environment, becoming a contemplative reader is about knowing when to hone one's attentional resources and to be patient with even the densest and most complicated texts.

In the context of a digital age, where numerous apps, devices, and notifications can make competing demands for our limited attentional resources, knowing when and why to adjust our focus is all the more important. When we read on screens, we can often feel as though our attention is fragmented as we flit from one app to the next, from one notification to another. After all, we read a substantial amount of text on digital devices every day, whether that's through text messages, e-mails, or social media posts. Although many of us can clearly articulate the purposes for reading in these spaces (staying in touch with a family member, for example, or keeping abreast of work communications), we can also frequently engage in all kinds of reading acts without really thinking about why we are doing so. In fact, some user research even suggests that the average American touches their phone over 2,000 times per day, a number that demonstrates a common compulsion to task switch, losing and breaking focus all the while (Winnick 2016). Although it is not always a bad thing to respond to updates and to check on new information, it is important to register and understand *why* we feel compelled to do so in particular moments. In other words, when we engage in contemplation as a reading practice, a likely outcome is the reminder that we may need to reread, rethink, and refocus on what we're reading, even when it's an online space where other notifications and novel pieces of information may be competing and vying for our time.

To that end, being a *contemplative* reader is not just about maintaining singular, dogged focus. It's also about understanding *why* it's important to maintain that focus with a particular text. Knowing when and why we should stick with or be patient with a text can also be understood as a form of practicing *metacognition*, or an ability to understand why you think about something in a particular way. Just as someone who practices meditation must know why they are seeking out meditative practice and must maintain a focus on that goal, so too must a contemplative reader know when to check in and be patient with a particular text. In other words, we must not simply practice focus for focus's sake; we must understand when it's appropriate to apply focus.

"Contemplation" is the last category for engagement in our digital reading framework because it is a practice that undergirds the other ways that we might engage with acts of reading. It is much more challenging to curate, connect, create, or contextualize reading without contemplating why you are engaging in that work in the first place. Contemplation is also an iterative process. We start a reading with an intention, but we need to check in with ourselves midway through about how the reading process is going. As we read, engaging in contemplation means considering what we're missing and what we're struggling with and asking ourselves why we're rapt with attention, or why we're veering away from the text at hand. Why are we bored? Why are we thrilled? Why are we apathetic or curious about what's in front of us? Our ability to answer these questions can help all of us more capably engage with the reams of text available to us online and otherwise.

We don't all have to be career yogis or full-time meditators to reap the benefits of a meditative practice in our everyday lives. Similarly, we don't *always* have to think about why we're engaging in reading in particular ways or why we're learning what we're learning. But even engaging in contemplation in small chunks, striving toward being reflective where and when we can, can offer us a tremendous service as readers. If we are to be critical of the environments we read in and thoughtful about the spaces we choose for our reading practice, we must also remain actively aware of our decisions and, at the same time, be intentional about when we choose to skim, to dive, and to surface in our reading experiences.

Scholarly Connections

Learning is not just being able to name what we know, but understanding how we know what we know. Contemplative pedagogy has, in fact, garnered increased interest in both K–12 and higher education over the past decade (Hart, 2004; Brady, 2007; Gunnlaugson, 2009; Franzese & Felten, 2017). Contemplative practices, broadly speaking, originate in wisdom and religious traditions, like Buddhist meditation, Hindu yoga, Jewish mysticism, and Christian prayer. Yet educators who practice contemplative pedagogy do not see the practice as intrinsically tied to these religious traditions and, instead, understand contemplation as activating a range of approaches that are "designed to quiet and shift the habitual chatter of the mind to cultivate a capacity for deepened awareness, concentration, and insight" (Hart, 2004, p. 29). Some examples of contemplative pedagogy include personal journaling, breathing exercises, listening exercises, body focusing, and guided imagery (Brady, 2007; Hart, 2004). What these kinds of exercises can potentially facilitate is renewed awareness of how the body and mind intersect to create meaningful, holistic learning experiences.

When it comes to practicing contemplative pedagogy as part of a reading praxis, many scholars have suggested that students simply slow down when they read. For example, Richard Miller (2016) suggests that instructors consider giving their students space to practice slow reading as a means of inviting wandering, ambiguity, and questioning. He makes the case that rereading and contemplation are, in and of themselves, critical reading practices that are not just about hunting for information, but about responding to what's on the page and inviting independent thought from that point onward. Thomas Miller and Adele Leon (2017) similarly invoke the concept of reading slowly to process and take stock of online sources that may evoke strong emotional reactions (p. 16). Although slowing down is likely not a complete solution to developing information literacy (see the last chapter on contextualization for some strategies to help students understand their informational environments), the act of taking a pause and taking stock of one's feelings and situations is a meaningful solution for overcoming emotionally overwhelming feelings.

The environment in which one reads can clearly affect part of one's embodied learning experience, so contemplative practices may also include inventorying or reflection exercises about reading spaces. Jonathan Alexander

(Alexander et al., 2013) suggests that readers take stock of how they move within and across multiple media and platforms as a means of managing the "steady stream of text" that they may encounter on a regular basis (p. 55). By describing the intentions for why he reads in different spaces and how the mediation in those spaces impacts the choices he makes and what he's understanding, Alexander develops a deepened awareness of how the reading environments and spaces shape his understanding of text. Hannah Rule (2018) complicates this process of reflecting on reading spaces by making the case that studying "embodied interaction with immediate material environments" also helps readers recognize both what's in their control to change, and also what's outside of their control (p. 405). Specifically, studying reading and writing spaces "helps budge the clingy assumption that composing processes are ultimately only rational, linear, goal-directed mental action . . . [and] illustrates instead how processes are susceptible to environmental forces and never in writers' full and autonomous control" (Rule, 2018, p. 405). By paying attention to the ways in which readers' and writers' bodies necessarily change how they are able to access texts, readers can develop a more intentional awareness of how their reading behavior emerges from a complex interplay of social, expressive, cultural, embodied, and material circumstances. Identifying these factors may help readers recognize what makes their own reading practices unique to their embodied and material circumstances.

Beyond taking stock of the environments in which reading can happen, another common approach to slowing down as a reader is through practicing close reading strategies. *Close reading* has been mostly commonly practiced in humanistic disciplines, like literature, but literacy scholar

Zhihui Fang (2016) makes the case that close reading could be effectively deployed in disciplines beyond literature. Because close reading is the "methodical analysis of words, sentences, paragraphs, and visuals to explore their significance in the text," a close reading pedagogy could be applied when it "takes into account all key elements involved in the reading process—including the reader, the text, the task, and the context . . . with a special emphasis on promoting students' understanding of how language and other semiotic systems construct meaning across genres, disciplines, and contexts" (Fang, 2016, p. 107). What this means is that close reading across the disciplines could look like a series of exercises in which instructors invite students to look closely at the sentence and word level of texts to deepen their understanding of both the text itself and the context in which this particular reading appears. Douglas Fisher and Nancy Frey (2014) offer a series of practical scaffolds that instructors have used to teach close reading successfully, including deliberate rereading, text-dependent questions (or questions that point students directly to aspects of the text that instructors want them to pay attention to or focus on), collaborative conversations in full-group or small-group discussions, and annotation practice.

At the level of higher education, it may seem like some of these scaffolds for close reading could be too labor intensive and may be challenging to implement if students are not completing the readings in advance or in the first place. Yet strategies like text-dependent questions especially, which may remind students why they are reading in the first place, may, in fact, encourage greater reading compliance. In other words, college students are more likely to complete and engage with required reading if they are asked to engage in contemplative practices, like close reading, that could be aligned with the course's learning goals and purposes.

Evidence from studies on reading compliance shows that students tend to be most motivated to read when they know how they will be applying the reading in the class or when they know what benefit the reading may have for them as learners (West, 2018; Bunn, 2013; Sharma, Van Hoof, & Pursel, 2013; Carney, Fry, Gabriele, & Ballard, 2010; Brost and Bradley, 2006; Burchfield & Sappington, 2000). For example, Jane West (2018) tried multiple reading compliance techniques in a 36-student under-graduate class she taught, and found that the majority of her students preferred taking individual reading notes as a motivating strategy instead of activities such as in-class quizzes, in-person discussions, and exams (p. 151). In qualitative student responses, West recorded students' interest in reading with purpose and direction as they pre-pared for class discussion and engagement. Similarly, Brost and Bradley (2006) found through undergraduate student surveys that students were most motivated to read when they had a personal interest in the material and when their instructor used the readings in lecture and discussion (p. 105). Both West's study and Brost and Bradley's suggest that when the instructor primes the students with an un-derstanding of what the reading will offer them and aligns what's in the reading with what they present in class, the exercise of exploring course concepts through reading becomes all the more compelling. It is important to note that other studies have shown the value in extrinsically motivating factors like quizzes (Culver, 2016; Hoeft, 2012; Clump, Bauer, & Bradley, 2004) and guided in-class activ-ities (Kerr and Frease, 2017; Starcher & Proffitt, 2011) to improve reading compliance too. What these studies on reading compliance may collectively demonstrate then is that offering students a clear sense of purpose for their readings is a consistently valuable way of encouraging engagement with reading tasks.

Engaging students in conversations about how they read what they read and how they engage in academic reading practices may also help boost students' confidence. A major reason that students don't read required texts is an expressed concern that they do not know how to read those required texts effectively (Smale, 2020; St Clair-Thompson, Graham, & Marsham, 2018). To that end, Daniel Schwartz, Jessica Tsang, and Kristen Blair (2016) suggest "self-explaining" as a strategy where students, when struggling, decide for themselves to pause and "regulate their reading by slowing down and looking back to earlier sentences to see if they can figure out how their earlier interpretations were incorrect" (p. 236). This ability not only for students to understand when something is unclear, but also to regulate their process and take action to resolve their lack of clarity is a key component of engaging in contemplative practice. Although not all students are always able to articulate why they're struggling to understand something, the mere act of pinpointing what moments may be challenging and may require further growth or thinking is a form of engaging in successful contemplative engagement.

Practicing slow reading, close reading, and self-explaining strategies are challenging pursuits, ones that our students probably won't master overnight. Indeed, understanding why we read, how we read, and when to read slowly is a challenge for even the most expert of readers. Yet if we are to take seriously the challenges inherent in digital reading environments, including the availability of distractions and the plethora of information available, practicing contemplation as a category for engagement is all the more important. Knowing how to organize our reading and when to organize our reading can help us find clarity, purpose, and direction to make sense of the many options and avenues for reading that are available.

CLASS ACTIVITIES

Contemplation is likely an iterative process for you and your students because opportunities for taking a step back, checking in, and slowing down can be valuable at any point in a given term. These particular activities may, in fact, be best facilitated in small ways throughout the term so that reflective, metacognitive practice is interwoven with the other ways of engaging with course material and reading. The goal of these activities is to get students to recognize what they're finding meaningful in their readings and why they're finding that work meaningful, so these activities can also be scaled down to allow students to consider these kinds of questions in short intervals at the beginning or end of a class session or term.

ACTIVITY #1: 3-2-1—3 INTERESTING MOMENTS, 2 CONFUSING MOMENTS, 1 QUESTION

ACTIVITY OVERVIEW

To help students reflect upon their experience with one reading, you can ask students to identify moments they found interesting and confusing. By giving students three interesting moments, two confusing moments, and one question to identify, you can get them to isolate and identify the moments they'd like to continue to question, discuss, and explore.

ACTIVITY GOALS

- Reflect upon salient moments in a single text.
- Ask questions and promote the development of inquiry-based thinking.
- Consider both the value of and challenges within a single text.

BEFORE THE ACTIVITY

Pick one reading for your students to complete for this activity. It is important that you delimit this activity to one particular reading so that students can really focus their moment of inquiry and be prepared to dig deeply into one set of ideas. Sometimes, less is more, and that can be particularly true for cultivating reflective thinking.

Note that this activity can be taught for a reading that is not available in a digital environment. The advantage of teaching this kind of activity for a text that is available in a digital environment is that it gives students opportunities to focus on and isolate key components of the text, thus helping them contemplate and isolate what they may consider some of the most important dimensions of their digital reading experience.

ACTIVITY STEPS

1. Invite students to engage in "3-2-1" thinking. Specifically, you can offer them the following prompts

either in worksheet form, as prompts in a discussion board (particularly if you are teaching an online or hybrid course), or as areas for them to explore in an individual assignment for submission:

a.   Identify 3 interesting moments in the reading. Submit these 3 moments as direct quotes, noting beneath each quote what you found interesting or why this moment was interesting to you.

b.   Identify 2 confusing moments. Submit these 2 moments as direct quotes, noting beneath each quote what you found confusing or challenging to you in these moments. Was it the vocabulary used? The concept mentioned? The argument itself?

c.   Ask 1 question. Your question can be about anything related to the reading, but it should be open-ended rather than a question that can be answered with "yes" or "no." An effective question can be a response to or an extension of something you found interesting; it can also be a question that might help you clarify one of the moments that you found confusing or just a question that you can imagine directly addressing to the author(s) of the text itself (rather than to your peers or to the instructor).

2.   Invite students to submit their "3-2-1" thinking. You then have several options for working through the submissions:

a.   For a small face-to-face course, you might invite students to share their "3-2-1" thinking in small groups (perhaps of three or four students). Each small group can then be tasked with nominating one person from their group to ask their 1 question or to put their 1 question into a shared classroom document. You can use the questions generated to build a class discussion or to design prompts for another activity.

b. For a large, lecture-based face-to-face classroom, an instructor can ask students to turn to a partner and share their "3-2-1" thinking with them. Time allowing, you can then invite a few of the pairs to share the most salient or thought-provoking parts of their conversation. Alternatively, you can invite the students in the large lecture to submit their one question to a polling or discussion board tool. You can then project the submitted questions and these questions as prompts for the lecture to come.

c. For a hybrid or online course, students can respond to another person's 1 question in a discussion forum or chat room; the first student can invite another student to take a stab at answering their question—or at least responding to and affirming that question—which should encourage deepened inquiry.

3. To end this activity, extend an invitation to students to continue "3-2-1" thinking by expanding upon the number of interesting moments, confusing moments, and questions they may encounter in subsequent readings.

ACTIVITY #2: CREATING A READING PROCESS JOURNAL

ACTIVITY OVERVIEW

Students create a reading process journal alongside their experience of either reading one text or a series of texts for a class environment. In this reading journal, they keep track of key insights and questions as well as the factors that either prevent them from understanding what they read or really help them develop a clearer understanding of what they read. In creating this process journal, students develop a more refined understanding of what they learn from the text they encounter.

ACTIVITY GOALS

- Develop a clearer understanding of one's own reading process and practices.
- Pinpoint areas that inspire further inquiry or investigation in a reading.

BEFORE THE ACTIVITY

Before you introduce the reading journal assignment to your students, decide whether you'd like your students to keep track of their reading experience for one text or for multiple texts over the course of the quarter. Some instructors may want students to maintain a regular journal with entries to cover each of their reading assignments over the course of the full term. Other instructors may have fewer readings in their class to cover but may want students to pay particular attention to how they're reading and what they're gleaning from one particular reading assignment. Students may absorb different insights from this activity if it is facilitated over the course of a term instead of for one assignment, but the goals should still be achievable regardless of the time-frame in which the activity is facilitated.

Because the reading journal is meant to be a reflective tool, this activity is best facilitated as a homework assignment or as an asynchronous activity. Once you decide on the scope of the activity, write the assignment instructions for your students so that they have a clear understanding of what exactly they need to accomplish, particularly since they are completing this activity in their own time.

As part of sharing the assignment instructions, invite students to maintain their reading journal in whatever space makes the most sense to them (a paper notebook, a word-processed document, a notes section in a digital note-taking application, etc.). Consider giving students a list of digital note-taking applications or digital word-processing options in case they're not aware of places where they can maintain a journal in a digital format (or on their mobile phones). See the appendix for a list of possible journal-keeping or note-taking tools.

ACTIVITY STEPS

1. Share the journal instructions with your students. You may use text like the following:

   a. To understand the main concepts from the assigned reading, you will maintain a journal that keeps track of some of the main points you're learning and questions that you have about the reading assignment. This journal is designed to help you *retain* what you're learning from the reading and also recognize what you might want to follow up on or learn more about. You may find it helpful to complete a table (as illustrated in Table 2) to keep track of and organize your thoughts.

2. When your students have completed a reading journal (like the one in Table 2 or one that has been modified to meet your individual class needs and purposes), engage in either a face-to-face conversation or a discussion forum (if teaching online) in which you debrief the results from the reading journal. Some questions for a debrief might include the following:

   - How did it feel to maintain this reading journal? Which parts were helpful? Which parts were challenging? Tedious? Engaging?
   - How did it feel to assess your expectations for reading before and after your reading experience? For how many did the expectations at the beginning align with the reality at the end?

3. Once students have discussed their experiences of maintaining the reading journal, their recorded responses can be a launching point for a larger class conversation or they can be starting points from which students can begin independent research or writing projects. If you are asking your students to maintain a log over the course of a full term, they can refer to the journal in subsequent class sessions. Expectations across a longer period of time can be compared while "stand-out" moments can also be compared across different readings to see what patterns of interest (or confusion) students notice in their reading processes.

Note: If your students are maintaining digital versions of their reading journals and are also completing the readings themselves in digital spaces, you can invite them to take screenshots of moments in the reading that stand out to them (or copy and paste text) for ease of reference. You still want to encourage them to keep track of citational information (e.g., page numbers, publication information), but a digital space may

Table 2. Reading Process Journal Example

BEFORE YOU START READING

Based on the title and abstract/summary for the reading, what kinds of things do I expect to learn from this reading?

WHILE YOU READ

Moments That Stood Out to You (because they were confusing, interesting, etc.)	Why?
[This can be a quote.]	[This response can just be a sentence or two about what you found interesting, confusing, etc. about this quote.]
[This can be a paraphrased version of a passage.]	[This response can just be a sentence or two about what you found interesting, confusing, etc. about this passage.]

AFTER YOU FINISH READING

Did you learn what you expected when you first began this reading? How did your expectations align or differ? (Look to what you wrote before you started reading for a reminder of your expectations!)

allow them to maintain an interactive record of reference. They can also maintain this reading journal in a citation management software program (see the appendix for a few examples of this kind of software, current as of this book's publication).

ACTIVITY #3: READ, LISTEN, LEARN: AN AUDITORY REFLECTION ACTIVITY

ACTIVITY OVERVIEW

Students take turns reading portions of a short, assigned text out loud in real time (this can be done over video chat if you are teaching a fully online course). When students are listening, invite them to annotate their readings and write down some key words or concepts that they heard. After the entire chosen text has been read aloud, students engage in a conversation about what they heard as listeners, contributing to a shared document or a whiteboard space some of the quotes, words, or ideas that stood out to them as they were listening. At the end of the activity, the class engages in a conversation about how being read to changed their experience of accessing and engaging with the reading (in comparison to silent reading experiences).

ACTIVITY GOALS

- Process information in differing modalities.
- Encourage sharing low-stakes and creative reactions to key concepts in a new text.
- Listen to other voices and process them alongside one's own reflections and reactions to a text.

BEFORE THE ACTIVITY

Pick a short text or segment for students to read aloud. Ideally, this should be a new text for the students, or one that you have not assigned at a prior moment in the class.

If you are teaching a face-to-face class, you may want to make the moment of reading aloud a component of the real-time class session. In this case, it is helpful to give students access to the document in advance of the read-aloud session so that interested students can pre-read the document before the live class session. You also want to give students the option to opt out of reading aloud in the live moment, give them time to prerecord themselves reading the text aloud, or give them the option to prepare the text to be read for them in a text-to-speech application. It is less important that students use their own voices and more important that students engage in an act of reading as an act of listening in some capacity.

If you are facilitating this activity outside of a live class session, assign students to prerecord one segment of the text and share their recording in a shared class space. Again, students may want the option of having their segment recorded by a text-to-speech application rather than by using their own voice.

Aim to pick a reading that is relatively short in length, depending on how much class time you can devote to this particular activity. In general, when students are reading aloud, less is more; the less text students have to wade through, the more they can concentrate on the most salient bits and get the most out of pulling out key concepts, ideas, and themes from something particularly targeted or relevant to your course content.

If you're teaching a small class, the read-aloud session can happen as a large group. However, if you're teaching a large class or are worried about the time it would take to have each student read a portion out loud, you can also have students get into smaller groups to conduct a read-aloud session.

ACTIVITY STEPS

1. Engage in the read-aloud moment, whether that's in a live class session (where students switch between reading/listening roles and/or listen to their peers' prerecordings or text-to-speech audio) or online (when students listen to short recordings of their peers' readings or text-to-speech application readings). Offer the students a few options for how they can spend the time as they're listening to their peers read. They can annotate the reading as they're listening. They can sketch, doodle, or make a map while they're listening. Or they can simply listen without doing anything. It may even help to give your students a range of things that they can do while they listen so that they know their options, but the core of the activity is simple: students need to read (or prepare their reading through a text-to-speech application) when it is their turn and listen when it is their peers' turn to read. The one thing you want students to keep in mind is that they will be discussing and sharing their understanding of key themes or ideas after the reading is over, so they may want to be primed and prepared to share their reactions and their identification of key ideas.

2. After the reading is completed, invite students to take a few minutes to write down what they heard or understood to be some of the key ideas from the

reading. Depending on the content, you might ask students to identify the argument that they heard, to identify evidence for that argument, or to identify themes or concepts that they heard repeated or acknowledged in the reading.

3. Invite students to share a component of what they wrote down in a collaborative space. What students write down varies depending on the writing prompt they received, but successful examples of what students share can include themes, key words, or even quotes that stood out to them. The shared space that you choose for students to collate these reflections may also depend on what you're having them write, but options for single-word responses or short phrases can be as low-tech as writing on a whiteboard or as high-tech as using a collaborative polling tool (see the appendix for polling tool options current as of this writing). If you're wanting students to share full quotes, excerpts, or sentences, a digital space like a class wiki or a collaborative note-taking document or chat space may be more appropriate to facilitate (see the appendix for note-taking tools current as of this writing). The purpose of having students work in a shared space is to see how multiple people understood, listened, and extrapolated ideas.

4. Depending on the prompt and what students contributed to the shared space, a discussion can take a number of different directions:

  - Option A: Students look at their peers' responses and find the common threads. As a facilitator, you can guide a conversation about those common threads and why they may be important for understanding core goals/outcomes in the course.

- Option B: Students identify common threads in their peers' responses and write about why those common threads are important or significant for another component of the course. Students can turn in these written responses or discuss the importance of these common threads.
- Option C: The activity ends here, and students look at the shared space as a homework or asynchronous assignment, reflecting on what they saw their peers record and how the themes/concepts/quotes identified in the shared notetaking document inform the further research, study, exploration, or project they will do in the course thereafter.

5. Either immediately after the activity is over or as part of a homework or asynchronous component of the course, it may help to invite students to reflect on how the experience of listening and slowing down their process of reading by reading aloud changed their reading experience. Some prompts you might use include these:

- How is it different to read aloud (or to read through a text-to-speech application) than it is to read silently? How is it similar?
- Would you choose to read aloud in the future? When would you choose to read aloud or to read silently?

KEY TAKEAWAYS

- To engage with contemplation, readers identify an intention for their reading practice and, therefore, understand why they are reading in the first place.
- Practicing contemplation encourages readers to be metacognitive or to understand why they think about what they learn from a reading in the way that they do.
- It takes attentional resources to be contemplative; practicing contemplation means being patient with one's self as a reader and knowing when a pause or moment of focus is appropriate.

PART 3

SURFACE

CRITICALLY APPROACHING THE ADOPTION AND
USE OF DIGITAL READING TECHNOLOGIES

CHAPTER 9

THE ETHICAL IMPLICATIONS OF DIGITAL READING

GRAPPLING WITH DIGITAL ARCHIVING, READERLY PRIVACY, AND EVIDENCE OF OUR READING

After each course I took in college, I accumulated stacks of papers, spiral-bound course readers, and books. Although I was not likely to use most of the materials in the next course, I could not quite part with the records of my learning. Yet I also didn't know *where* to put all of the things I had to store. Because I lived in a small apartment, space was limited, so I did what so many of us do when we don't want to make a choice: we push the problem elsewhere and delay the decision-making. I proceeded to take all of the papers to my childhood bedroom at my parents' house, a conceivably more stable space to store such things.

Eventually, my parents got a little fed up with the stacks of papers towering in my childhood closet. Each time I returned home, my parents (gently) asked me to go through what I had stored to see what I actually wanted to keep. I found myself spending hours thumbing through the old content, deciphering my notes like a detective for my past self, revisiting what I had learned in my seminar on *The Canterbury Tales* or my critical theory class's discussion of the male gaze. I often couldn't quite track the notes I had taken on my readings or what they meant and, more often than not, I wound up simply throwing away the stacks upon stacks of papers I had stored.

Very little evidence of my learning in college remains, and although it was not exactly practical to keep every single notebook, course reader, and textbook, I regret that I didn't have a better way of storing, archiving, and maintaining a path of my knowledge that I could look at today. Although I'm no longer studying literature in the way that I was as an undergraduate English major, there are, I suspect, many ways of thinking that I developed in college that I'd probably still find useful today. Even if I had not gone into higher education, I may still have found value in archiving what I learned in clearer ways so that I could track the transferable ideas. Even just remembering what ideas made an impression on me or changed my view of the world would have been interesting for me to consider later in life.

Memory has been at the center of concerns with reading since the beginning of reading as we know it. Remember how Socrates's primary concern with writing was that it would undermine our ability to remember what we know? As we've come to accept putting more of our thoughts in writing and relying less on oral modes of transmitting and remembering information, our concern with memory has become all the more acute. Reading for learning involves being able to recall how a specific fact or moment in a text may impact prior knowledge or may change the reader's assumptions about a particular topic. Further still, reading for knowledge also requires us to have the ability to refer back to particular moments or to put a pin in an idea so we can return to it at a later date. And this all requires that we have ways to remember the totality of important points from a text in order to use and apply that knowledge appropriately. Ways to create mnemonics for improving what we remember from readings are applicable across print and digital spaces. But we may need to be especially attentive to some more specific qualities about reading in digital spaces if we want to retain and also review and reflect back on what we've learned as well.

Specifically, when it comes to storing and keeping track of what we've read in online spaces, we have to be attentive to the infrastructure(s) in which we encounter readings in the first place and we have to know how our practices may align (or clash) with those infrastructures. For example, the ways that we might store reading that we've found on the web may be very different from how we choose to store what we've downloaded from an external hard drive; we make these choices not just because of the technical capacity to store in and across those spaces, but also because of the ways we access information and data on the public web or in private file storage.

Hopefully you have found that the strategies in Part 2 have already offered you some different ways to help students remember what they've read even without the strategies for remembering particular locations or moments that we've come to rely upon with printed books. But mnemonic or pedagogical strategies alone won't help us remember everything. At a certain point, we also need to make sure that we have mechanisms for recording, storing, and documenting all of the important activities that we have done. It is one thing to have a conversation about what works and what doesn't, and to ask students to reflect and write and keep track of what they've read and consumed. But how do we ensure that all of the work we're doing around a text survives? How do we keep track of all of those notes, readings, documents, and conversations in ways that can make sense to us later? How do we ensure that we all maintain records and archives of our reading so that all of that labor doesn't just disappear? And how do we be deliberate in allowing certain ideas to disappear if we want them to?

Technologies inevitably change over time and so this chapter may eventually feel dated in its approaches to familiarize readers with the critical differences around digital infrastructure that exist at the time of this writing. However, even if the specifics of how we handle and distinguish between different forms of digital infrastructure may change, the goal of this chapter remains to raise some questions and concerns about what it means to archive evidence of reading long-term and to provide some strategies for guiding students through understanding how they can maintain or destroy archives of their learning. After all, what we must keep at the fore of any conversation about maintaining records of our reading is that each individual should have the agency and freedom to decide how and where they want those records maintained. As instructors, we can create spaces to receive and share our students' work, but we ultimately have to offer our students choice in where they decide to take their work after our courses and beyond.

The Lifespan of Digital Archives

Long-term compatibility of digital documents and file types with future operating systems or software is a major archival concern. Many digital files have become obsolete with unreadable file extensions and the contents of boutique file types wither into obsolescence. Keeping track of which file types can open in which applications may feel like a struggle, and I can see why many readers may feel reluctant to move their reading practices to digital spaces. After all, nothing is quite as easy (and perhaps even as safe) as storing some notes in a paper filing cabinet or on a bookshelf: look up or pull open a drawer, locate the file or the book with the appropriate information, and voila! You're done. Plus, you can lock a filing cabinet, keep the key in a protected space, and move along with piece of mind. Yet physical space is a precious commodity. We can't assume that all of our students can keep cabinets and shelves of things. Many of them may be in living situations where they are constantly economizing space and only keeping the material goods that they absolutely know that they would like to hold on to forever. In those cases, the value of storing documents from class work may not seem immediately evident and the lifespan of documents becomes rather short indeed. Not to mention that paper itself is also a fragile technology. An accidental coffee spill or a significant tear can render paper documents completely unreadable.

Some file types have become more standardized across platforms, operating systems, and devices over the years, and it's likely that as a reader, you will instantly recognize many of them. You can invite your students to store files in these file extensions. For example, PDFs, or portable document files, are readable across devices and operating systems and can be read in a variety of software applications. Similarly, files with .html extensions can be read in any browser, since they are file types designed to be read within a universal web interface. If users have the option to download and extract the source code from their files, they have an even more secure solution; although reading source code requires the ability to understand how the language of source code operates, source code itself is the most "original" form a file type can take. The point is that many files don't necessarily have to be lost and gone forever as long as consumers understand how to save and export their files in a variety of formats. Plus, with cloud-based storage, storing standard archivable files is getting easier than it has been in the past.

Part of our task as educators who are asking students to produce, comment upon, and store their readings is to grow increasingly aware of what steps we all may need to take to preserve and move our documents across different spaces rather than simply expect our digital files to stay the same over time. This is, perhaps, not all that different than the steps we may need to employ to store paper in some ways; if our own paper copy of a handout or article gets damaged by a coffee spill or an unfortunate tear and we have no other backup copies, we lose access to that article. Just as we would rely on a backup to avoid having to rely on the coffee-stained or torn copy, we also need to make sure we have ways to back up and restore digital files from inevitable material wear and tear. To put it another way, museum archivists must preserve papers under glass so they do not degrade entirely; we must become the museum archivists of our digital work. We have to learn about our preservational environments to ensure that the things that really matter to us are preserved and stored in spaces that we can remember, that we can understand, and that, importantly, we can control as consumers and archivists.

The *control* piece is what gets complicated by the constantly shifting landscape of who or what has access to the spaces and tools for preserving digital documents. In fact, while teaching in higher education, I've noticed an odd paradox in how we talk to students about the permanence and agency of their work. On the one hand, we warn our students that anything and everything they compose online is relegated to permanence. Post a picture of yourself at a wild party? That image might impact your ability to find employment forever. But on the other hand, when we ask our students to turn in work to our learning management system or put it in some other online storage space, we somehow forget that this work is just as permanent. In this case, however, we don't ascribe students with the agency to determine where their work winds up. Many students, I suspect, simply trust that their instructors are making a choice for their benefit about where their work goes. That may often be true, but as educators, we need to understand how to maintain that trust and not unwittingly violate it.

To be clear, I don't think it's a bad thing for instructors to navigate how students submit, share, and distribute their work in the space of a class. In fact, part of creating a learning experience for students is giving them some orientation to how they need to engage in digital spaces to contribute successfully. But what I think we as instructors must do a better job of is (1) understanding the tools our campus has purchased licenses to (e.g., the learning management system, third-party file storage solutions) and (2) giving students options about where and how they can submit and store their work so that they can opt out if they have concerns.

If I think back to what I would have done in college if I had been given a clear opportunity to digitize my reading notes or evidence of my learning, I'm not sure I would have understood the implications of the decisions I would have had to make to do so. Indeed, I imagine that any concerns with privacy or the possibility of my writing becoming data for an educational technology company's profits would not have crossed my mind. Of course, those thoughts wouldn't have crossed my mind partly because conversations about data privacy and online surveillance were not really happening in popular media when I was a college student (or at least not in the circles I was part of). But I think even if those conversations had been happening at the time, the connection may still not have been clear for me.

It's possible that I may have understood some of the implications of my academic data being generalized for company profits. But in all likelihood, I probably would not have wrapped my head around the fact that when I consented to a company's data policy, it often meant I was making my content visible to millions of bots, which then isolate patterns and trends that could be generalized to reduce my own agency in what information I would like revealed about my work (or myself) moving forward. To that end, I also don't think I would have had the skills or insight to decide how I could make choices to store my data in safe ways. Although being online is an activity that, in and of itself, means giving up more privacy about our personal lives than many consumers think it does, there are some ways that we can control where and how our information gets stored, shared, and accessed. Unfortunately, the reality, as of this book's writing, is that consumers themselves bear the burden of educating themselves about what it means to control one's own privacy on the web. That said, if we can help students recognize some of the small ways that they can reclaim some agency over their personal information online, and particularly the kind of information that aligns with their learning, the better.

You can see, perhaps, that I'm wrestling with a major conundrum about reading online today. I see the tremendous potential in being able to store, track, and archive records of what we read and how we read online, especially when it comes to reflecting on what we've read or how particular moments of reading may shape how we understood what we read. I also think that reading online can be considered an equity opportunity for our institutions, to make sure that students can access the same information across the platforms and devices that we know they have access to. Yet I recognize the potential danger in encouraging students, and anyone really, to maintain records of reading in spaces where those records may be exploited. Understanding how and where that exploitation can happen is perhaps a first step in acknowledging and responding to this potential danger.

Understanding How Privacy Matters for Reading Online

When it comes to reading, concerns with the privacy of our archives and potential annotations therein may not necessarily be at the forefront for either students or educators. In fact, because silent reading is often perceived as an intensely private and internal process, we may not even consider how our reading behaviors can, in fact, be very public, especially when they happen online. Yet online reading can be tracked and remembered in several ways, for better or for worse. For example, when you read an article on a web browser, the web browser you're using maintains a history of everything you've accessed. That might not necessarily be a bad thing; I've often used the History feature in my web browser to recover the link to an article I accidentally closed without saving.

But accessing what users have read via browser history can be weaponized. In the K–12 education system especially, school districts are increasingly adopting surveillance solutions where students' web browser searches are flagged for disturbing content. Depending on the severity of the flagged content, students' families may be contacted or the system may route the student directly to the police or other law enforcement (Beckett, 2019; Haskins, 2019). Although school systems tend to adopt these surveillance solutions as a "safety" measure, privacy experts and educators alike are concerned that these kinds of surveillance mechanisms could reinforce the many biases that schools may already have toward over-disciplining students of color and/or students with disabilities (Beckett, 2019; Balingit, 2018). Chris Gilliard has pointed out how a web based on surveillance and personalization algorithmically reinforces biased assumptions, particularly about people of color and low-income individuals. In fact, he coined the term *digital redlining* to describe the ways in which "technological policies, practices, pedagogy, and investment decisions . . . enforce class boundaries and discriminate against specific groups" (Gilliard, 2017) He gives several examples of what digital redlining can look like in practice: locking students out behind information paywalls that prevent students from accessing information, "customizing" particular Google search results based on IP addresses from particular regions or devices, and controlling the visibility of particular kinds of information via platform algorithms in social networks.

Social networks keep careful track of user engagement within the network, down to every individual click that users make, in order to change its algorithms and to "personalize" the kind of content that users see the next time that they log in. Similarly, publishers of online articles (from popular magazines, newspapers, and blogs to library databases and scholarly warehouses) track where users find their articles via small pieces of data, called cookies, which follow users across the web. Although algorithmically generated recommendations can be useful for finding related articles and resources, social networks especially profit off of knowing where, when, and how users interact on their platforms, often selling that data to other third-party ventures to secure more profit. Our reading behaviors, in other words, can generate a lot of capital for others while also impacting what our informational landscapes look like. More importantly, surveillance acts both within school systems and outside of them contribute to algorithmic discrimination, wherein problematic assumptions are made based on what readers are accessing. Reading is not safe to everyone, precisely because of the ways in which simply clicking on and accessing particular pieces of information can shape the kinds of stories that may be visible thereafter. And that should, rightfully, make us feel angry.

Although institutional learning management systems (LMSs) are protected behind institutional log-ins, which is more private than using publicly available cloud storage (at the moment of this writing, name brand examples of this include Box, Dropbox, and Google Drive), even LMSs themselves operate under data policies that may not necessarily keep work entirely within the student's or even the instructor's control. When a student graduates from an institution, they lose access to the work that they submitted to the LMS. Instructors, too, lose access to their past course content as they move to a different institution. Many educators argue that the LMS is designed to be an extractive system that creates walls around student data to limit and reduce access to their intellectual property (Beck, Grohowski, & Blair, 2017; Stommel, 2017; Watters, 2014). As data becomes a more valued commodity, many corporately owned institutional learning management systems extract data inputted into the learning management system to engage in machine learning approaches and generate data profiles that may allow the companies to sell said data to third-party educational technology vendors interested in developing ever more digital solutions for student learning (Hill, 2019). Although the field of LMS operations continues to change quickly, I encourage all educators to research their institution's LMS and look for as much information as you can about privacy policies therein.

I'm not going to mince words here: data collection in educational environments is predatory *unless* students and instructors have full and equal access to the data collected. Unless students and instructors can review, revise, and redact whatever they've shared and submitted within institutional learning management systems and have full control over how their data is being used, processed, and disseminated, we have to be extremely wary of educational technology solutions for storing student work. To the extent that we can, we may aspire to building what Amy Collier (2017) calls a *digital sanctuary*, or spaces in higher education institutions where students can be free of constant device surveillance and an invasion into their privacy and intellectual property.

As instructors, we need to be vigilant about protecting our students' privacy, ensuring that they have options for how their work is shared with others and how permanent that work might appear to people outside of the university setting. It is, in fact, law—Family Educational Rights and Privacy Act (FERPA), if you're not familiar—that we keep students' grades and assessments private. But beyond the law, we have an ethical obligation to give students agency over how their intellectual work is shared, disseminated, and stored. I say deliberately that this is an ethical obligation because instructors wield power in a student-teacher relationship; within this hierarchy, instructors must be mindful of that power's impact on how students perceive of doing work for our classes. We must not abuse that power by requiring all students to share their work in public venues or in permanent spaces, even if we think that it will expand their notion of what's possible in terms of producing and sharing valuable intellectual labors. We can't portend to know our students' relationships with public discourse and, more seriously, we can't make choices for them if casting our students' engagement in broader publics may, in fact, be dangerous to them.

When students are producing academic work, they are often experimenting with new ideas. Regardless of the discipline students are in or the work they're producing, we certainly don't want students to feel like their works in progress or the evidence of their learning process are both immutable and publicly available. Indeed, we want students to feel like learning is, indeed, a *process* where the evidence of that learning can change and the products created from that learning remain under the student's control. Further still, no one moment of learning necessarily needs to be ossified in time and, in fact, it's often better when that learning is *not* created as or perceived as an artifact completely ossified in time. Nothing is perhaps more paralyzing for a good learning process than feeling as though one's initial, rough thinking is getting scrutinized by someone, or that there's no way to revise work that remains in progress.

We have to show that our perceptions of what's permanent online and what isn't are largely driven by the social contexts of where, how, and why we produce certain kinds of intellectual work. In that process, we also have to help students understand just *how* they can keep track of the evidence of their learning and give them options, should they so value them, for keeping track of their own learning as it's happening. It is our ethical obligation as instructors to help students know how they can collect the work they've done and how they can maintain control over that work in their own spaces.

How We Empower Students to Make Choices about Archiving Digital Reading

For so many of our students, academic spaces, particularly in higher education contexts, are extremely unfamiliar and intimidating; it should come as no surprise to anyone reading this book that colleges and universities are not always welcoming places to all students. Encountering the new technologies that instructors expect them to use can make adjusting to a university environment even harder for some students. Even for those students who have had ample exposure to using technology for learning, their prior learning environments may have approached using technology differently than university classroom environments do. Inevitably, students also have had different levels of exposure to and experiences with understanding how and whether their data is stored and tracked within different kinds of learning management systems and educational environments. It is important to assume the best in our students because anyone who consumes and shares information online is continuing to learn about the best ways to do so. Given all of these differing experiences, contexts, and orientations to learning in digital spaces, it is all the more important that we begin conversations about storage, archiving, and data privacy by showing that we trust our students. But what does it mean to put trust in our students exactly?

For starters, it means being transparent about why we've built the online learning spaces we have or why we've distributed digital readings in particular platforms. Showing transparency does not have to take a long time: it simply means we acknowledge and name how we've chosen to distribute readings for our students and how, in kind, we've made choices about where they might store and keep track of notes or thoughts on their readings throughout our courses. Describing our rationale for where, when, and why we want students to archive their learning and explaining the value of building that archive is part of how we can build shared understanding and trust with our students. By making our decisions about how we design classes and select reading assignments visible to our students, we also help students more clearly see the value of reading activities.

Another component to building trust around creating archival spaces for reading may also mean being vulnerable and sharing with students what our own practices and decisions are around how we store, archive, and maintain records of our own reading. I think it is easy for our students to forget that, as instructors, we are also often active readers. Even if it is not explicitly our job to do *research* as part of our job titles or responsibilities, we are all necessarily reading, writing, and exploring new ideas as part of our everyday work as educators (you're definitely one of these people if you're reading this book!). To that end, we can help students better understand what it *looks* like to do this work at the nuts-and-bolts level if we share our own tools, workflows, and practices.

I realize that perhaps the idea of sharing your own reading workflows and processes (digital and otherwise) can strike a pang of anxiety in your heart. "What if my own workflow is messy and unclear?" you might wonder. "What if I don't fully understand the implications of where I store and disseminate my own intellectual work? What if I don't see myself as a model of digital research and writing work for my students? What if I'm still refining my approaches to reading and writing in digital spaces?"

There's a short answer to all these questions that I hope is a comfort: don't worry about it. There remains tremendous value in helping your students understand how you work, archive, and take notes on your ideas no matter how messy, complicated, and convoluted your workflow is. Integrity and vulnerability go a long way toward building trust in pedagogy, so if you feel like your own research and writing workflows could use some overhaul, or you could develop a greater understanding of the platforms you're using and how those platforms handle data privacy, great! Sharing your own uncertainty and your own critical questions creates valuable bonds with your class community and helps raise the kinds of critical questions that students did not even know that they could ask. In other words, simply talking about what it means to archive our own work, including the challenges, the limitations, and the affordances we face, is valuable. If we want our students to make thoughtful choices about how, where, and why they work in particular ways, we have to model that thoughtfulness ourselves.

Where and how we spend our screen time is an intensely contested issue because it comes down to what our values are and what material conditions are available to us that shape those values. If we are privileged enough to have options about where and how we produce particular kinds of work, we have to weigh the implications of our choices and what they might mean for our ability to complete work in sustained ways. If we are not privileged enough to have these options about where and how we produce work, we *still* have to weigh the implications of our choices while also finding ways to compensate for the inherent limitations of whatever choice we make.

I wish that I had an answer for archiving our work that was as simple as: "Here's the one surefire way to ensure that your workflow is engaged, sustained, well managed, and well archived." I'm afraid I don't really have an answer to that question because our technology continues to change. Plus, the more options we have available to us, the more choices we have to weigh. As long as surveillance capitalism dictates much of the educational technology market, we also have to remain vigilant about researching where and how our data gets used.

Sometimes it's simpler to ignore the options, to continue tried and true workflows. I'm sympathetic, after all, to the concept that if something is not broken, there is no need to fix it. And I also don't want to advocate for changing how we work and store ideas just because there *are* other solutions available. With that said, I think that there is a benefit in keeping an open mind to options for learning and working, and for exploring new ways of doing work, particularly if we recognize that our own methods have critical limitations or if our own methods close us off to an understanding of how our students, colleagues, or collaborators may be working.

The value in exploring new ways of storing, archiving, and tracking our knowledge is simple: it allows us to understand the people who use a diverse array of techniques. When we are in the role of educators, we are, perhaps, in the most critical position of all to examine, evaluate, and experience new ways of working and learning for ourselves so that we can better understand how to help the myriad, diverse students we see in our classrooms.

Strategies for Archiving Evidence of Learning and Reading Online

We've weighed a lot of the challenges and complexities of storing evidence of reading online already, and we've covered some of the ways in which you might empower students to make some of their own choices about reading and archiving evidence of their reading online. I think it is still important, however, to offer some really concrete advice to students who want to carefully track their reading about some ways they can do this without too much additional stress. Let me first say that the student suggestions I provide here about archiving evidence of learning and reading online are very much grounded in the moment in which I'm writing this book. Because our materials can have such a tremendous impact on our techniques, my perspectives and strategies are shaped by this moment in time when cloud-based computing is ubiquitous; files are now available anywhere there's an internet connection. Although we cannot always count on having documents from the internet at our fingertips, the current conditions seem to suggest that we can count on having access more often than not. What this means is that our perspective toward archives is largely shaped by an understanding that cloud-based storage is a stable way of ensuring that documents can be shared, accessed, and preserved anywhere that internet access is available.

With this perspective on the material conditions (and limitations) in mind, I offer a few suggestions for how we might have conversations with our students about archiving evidence of our reading and learning:

- *Encourage students to come up with a clear and consistent way of storing files, documents, and activities for a particular class context.* How many of us are guilty of downloading files from the internet and then simply saving them to a desktop or to the generic Documents folder on the hard drive? Or how many of us let downloaded documents simply languish in a temporary Downloads file in the internet browser? It is all too easy for us to forget that digital documents often need to be sorted and stored in order for us to keep track of them. The same goes, of course, for any readings and reading notes that we may take over the course of a class. Therefore, at the very beginning of a course term, I'd encourage you to include a specific note to students somewhere that encourages them to label and develop clear and consistent ways of storing and tracking documents. Not everyone necessarily wants to store and file documents in identical ways, but a core digital competency is understanding where files go and how to find and restore usable and productive files. Although it is too heavy-handed and didactic to require students to name and file documents, you can provide a reminder for students, drawing explicit attention to how important it is for them to develop an organizational file system so they can track the learning they glean from readings in your class.

- *Develop mindfulness around metadata and how that metadata might impact future storage or understanding of the document (and its annotations).* Metadata is often something that we ignore in our documents, especially when we're focusing on the *content* of the document rather than how or when the document was created. For the most part, those most interested in metadata on college campuses are librarians, but as the lifespan of our documents grows longer online, and as the origins of digital documents become of even greater critical interest, spending just a bit more time helping our students identify the metadata of their documents may help them stay better organized. For example, a short amount of time in class might be spent showing students how to access the About information on a word-processed document so that they can see when and how the document was produced and how large the file size is. If students know this information, they may also understand where they want to store the document for their own files or how they want to keep track of multiple versions of a particular document. By helping students orient to the metadata of their documents, we may also help them better understand the metadata of *other* documents, too, a skill that may help them interpret the context for other documents that they may encounter online and in their research.
- *Offer students a list of tools or resources for storing, sharing, and archiving documents and notes.* Our students' reading, archiving, and note-taking practices typically stem from whatever experiences they cultivated during high school. To that end, some students have experienced a wide range of exposure to various tools and technologies for storing

and annotating their readings, whereas others have had limited access to particular learning tools. As an instructor, curating a list of resources that students may use to store, share, and archive documents and notes ensures that students are equally aware of how to access information or resources that may benefit their learning. Whereas tools alone will not necessarily make students good readers, these tools may offer students some avenues for exploring their thinking and deepen their insights in ways that may not have been possible before with the resources available to them. I have a recommended list of tools, current as of the publication in this book, in the appendix, but you may find it useful to create your own. A resource list may be something you include in a syllabus or it can be an additional document you give to your students at the beginning of a term. Just as you might direct students to resources on campus, like a tutoring center, a list of online tools may give them avenues for supporting their work in your class.

It is worth noting that archiving evidence of learning has most visibly taken form in a particular pedagogical framework: ePortfolio pedagogy. ePortfolios (electronic portfolios), broadly defined, take the form of web spaces, like a blog or a website, that students populate with artifacts of their learning from either a particular course or a group of courses they've taken during their college career. ePortfolios empower students to collect, curate, and reflect upon anything from research papers to low-stakes writing assignments to lab reports to problem sets. Exactly what goes into the ePortfolio is up to the student and is often framed by how the instructor introduces and integrates the ePortfolio assignment into a particular course or term. ePortfolios often take the form of a final capstone project in a particular course, but they can also be used as low-stakes interventions for students, merely allowing them to keep track of what they're producing, reflecting on, or working on throughout a course. Instructors can also use ePortfolios for student advising to help students reflect on how the courses they've taken throughout college may reflect their values, interests, and goals. The possibilities for ePortfolios are many, but primarily, they all invite students to be conscious of what they've learned throughout a course and of how their learning can be transferred to contexts both within and beyond the course itself.

An ePortfolio is but one powerful tool students can use to create a mindful, structured archive of reflections on course readings or other kinds of work they produced throughout a term. Using an ePortfolio is a powerful technique, and for it to be successful, it is essential that you carefully scaffold class activities and frame the value of ePortfolio as a project (see Eynon & Gambino, 2017; and Penny Light, Chen, & Ittelson, 2011, for more on this). Regardless of how instructors encourage students to archive their work, whether it is through ePortfolio pedagogy or through smaller technical interventions, one thing is clear: encouraging students to keep records of their work and to look back on it is critical to making learning experiences memorable, transferrable, and, above all, accessible to diverse groups of learners.

Looking Ahead

Students learn and remember content in a variety of ways and, as instructors, it is not up to us to dictate the terms for how students retain and transfer understandings that they glean from particular reading assignments. What we can make space for, however, are a variety of avenues through which students can work to apply, reflect upon, and remember what they learn from their readings. By opening up options for reading, storing, and archiving ideas in digital spaces, we move students closer to participating in Universal Design for Learning (UDL) pedagogy, a framework that invites flexible learning environments for our neurodiverse students. It is simply not possible for every pedagogical strategy we take to reach every single learner, but the more options that we can reasonably provide to our students, the more equitable we make our educational practices and the more students we can reach. Helping students understand how they can archive their work is but one way to reach more of them where we are. As we continue to think more about the possibilities of reading in digital spaces, we get even closer to finding more ways that students can become engaged in reading.

PRINCIPLES, PRACTICES, AND FUTURES FOR DIGITAL READING

I often find myself thinking at the intersection of techno-optimism and pessimism: my instructional design peers often want to talk about the latest and greatest learning gadgets to inspire their faculty and to "optimize" their workflows. The faculty I support often just want learning solutions with the least amount of technical overhead. My instructional design peers remain hopeful for the next great development in online learning, convinced of the value that digital spaces can have for our students. The instructors I support worry about whether our students will be oversaturated in media, concerned that yet more exposure and incorporation of digital tools in their classes simply reinforces an "always-on" culture (with credit to danah boyd 2012 for this phrase), a space where being disconnected just ceases to exist.

I am deeply sympathetic to both of these perspectives. My optimistic side wants to find promise in the digital developments happening all around us. The tools we use, the technologies incorporated in our lives, are such inseparable parts of our learning experiences. I'm inclined to suggest that we grapple with these tools, look at them critically, determine what's useful, and discard the rest rather than ignore them or excise them from our learning situations entirely. My pessimistic side wonders if the optimistic side is naive. The last thing I want to do is make my students' work vulnerable to exploitation or to lock my students out from accessing the kind of work that they've spent so much time and energy completing.

We obviously cannot accept all tools for learning, and as educators, our job is to both develop our own digital literacy, enough to be critical of the tools that we select, and to understand the implications of what we select both for ourselves and for our students. It sounds challenging to do this, and it is. But we can find ways to make peace with the tools in our lives as long as we select ones that support the work we want to do. Our work needs to drive the tools we use, not the other way around.

To that end, this final chapter takes us right back to the tensions that we've been navigating throughout this book: between adapting to the conditions of our constantly changing technologies and teaching the ways of reading that remain critical to knowledge consumption and analysis. Perhaps it is better that this tension remains unresolved because its existence means that, as educators, we remain constantly mindful of and flexible toward the materials that shape our teaching and learning while also keeping our own learning goals and objectives at the heart of the work that we do. Even for those of us who are educators and not necessarily teachers, keeping this tension in the forefront of our minds allows us to remain nimble in our learning and our own ability to adapt to the ways in which information is consumed, exchanged, and produced in our various disciplines.

So, what do we do with the knowledge of this tension? What does remaining mindful of this tension look like? How do we help our students understand and process this tension for themselves in ways that do not pathologize their own device usage or learning? To answer these questions, I offer three remaining principles for readers of this book to practice as they consider the importance of reading in digital spaces moving forward.

Principle #1: Remain Flexible and Open-Minded, Yet Critical

Digital tools are another avenue we can use to open up and explore new possibilities in learning. I don't see educational technology as the solution to problems in learning, but I don't see it as a barrier to learning either. The analogy I like to make is a simple one: in a classroom, you're able to do certain activities if you have a whiteboard at the front of the room and the students are seated at desks. Imagine you now have a chalkboard in addition to the whiteboard. You may be able to do some slightly different things now that you know that you have additional writing space. Now imagine that you also have a projector in that room. You now have three options: the whiteboard, the chalkboard, and the projector. You suddenly have several options for displaying and communicating information. Will you use all three tools all the time? Probably not. Some days you may only need the projector or only the chalkboard. But it's nice to know that you have the options of using all three.

Although chalkboards, whiteboards, and projectors are

not very fancy, they all remain examples of educational technology. I view all tools, from the extensive and elaborate to the simple and straightforward, as possibilities. Until a tool is proven to be *detrimental* to learning, which some tools can be (more on that in a moment), I like to look at tools with a glass-half-full approach. What can this tool do? What does it offer?

Over the years that I've been assessing which educational technologies instructors in my institution might want to adopt, I've developed an internal heuristic that I'll share now as part of this first principle of being flexible, open-minded, and critical. This heuristic is just one way of following this first principle, but it is the approach, I hope, that at least gives you some groundwork for doing the important work of considering the options for educational technology while also remaining critical enough to reject tools that may harm student learning or discriminate against particular student populations.

A.   What does this tool do? What are its core functions?

This is an obvious question to ask when you are considering whether to adopt a particular tool, but it's an important one to consider and try to break down into the simplest of terms nonetheless. For some tools, especially digital learning ones, it can be hard to understand what the tool actually *does* and how it actually works. So, when you are trying to decide which tool to use, try to think through how it would work in a classroom. What would you do with it? What kinds of activities would be possible with it? How would you imagine doing certain learning activities with this tool at your disposal?

For instructors in my program, I designed a grid (see Table 3) to help them think this through.

Table 3. Learning Activity Chart: A Graphic Organizer That Instructors Can Use to Consider How Learning Activities Might Align with Different Spaces, Modalities, and Learning Contexts

LEARNING ACTIVITY TYPE	WHY?	WHERE?	TOOLS NEEDED	ALTERNATIVES	YOUR QUESTIONS
(e.g., large-group discussion, small-group activity, individual writing, think-pair-share)	(e.g., "this activity tindependent reflection before students share their ideas.")	(e.g., In the classroom at tables, in the classroom on computers, outside in the quad, at home on Canvas)	(e.g., tables, whiteboards, computers, collaboration stations, Google Docs, etc.)	(e.g., this type of activity could be conducted out of class OR this type of activity could be done in a discussion forum rather than on a whiteboard.)	(e.g., "Is it possible to do this kind of activity online?" OR "How might this activity be better designed to center the student?")
....	....	....	....	....	....
....	....	....	....	....	....
....	....	....	....	....	....
....	....	....	....	....	....
....	....	....	....	....	....
....	....	....	....	....	....

B.   Where does this tool work? On a Mac, PC, or Linux lap-
     top? On a Chromebook (i.e., a laptop that can only use
     Google Chrome and no other software or applications)?
     On a smartphone? On a tablet? Can components of this
     tool be exported to file formats (like PDFs or images) so
     that they can be printed out on paper if need be? Can
     components of this tool be used with assistive/adaptive
     technology, like speech-to-text tools or screen readers?

     Not all tools are usable on all devices, so it's important
to keep in mind what your students have access to when
you pick a tool for them to adopt. Bear in mind that 95% of
college students have access to smartphones (99% of whom
own the smartphones themselves) and 91% own laptops
(97% of whom own them personally) (Gierdowski, 2019a).

     The question of what devices students will use to ac-
cess their learning causes a lot of technologists and teachers who use technology to throw up their hands and say,
"Why bother using new tools if I can't find one that's
compatible with all of these various devices?" Indeed, if
a particular tool or application only works on one kind
of device, it should be a deal-breaker. But you may find a
cluster of tools that do some roughly similar operations,
and those operations—those options—may still be of
value to you and your students for the learning experience you hope to develop and curate.

     Another way to respond to this question is to consider
how you can accommodate multiple devices using the
same tool in the room. Does the version of the tool on a
laptop seem really different than the version of the same
tool on the smartphone or the tablet? Or are these tools
similar enough that you can facilitate an activity with this
tool and invite students to use any kind of device they
bring into the classroom?

C. Does this tool require a stable internet connection to work or can it work offline?

We can't always rely on a stable internet connection to do our teaching. According to recent EDUCAUSE survey data collected and analyzed by Dana Gierdowski (2019b), 24% of college students report having fair to poor Wi-Fi access on their college campuses (p. 15). In fact, even for me, teaching at a university in Silicon Valley, a place where you would expect the highest speed and most reliable wireless internet out there, not all of our students have regular and consistent internet connections either, even on campus. The tremendous lack of access to reliable Wi-Fi networks became all the more acute in the wake of the COVID-19 pandemic in 2020 when undergraduate students had to join classes remotely. Some students remained on campus, but many others returned to homes where Wi-Fi access was limited to nonexistent (Casey, 2020; Kelly, 2020; Woolley, Sattiraju, & Moritz, 2020). Therefore, it's important to consider whether a tool functions successfully offline if a connection gets lost.

If the tool only functions when students are online, another question to consider is how disruptive temporarily losing a connection may be. For some tools, going offline may just mean that the tool freezes for a moment until a connection is reestablished. Other times, losing a connection may mean that information gets lost in the process. If you are assessing whether to adopt a particular tool, you may want to test out this issue by turning the internet on your device off and then turning it back on again to replicate what it looks like to that device when the internet cuts out. Your experience navigating between the offline and the online experiences may determine the extent to which you wish to integrate that

particular tool into your students' learning experience
and how well it fits their needs.

D. Who is using this tool? If students are the intended users,
    how well does this tool help reach this audience?

Not all possible learning tools are built for educational
environments and contexts. For example, most word-
processing tools were not exclusively designed with educational contexts or audiences as the primary users. That
doesn't mean that these tools aren't useful, but you'll
want to consider, when assessing the tool, how its functionality and user interface may or may not be under-
standable for a student audience.

As a concrete example, I often browse around for various PDF editors for students to use when they're reading
and annotating PDF documents. Some PDF editors tend
to be built more for a business audience than an educational one, which means that some of the functionality
that students frequently use, like applying sticky notes,
might be harder to find in the user interface than tools
that a business audience might use, like creating a form
in the PDF. I tend to try and find PDF editors that are
geared more toward student usage so that the functional-
ities students may want are apt to be more visible.

E. How is the audience's privacy protected when using this
    tool? How is/isn't the data that users enter used to power
    the tool and its functionality?

We are all becoming increasingly aware of the fact
that efforts to protect our personal information are critical to feeling safe and protected when we are working
online. While Chapter 9 spent more time emphasizing
thinking critically about the importance of protecting
user privacy online, it is important to reiterate the value
of checking in on privacy and data concerns when you

are selecting a new tool for students to engage with in their digital reading practice. Some users may not have a clear sense of why data and privacy might matter for them, while some might struggle to understand why privacy matters to others, even if it's not of great importance to them individually. Autumm Caines and Erin Rose Glass (2019) suggest that to invite conversations about data privacy and to show your support for students who may have concerns, you should include a statement in the course syllabus that invites students to assess whether using a particular classroom technology infringes upon their privacy. Caines and Glass suggest the following questions for instructors to include in their syllabus:

- What types of personal data do you think are collected through your use of digital tools for educational activities?
- What value does your personal data have for different contexts and entities? Consider how your data might be valued by your instructor, the institution, yourself, and companies.
- Who owns your personal data, who can sell it, and who can use it?
- Do you have concerns about how your personal data can be used? If so, what are they?
- Are there aspects of your identity or life that you feel would put you in a place of special vulnerability if certain data were known about you or used against you?

Caines and Glass (2019) acknowledge that not all students read or engage with such statements and others may still need guidance through these statements, but their point is sound: instructors should make some kind of statement to acknowledge that they understand that data is not neutral and that privacy should not be taken for granted. Instructors may help guide students through these kinds of questions or attempt to answer these questions for themselves as part of selecting tools for engaging in a digital reading practice.

F. How would this tool be used for assessment? What attitude toward assessment does this particular tool communicate?

Whenever we adopt a new tool, we have to consider assessment within the tool from two perspectives: how might we assess student work within the tool and how might the tool's framework frame student assessment for us?

As one caveat here, *assessment* does not necessarily mean "grading." Whenever we adopt a tool for something, reading in particular, we likely won't want to give students a grade for how well they've read something; by many instructors' standards, that would probably be far too controlling and detrimental to students' willingness to read in whatever ways make the most sense to them. Plus, much recent higher education conversation and literature about grading practices suggests that grading can make learning feel like a punishment, resulting in students being highly demotivated to learn (Supiano, 2019; Stommel, 2018; Kohn, 1993).

That said, assessment means gauging student engagement with a particular tool. It means looking at what students are able to do in the tool and determining how well they do that work. Assessment may also mean giving feedback to students on their work, even when that feedback is mostly meant to be encouraging. For example, when we're picking new tools, we want to consider how we can assess their efficacy. In what ways will we gather and give feedback? What will that process look like?

Many tools built for educational purposes also have assessment mechanisms built in, and as an instructor, you want to consider what those mechanisms communicate. For example, if the tool includes a space to give a student a particular grade, you want to consider, as an instructor, whether you want to engage with that grading dynamic. Does the grading dynamic only allow you to give numerical scores? Or holistic letter grades? Or something else? Consider how the tool's grading mechanism aligns with your own grading philosophy.

G. What kinds of bodies can use this tool? Which bodies are included/excluded through using this particular tool?

When we're picking an educational technology, we need to consider accessibility for different kinds of users. Specifically, we need to consider whether disabled users may be able to access and engage with the tool. For example, is the tool screen-reader compatible? Is the text searchable in the tool? Is there enough color contrast in the tool so that particular buttons and operations are visible to everyone? When assessing every tool, you should engage in some dialogue around who may be excluded by a tool's interface; interested readers may want to look to more in-depth engagements with Universal Design for Learning (UDL) to learn more about how to assess tools for accessibility (Murawski & Scott, 2019; Tobin & Behling, 2018; Baglieri and Shapiro, 2017; Dolmage, 2014 Womack, 2017; Oswal and Meloncon, 2014). When implemented thoughtfully, UDL should make learning more accessible to all learners, not just those with disabilities, and all students may find value in lessons designed with UDL. We may not necessarily be able to accommodate or anticipate all possible needs, but as we search for different tools, we should aim to keep student's needs forefront in our minds.

H. How can the users back up or export their own intellectual property while or after they use the tool?

Keeping content locked within a third-party tool may not necessarily be a problem, but when students are doing intellectual labor within the tool, it is better to give them the option to transfer or transport that information in whatever ways they would like. Think about how you would feel if your content was only accessible in one particular platform; you might feel frustrated that you couldn't move, change, or transfer that content to another place when you saw fit. For students, this situation is exacerbated when they may want to access material they've produced for a class, but are unable to do so—if they lose access after graduation, for example. Make sure any third-party tool you choose does not prevent students from accessing or engaging with material, even when they are no longer a student at the university.

Other factors that you may want to include in your own tool assessment metrics may center around cost, for example, or learning management system integration (otherwise known as *learning tools interoperability*, or *LTI*) if you are concerned about embedding your tools directly into your university's learning management system space. I chose to leave these factors off of this particular heuristic because orientations to these kinds of concerns may differ from institution to institution. Instead, this heuristic offers some grounding principles to narrow the field of options and help you to select tools with your students' learning needs in mind. I suspect that some factors in this heuristic may change in time, especially if (and when) some of these orienting principles to our technologies change. But what I want to emphasize above all, and at a bare minimum, is that our students' concerns should always be the ones that we center when we consider technology choices.

Principle #2: Listen to Your Students

As an instructor, it can be easy to convince yourself that any activity you spend a significant amount of time designing is going to work. When you're someone who thinks carefully about an activity's learning outcomes and what kinds of steps you'll help your students get to in order to achieve those outcomes, you probably feel pretty confident that the activity is going to meet those students exactly where they are. Incorporating new educational technologies into these activities adds yet another layer of complexity to the activity: if you've taken the time to select a particular tool and to apply it into your pedagogy carefully, you must feel pretty confident in the value of the tool.

Every bit of planning can go out the window, however, if you start to hear that something in your classroom is just not landing the way that you expected it to. I once organized a fairly complicated activity in one of my classes where students had to rotate between different computer stations around the classroom (I was teaching in a classroom with five built-in computers known as collaboration stations) and access a different set of materials at each station. When each group went to each station, they would then do two things: enter some notes into a Google Doc on the station and add some highlights to a PDF-based reading within a shared annotation tool. The idea was that even though students would be at different stations they would all still be collaboratively working together to build a shared resource and to build comments on shared readings together. In theory, the idea was brilliant: student-centered, active, engaged, and networked.

I wouldn't call the activity a disaster exactly, but it was chaotic to say the least. Students were confused about all of the different moving parts of the activity. They weren't sure where to post which pieces of information and the timing was way too tight. I was asking students to move pretty quickly around the room, and they barely had any time to engage with the task. I found myself running from station to station, needing to explain a lot more than I had anticipated.

But there was a silver lining: one group, of their own accord, decided to change the activity. One of the group members beckoned me over, complaining that the computer had frozen when they tried to access the Google Doc. I hopped onto the computer station and attempted to fix the situation. At first, I tried to get the students to pivot by accessing the Google Doc on one of their laptops instead. However, one of the students spoke up: "Can we just use the whiteboard to take the notes?" gesturing to the whiteboard behind the computer station. At first, I hesitated: I wanted everyone to be able to see each other's notes outside of the classroom. I found myself at first trying to convince them to get back into a different Google Doc, but then it hit me: why was I so insistent on having them complete the activity in exactly this one way?

So, I listened and I let go. They soon started to scribble away on the board behind the computer. Another group noticed what the enterprising group began and started to do the same thing (even though their computer was functioning normally). Eventually, the walls were filled with whiteboard drawings and notes. Some groups still worked in the Google Doc and the PDF; indeed, the online notes still wound up being pretty robust. But students gave themselves greater options: some groups found the online note-taking a lot more intuitive while others found the whiteboard easier to access. Everyone found a way to engage, but the pathways just looked more diverse and more variable than I had anticipated. Although I had initially felt frustrated that my elaborate activity bombed, I left the room impressed that my students had stripped away the unnecessary complexities while keeping the goals of the activity in mind.

That moment transformed my teaching in two ways: first, it was a good reminder to simplify my lesson plans and not to try to pack in too much. But second, and more importantly, the experience also showed me that if I listened to my students when they identified alternative pathways, they could be a lot more proactive and engaged than if I simply kept them all working in lockstep. As a learner, I tend to thrive off of a lot of structure and tend to do better if I'm following the same instructions as everyone else, but as an instructor, I've realized that the ways that I love to learn are not the ways that everyone else loves to learn. As much as I enjoy rules and structure, lots of students out there thrive with more open-ended prompts. There's no real way to reach everyone equally all the time, but there are lots of ways to be empathetic and to provide multiple options and pathways into learning. Even in a fully online environment, many students find their own pathways and options for engaging in their spaces.

So, be flexible. Listen to what your students are telling you. And don't just listen and dismiss: really listen. Then, adapt.

It's not that you have to abandon your goals altogether; if you communicate your goals clearly and give students various avenues to meet those goals, they will trust you. Indeed, students are in a position where they want guidance and structure from you, but they also want agency within that structure. That, ideally, is what all of us want: a way into something new that we can also make our own. Reading, writing, communicating, and learning are no different.

Principle #3: Trust Your Students and Their Motivation to Learn

When I was a graduate student, I remember overhearing so many frustrated hallway conversations among my fellow graduate student teaching assistants and instructors about student motivations.

> "They don't want to read anything!"
> "I can barely get them to read a five-page article, much less a novel!"
> "I just don't know what will *motivate* them other than grades."

They weren't wrong. Some students don't want to read anything and they may not be motivated beyond grades. We can't fundamentally change some students' orientation to learning if they're not interested in changing that orientation for themselves. Instead, I argue that, as educators, it's also not really our jobs to convince anyone to love something that they don't inherently love.

What we can do, however, is trust that our students are coming into the room with the best of intentions. Sure, it may frustrate us that they don't want to read the thing that we love reading. But we can also probably remember our own educational experiences when we felt completely unmotivated by what was in front of us. For instance, I wanted absolutely nothing to do with math classes after I took a statistics class in high school. Even in my humanities classes, I found myself bored to tears (at one point, *literal* tears) by critical theory. But I found it within myself to find the motivation somewhere, somehow, to engage with my instructors at a certain point. I wasn't always the ace student in everything, but I didn't always want to be. The point is that I found my way into the assignments, the activities, and the classes in the ways that made sense to me. Being able to articulate that was a form of motivation even if it wasn't necessarily giving my class the 100% effort that I might have done for something that I really cared about.

We need to remind ourselves that motivation can take different forms and appearances. It does not have to look like all-out effort. We may not always be able to see motivation by looking at our students from the outside. Although motivation can look like seeing our students' faces buried into books, barely coming up for air, it may not look that way for everyone. It's the same principle I touched on earlier in this book: attention may look like staring attentively at a professor during a lecture, but it also may look like students typing notes into their laptops, perhaps with several windows open so they can check sources or define words that they hear along the way. What works for us may not work for others.

Of course, at times it will be glaringly obvious that our students truly lack motivation. An averted gaze, a slumped body in a chair, or a beleaguered sigh coming from a student can feel discouraging. How do we reach people who don't want to be reached? How do we respond to negativity and frustration in ways that don't simply replicate the negativity or exacerbate the frustration?

I'll tell one other story of my own experience working with a student who just did not want to read or write. When I was a tutor in the college writing center as an undergraduate, a student came into the center for an appointment with me, sat down at a table across from me, slumped into his seat, and then turned *his whole body* completely away from me. When I asked him how he was doing and what he wanted to work on for the day, he paused, took his paper out of his backpack, slammed it on the table and simply said, "Here's the essay I have to write." I didn't quite know what to do. I tried to maintain a chipper tone, and I leaned across the table to take a look at the essay. I could tell that a lot of work still needed to be done on it, but my writing center training told me that I should not just take the essay and do the work for him; rather, I should engage in a conversation with him about his work. I had to find a way to reach him somehow. At the time, I didn't know how to do it.

I asked around for advice later and got a brilliant suggestion from a colleague: if a student is completely unmotivated to work, just start a conversation about something unrelated to the project or the work. Ask about something he has really been enjoying doing lately. Ask him about a recent event on campus and his reaction it. Ask him about a cool button on his backpack. In other words, try to find where he *is* motivated and see how cultivating that positive attitude might tap into a more productive line of conversation. This might mean going off topic from the task at hand and veering into a completely different conversation, but at least the conversation is moving rather than remaining stagnant. In other words, giving students space just to talk about whatever is on their minds and finding an area of interest to them is often better than brute forcing a path through to get a particular task accomplished.

In short, what that experience revealed to me is that, even when students are unmotivated, we can aim to meet them where they are. It may not be possible to *convince* a student to be motivated to learn exactly what we may have to teach, but we can at least reach out, show that we care about who they are, and see what choices they decide to make from there. It's important not to deny the inevitable feeling of frustration we may experience when we try hard, prep a lot, and then reach out to our students and receive little in return. But rather than stewing in negativity over students who will not change or who will not do the assignment, we are better off staying positive, trusting that students will find their way, whether their path looks like ours or not.

Further still, we have to trust students to develop their motivation in ways that make the most sense to them at different moments in their educational trajectories. We can be encouraging and supportive while also being realistic. We can help them see the consequences of their motivation (or lack thereof) and guide them through their choices thereafter. In short, even if students are unmotivated, we have to trust the choices that they make for themselves even when they don't look like our choices.

What Do We Do about Digital Reading Now?

What I hope this book has made clear is that understanding reading means understanding how we consume, produce, and share information. Reading has never just been about contrasting the media itself, the books versus scrolls or the books versus screens; reading is about *listening* and *seeing* other people's stories. Reading is about getting access to new worlds, new minds, and new experiences. Reading gives us a unique window into the inner consciousness of others, a window that we so rarely get to see. We know that reading builds empathy, critical thinking, and deepened awareness. To that end, reading encompasses a wide range of possibilities and practices. When we close off choices for *how* we read, we may also close off what we can read and access. For the students that we support, closing off this access in our classrooms may mean closing off access for an even longer period of time after that. I can't tell you how many people I've met who have said that the most influential books they've read have been ones they encountered in high school or college. Schooling spaces, as discriminatory and inequitable as they can be, have a tremendous impact on what people read in the years beyond.

The more open-minded we can be, the more we can expose our students to the range of possibilities inherent in reading. The more we may encourage exploration, experimentation, and exposure to new ideas, the more we open up new ways of thinking. We can skim, we can dive, and then we can surface when we read, moving between the many worlds of knowledge that reading helps us enter. Reading, regardless of where it's happening, is an invitation to learn, to grow, and to excel. That's something that I hope for everyone to access through every media change we may encounter in the years to come. Everyone can be a reader, and we make that invitation all the more visible when we understand the diverse and compelling forms that reading takes.

TOOLS FOR DIGITAL READING

. . . .

This list of tools is for those of you who are interested in trying out applications of the digital reading approaches mentioned within this book. This tool list is current as of 2020 so be aware that some of these tools may no longer exist or may no longer be functional by the time you are reading this. That said, this starting list may offer you either a current or historical understanding of the applications available for fostering digital reading practices. This is not intended to be a comprehensive list; it is intended to offer a starting point for exploration of particular tools and applications.

Note that I've primarily selected tools that are available for students and instructors to use for free. However, some tools on this list are not freely available or are available on *freemium* models, where users can only engage with the tool in a limited capacity for free. I indicate which tools are free, freemium, or require subscription.

PDF Annotation Tools (for online desktop/laptop and mobile application usage)

....

- PDFescape (free): https://www.pdfescape.com/
- Scrible (freemium): https://www.scrible.com/
- PowerNotes (subscription required): https://powernotes.com/

PDF Annotation Tools (for offline desktop/laptop and mobile application usage)

....

- Foxit Reader (free): https://www.foxitsoftware.com/
  pdf-reader/
- Notability (freemium): https://www.gingerlabs.com/
- Adobe Acrobat Reader (freemium): https://acrobat.adobe.
  com/us/en/acrobat/pdf-reader.html

Social Annotation Tools (for online desktop/laptop and mobile application usage)

....

- Hypothes.is (free): http://hypothes.is
- NowComment (free): https://nowcomment.com/
- VoiceThread (freemium): https://voicethread.com/
- Perusall (free): https://app.perusall.com/
- PowerNotes (available by license): http://www.powernotes.
  com

Collaborative Document Composing Tools (for online desktop/laptop and mobile application usage)

....

- Google Drive/Docs (free): https://drive.google.com
- MediaWiki (free): https://www.mediawiki.org/wiki/
  MediaWiki
- Etherpad (free): https://etherpad.org/

Tools for Improving Accessibility (for online and offline access)

- Convert image-based PDF documents into text-based PDFs (online OCR conversion via Online OCR) (free): https://www.onlineocr.net/
- Text-to-voice application and mobile video editor (via Kinemaster) (free): https://www.kinemaster.com/

Content Curation and Bookmarking Tools (for online desktop/laptop and mobile application usage)

- Diigo (freemium): https://www.diigo.com/
- Pocket (free): https://getpocket.com/
- Padlet (freemium): https://padlet.com/
- Microsoft OneNote (part of the Microsoft 360 suite): https://onenote.com
- PowerNotes (available by license): https://www.powernotes.com
- Wakelet (free): https://wakelet.com/
- Pearltrees (free): https://www.pearltrees.com/

Citation Management Tools (for online and offline desktop/laptop access)

- Zotero (free): https://zotero.org
- Mendeley (free): https://www.mendeley.com
- EndNote (subscription required): https://endnote.com/

Visualization Tools (for online desktop/laptop and mobile application usage)

- Lucidchart (freemium): https://lucidchart.com/
- Piktochart (freemium): https://piktochart.com/
- Venngage (freemium): https://venngage.com/
- Aww App (free): https://awwapp.com/

- Canva (freemium): https://www.canva.com/
- Google Jamboard (part of enterprise Google license): https://jamboard.google.com

Slideware Creation Tools (for online and offline desktop/laptop access)

- PowerPoint (subscription required): https://products.office.com/en-us/powerpoint
- Google Slides (free): https://slides.google.com
- Adobe Spark (freemium): https://spark.adobe.com
- Canva (freemium): https://www.canva.com

Journaling or Note-Taking Tools (for online desktop/laptop and mobile application usage)

- Google Drive/Docs (free): https://drive.google.com
- Etherpad (free): https://etherpad.org/
- Evernote (freemium): https://evernote.com/
- Google Keep (free): https://keep.google.com/u/0/
- Microsoft OneNote (part of Microsoft 360 suite): https://onenote.com

Polling Tools (for online desktop/laptop and mobile application usage)

- Poll Everywhere (freemium): https://www.polleverywhere.com
- Kahoot! (freemium): https://kahoot.com/
- Mentimeter (freemium): https://www.mentimeter.com
- Top Hat (available by license): https://tophat.com/

REFERENCES

Ackerman, R., & Goldsmith, M. (2011). Metacognitive regulation of text learning: On screen versus on paper. *Journal of Experimental Psychology: Applied*, *17*(1), 18.

Adams, M. J. (2000). Theoretical approaches to reading instruction. In D. A. Wagner, R. L. Venezky, & B. V. Street (Eds.), *Literacy: An international handbook*. Boulder, CO: Westview Press.

Aguilar-Roca, N. M., Williams, A. E., & O'Dowd, D. K. (2012). The impact of laptop-free zones on student performance and attitudes in large lectures. *Computers & Education*, *59*(4), 1300–1308.

Ahmed, S. (2014). *The cultural politics of emotion*. United Kingdom: Edinburgh University Press.

Ainsworth, B., Allen, N., Dai, J., Elder, A., Finkbeiner, N., Freeman, A., Hare, S., . . . Thompson, L. (2020). *Marking open and affordable courses: Best practices and case studies*. Retrieved from https://uta.pressbooks.pub/markingopenandaffordablecourses/

Alexander, J., Micciche, L. R., & Rhodes, J. (2013). Indirection, anxiety, and the folds of reading. *Reader: Essays in Reader-Oriented Theory, Criticism, and Pedagogy*, *65/66* (Fall 2013/Spring 2014), 43–71.

Alexis, C. (2017). The symbolic life of the Moleskine notebook: Material goods as a tableau for writing identity performance. *Composition Studies*, *45*(2), 32–54.

Allen, I. E., & Seaman, J. (2017). *Digital learning compass: Distance education enrollment report 2017*. 1–39. Retrieved from https://onlinelearningsurvey.com/reports/digtiallearningcompassenrollment2017.pdf

Alter, A. (2018). *Irresistible: The rise of addictive technology and the business of keeping us hooked*. New York, NY: Penguin Random House.

Altick, R. D. (1998). *The English common reader: A social history of the mass reading public, 1800–1900*. Columbus: Ohio State University Press.

Alves, J. (2013, June 23). Unintentional knowledge. *Chronicle of Higher Education*. Retrieved from https://www.chronicle.com/article/Unintentional-Knowledge/139891

Alzain, A., Clark, S., Ireson, G., & Jwaid, A. (2018). Adaptive education based on learning styles: Are learning style instruments precise enough? *International Journal of Emerging Technologies in Learning (iJET), 13*(09), 41–52.

Amadieu, F., Tricot, A., & Mariné, C. (2009). Prior knowledge in learning from a non-linear electronic document: Disorientation and coherence of the reading sequences. *Computers in Human Behavior, 25*(2), 381–88. doi:10.1016/j.chb.2008.12.017

Ambrose, S. A., Bridges, M. W., DiPietro, M., Lovett, M. C., & Norman, M. K. (2010). *How learning works: Seven research-based principles for smart teaching.* San Francisco, CA: Jossey-Bass Education.

American Press Institute (2015, March 16). How millennials get news: Inside the habits of America's first digital generation. Retrieved from https://www.americanpressinstitute.org/publications/reports/survey-research/millennials-news/single-page/

Anderson, S. (2015, June 17). My approach to digital content curation. TeachThought [blog]. Retrieved from https://www.teachthought.com/technology/my-approach-to-digital-content-curation/

Archibald, T. N. (2010). *The effect of the integration of social annotation technology, first principles of instruction, and team-based learning on students' reading comprehension, critical thinking, and meta-cognitive skills.* (Doctoral dissertation, Florida State University). Retrieved from https://fsu.digital.flvc.org/islandora/object/fsu%3A168354

Arola, K. L., & Wysocki, A. (Eds.). (2012). *Composing media = composing embodiment.* Boulder: University Press of Colorado.

Association of College and Research Libraries (ACRL). (2017). Framework for Information Literacy for Higher Education. Retrieved from http://www.ala.org/acrl/sites/ala.org.acrl/files/content/issues/infolit/Framework_ILHE.pdf

Athreya, B. H., & Mouza, C. (2017). *Thinking skills for the digital generation: The development of thinking and learning in the age of information.* Cham, Switzerland: Springer International Publishing.

Augustine, St. (1993). *Confessions: Books I–XIII.* (F. J. Sheed, Trans.). Indianapolis, IN: Hackett.

Azmuddin, R. A., Nor, N. F. M., & Hamat, A. (2017). Metacognitive online reading and navigational strategies by science and technology university students. *GEMA Online Journal of Language Studies, 17*(3).

Baglieri, S., & Shapiro, A. (2017). *Disability studies and the inclusive classroom: Critical practices for embracing diversity in education* (2nd ed.). New York, NY: Routledge.

Balingit, M. (2018, April 24). Racial disparities in school discipline are growing, federal data shows. *Washington Post.* Retrieved from https://www.washingtonpost.com/local/education/racial-disparities-in-school

-discipline-are-growing-federal-data-shows/2018/04/24/67b5d2b8
-47e4-11e8-827e-190efaf1f1ee_story.html

Balogh, J. (1927). IX: Voces paginarum. *Philologus*, *82*(1–4), 84–109.

Baron, N. (2015). *Words onscreen: The fate of reading in a digital world*.
United Kingdom: Oxford University Press.

Baron, N. S., Calixte, R. M., & Havewala, M. (2017). The persistence of
print among university students: An exploratory study. *Telematics and
Informatics*, *34*, 590–604.

Bartholomae, D., Petrosky, A., & Waite, S. (2017). *Ways of reading: An
anthology for writers* (11th Edition). Boston, MA: Bedford St. Martin's.

Beck, E., Grohowski, M., & Blair, K. (2017). Subverting virtual hierarchies:
A cyberfeminist critique of course-management spaces. In J. P. Purdy
& D. N. DeVoss (Eds.), *Making space: Writing instruction, infrastructure,
and multiliteracies*. Ann Arbor: University of Michigan Press.

Beckett, L. (2019, October 22). Under digital surveillance: How American
schools spy on millions of kids. *The Guardian*. Retrieved from https://
www.theguardian.com/world/2019/oct/22/school-student-surveillance
-bark-gaggle

Berry, M. J., & Westfall, A. (2015). Dial D for distraction: The making
and breaking of cell phone policies in the college classroom. *College
Teaching*, *63*(2), 62–71.

Birkerts, S. (1994). *The Gutenberg elegies: The fate of reading in an electronic
age*. New York, NY: Farrar, Straus, and Giroux.

Blair, A. M. (2010). *Too much to know: Managing scholarly information before
the modern age*. New Haven, CT: Yale University Press.

Bowman, L. L., Levine, L. E., Waite, B. M., & Gendron, M. (2010). Can
students really multitask? An experimental study of instant messaging
while reading. *Computers & Education*, *54*(4), 927–31.

boyd, d. (2012). Participating in the always-on lifestyle. In M. Mandiberg
(Ed.), *The social media reader* (pp. 71–76). New York, NY: New York
University Press.

Brady, R. (2007). Learning to stop, stopping to learn: Discovering the
contemplative dimension in education. *Journal of Transformative
Education*, *5*(4), 372–94.

Brandt, D. (1990). *Literacy as involvement: The acts of writers, readers, and
texts*. Carbondale: Southern Illinois University Press.

Brandt, D. (2015). *The rise of writing: Redefining mass literacy*. United
Kingdom: Cambridge University Press.

Brost, B., & Bradley, K. (2006). Student compliance with assigned reading:
A case study. *Journal of the Scholarship of Teaching and Learning*, 101–11.

Bunn, M. (2013). Motivation and connection: Teaching reading (and
writing) in the composition classroom. *College Composition and
Communication*, *64*(3), 496–516.

Burak, L. (2012). Multitasking in the university classroom. *International Journal for the Scholarship of Teaching and Learning, 6*(2). doi:10.20429 /ijsotl.2012.060208

Burchfield, C. M., & Sappington, J. (2000). Compliance with required reading assignments. *Teaching of Psychology, 27*(1), 58–60.

Caines, A., & Glass, E. R. (2019, October 14). Education before regulation: Empowering students to question their data privacy. *EDUCAUSE*. Retrieved from https://er.educause.edu/articles/2019/10/education -before-regulation-empowering-students-to-question-their-data-privacy

Carillo, E. C. (2017). *A writer's guide to mindful reading: Practices & possibilities*. Fort Collins, CO: The WAC Clearinghouse and University Press of Colorado. Retrieved from https://wac.colostate.edu/books /practice/mindful/

Carillo, E. C. (2019). Navigating this perfect storm. *Pedagogy, 19*(1), 135–59.

Carney, A. G., Fry, S. W., Gabriele, R. V., & Ballard, M. (2010). Reeling in the big fish: Changing pedagogy to encourage the completion of reading assignments. *College Teaching, 56*(4), 195–200.

Casey, N. (2020, April 4). College made them feel equal. The virus exposed how unequal their lives are. *New York Times*. Retrieved from https:// www.nytimes.com/2020/04/04/us/politics/coronavirus-zoom-college -classes.html

Caulfield, M. A. (2017). *Web literacy for student fact-checkers*. PressBooks. Retrieved from https://webliteracy.pressbooks.com/

Cavanagh, S. R. (2016). *The spark of learning: Energizing the college classroom with the science of emotion*. Morgantown: West Virginia University Press.

Chartier, R. (1994). *The order of books: Readers, authors, and libraries in Europe between the fourteenth and eighteenth centuries* (L. G. Cochrane, Trans.). Cambridge, United Kingdom: Polity Press.

Chen, B., Seilhamer, R., Bennett, L., & Bauer, S. (2015). Students' mobile learning practices in higher education: A multi-year study. Retrieved from https://er.educause.edu/articles/2015/6/students-mobile -learning-practices-in-higher-education-a-multiyear-study

Chick, N. L., Hassel, H., & Haynie, A. (2009). "Pressing an ear against the hive": Reading literature for complexity. *Pedagogy: Critical Approaches to Teaching Literature, Language, Composition, and Culture, 9*(3), 399–422.

Claxton, G. (2011). *Intelligence in the flesh: Why your mind needs your body much more than it thinks*. New Haven, CT: Yale University Press.

Clump, M. A., Bauer, H., & Bradley, C. (2004). The extent to which psychology students read textbooks: A multiple class analysis of reading across the psychology curriculum. *Journal of Instructional Psychology, 31*(3).

Cochrane, D., & Ahlman, L. (2017, April 27). College costs in context: A state-by-state look at college unaffordability. The Institute for College Access and Success, 1–12. Retrieved from https://ticas.org /affordability-2/college-costs-context/

Cohn, J. (2016a). "Devilish smartphones" and the "stone-cold" internet: Implications of the technology addiction trope in college student digital literacy narratives. *Computers and Composition, 42,* 80–94.

Cohn, J. (2016b). *The books that bind us: Remediation of the printed book as social practice in the 21st century.* University of California, Davis.

Collier, A. (2017, August 28). Digital sanctuary: Protection and refuge on the web? Retrieved from https://er.educause.edu/articles/2017/8 /digital-sanctuary-protection-and-refuge-on-the-web

Collins, J. (2010). *Bring on the books for everybody: How literary culture became popular culture.* Durham, NC: Duke University Press.

Coiro, J. (2015). Purposeful, critical, and flexible: Vital dimensions of online reading and learning. In R. J. Spiro, M. DeSchryver, M. S. Hagerman, P. M. Morsink, & P. Thompson, (Eds.), (2015). *Reading at a crossroads? Disjunctures and continuities in current conceptions and practices.* New York, NY: Routledge.

Coiro, J., & Dobler, E. (2007). Exploring the online reading comprehension strategies used by sixth-grade skilled readers to search for and locate information on the internet. *Reading Research Quarterly, 42*(2), 214–57.

Corlett-Rivera, K., & Hackman, T. (2014). E-book use and attitudes in the humanities, social sciences, and education. *Portal: Libraries and the Academy, 14*(2), 255–86.

Cornelius, T. L., & Owen-DeSchryver, J. (2008). Differential effects of full and partial notes on learning outcomes and attendance. *Teaching of Psychology, 35*(1), 6–12. doi:10.1080/00986280701818466

Corrigan, P. T. (2012). Painting as a reading practice. *Pedagogy: Critical Approaches to Teaching Literature, Language, Composition, and Culture, 12*(1), 168–75.

Corrigan, P. T. (2013). Attending to the act of reading: Critical reading, contemplative reading, and active reading. *Reader, 65/66,* 146–73.

Craig, J. W. (2019). Affective materialities: Places, technologies, and development of writing processes. *Composition Forum, 41*(1). Retrieved from http://compositionforum.com/issue/41/affective -materialities.php

Craig, J. W., & Davis, M. (2019). A difference in delivery: Reading classroom technology policies. In M. R. Lamb & J. R. Parrott (Eds.) *Digital reading and writing in composition studies.* New York, NY: Routledge.

Crain, P. (2013). Reading childishly? A codicology of the modern self. In N. K. Hayles & J. Pressman (Eds.), *Comparative textual media:*

Transforming the humanities in the PostPrint era. Minneapolis: University of Minnesota Press.

Crary, J. (2001). *Suspensions of perception: Attention, spectacle, and modern culture*. Cambridge, MA: MIT Press.

Culver, T. F. (2016). Increasing reading compliance and metacognitive strategies in border students. *Journal of College Reading and Learning*, *46*(1), 42–61.

Cunningham, B. (2007, December). Digital native or digital immigrant, which language do you speak? *Academic Advising Today*, *30*(4). Retrieved from https://nacada.ksu.edu/Resources/Academic-Advising -Today/View-Articles/Digital-Native-or-Digital-Immigrant-Which -Language-Do-You-Speak.aspx

Daniel, D. B., & Woody, W. D. (2013). E-textbooks at what cost? Performance and use of electronic v. print texts. *Computers & Education*, *62*, 18–23. doi:10.1016/j.compedu.2012.10.016

Darnton, R. 1982. What is the history of books? *Daedalus*, *111*(3): 65–83.

Dehaene, S. (2009). *Reading in the brain: The new science of how we read*. New York, NY: Penguin Books.

Delgado, P., Vargas, C., Ackerman, R., & Salmeron, L. (2018). Don't throw away your printed books: A meta-analysis on the effects of reading media on reading comprehension. *Educational Research Review*, *25*, 23–28.

DeMartini, B., Marshall, J., & Chew, M. (2018). Putting textbooks in students' hands. *Technical Services Quarterly*, *35*(3), 233–45.

DeRosa, R. & Robison S. (2017). From OER to open pedagogy: Harnessing the power of open. In R. S. Jhangiani & R. Biswas-Diener (Eds.), *Open: The philosophy and practices that are revolutionizing education and science*. London, UK: Ubiquity Press. doi:10.5334/bbc.i

Deschaine, M. E., & Sharma, S. A. (2015). The five Cs of digital curation: Supporting twenty-first-century teaching and learning. *InSight: A Journal of Scholarly Teaching*, *10*, 19–24.

Diaz, J. T. (2012). The digital archive as a tool for close reading in the undergraduate literature course. *Pedagogy Critical Approaches to Teaching Literature Language Composition and Culture*, *12*(3), 425–47.

Dolmage, J. T. (2014). *Disability rhetoric*. New York, NY: Syracuse University Press.

Eisenstein, E. L. (1980). *The printing press as an agent of change*. United Kingdom: Cambridge University Press.

Elliott-Dorans, L. R. (2018). To ban or not to ban? The effect of permissive versus restrictive laptop policies on student outcomes and teaching evaluations. *Computers & Education*, *126*, 183–200.

Eynon, B., & Gambino, L. (2017). *High impact e-portfolio practice: A catalyst for student, faculty, and institutional learning*. Stylus Publishing LLC.

Fadiman, A. (2000). *Ex Libris: Confessions of a common reader*. New York, NY: Macmillan.

Fairfax, T. (1691). *Advice to a young lord*. For R. Baldwin.

Fang, Z. (2016). Teaching close reading with complex texts across content areas. *Research in the Teaching of English*, *51*(1), 106.

Farinosi, M., Lim, C., & Roll, J. (2016). Book or screen, pen or keyboard? A cross-cultural sociological analysis of writing and reading habits basing on Germany, Italy and the UK. *Telematics and Informatics*, *33*(2), 410–21.

Fischer, S. R. (2003). *A history of reading*. London, UK: Reaktion Books.

Fisher, D., & Frey, N. (2014). Contingency teaching during close reading. *The Reading Teacher*, *68*(4), 277–86. doi:10.1002/trtr.1298

Fleckenstein, K. S. (1999). Writing bodies: Somatic mind in composition studies. *College English*, *61*(3), 281–306.

Franzese, A. T., & Felten, P. (2017). Reflecting on reflecting: Scholarship of teaching and learning as a tool to evaluate contemplative pedagogies. *International Journal for the Scholarship of Teaching and Learning*, *11*(1). doi:10.20429/ijsotl.2017.110108

Friesen, N. (2017). *The textbook and the lecture: Education in the age of new media*. Baltimore, MD: Johns Hopkins University Press.

Froese, A. D., Carpenter, C. N., Inman, D. A., Schooley, J. R., Barnes, R. B., Brecht, P. W., & Chacon, J. D. (2012). Effects of classroom cell phone use on expected and actual learning. *College Student Journal*, *46*(2), 323–32.

Galanek, J. D., Gierdowski, D. C., & Brooks, D. C. (2018, October 25). ECAR study of undergraduate students and information technology, 2018. *EDUCAUSE*, 47. Retrieved from https://www.educause.edu/ecar/research-publications/ecar-study-of-undergraduate-students-and-information-technology/2018/introduction-and-key-findings

Gao, F. (2013). A case study of using a social annotation tool to support collaborative learning. *Internet and Higher Education*, 17, 76–83.

Gierdowski, D. C. (2019a, May 28). ECAR study of community college students and information technology, 2019. *EDUCAUSE*, Retrieved from https://library.educause.edu/resources/2019/5/ecar-study-of-community-college-students-and-information-technology

Gierdowski, D. C. (2019b, October 30). ECAR study of undergraduate students and information technology, 2019. Research report. *EDUCAUSE*. Retrieved from https://library.educause.edu/resources/2019/10/2019-study-of-undergraduate-students-and-information-technology

Gierdowski, D. C., and Galanek J. D. (2020, June 1). ECAR study of the technology needs of students with disabilities, 2020. *EDUCAUSE*. Retrieved from https://er.educause.edu/blogs/2020/6/ecar-study-of-the-technology-needs-of-students-with-disabilities-2020.

Gilliard, C. (2017, July 3). Pedagogy and the logic of platforms. *EDUCAUSE*. Retrieved from https://er.educause.edu/articles/2017/7/pedagogy-and-the-logic-of-platforms

Gitelman, L. (2014). *Paper knowledge: Toward a media history of documents*. Durham, NC: Duke University Press.

Glass, A. L., & Kang, M. (2019). Dividing attention in the classroom reduces exam performance. *Educational Psychology*, *39*(3), 395–408.

Goldrick-Rab, S. (2016). *Paying the price: College costs, financial aid, and the betrayal of the American dream*. Chicago, IL: University of Chicago Press.

Gose, B. (2017, September 17). A new generation of digital distraction. *Chronicle of Higher Education*. Retrieved from https://www.chronicle.com/article/Gen-Z-Changes-the-Debate-About/241163

Green, J. (2001). Spelling chuckers. *Critical Quarterly*, *43*(3), 147–51.

Gregory, C. L. (2008). "But I want a real book": An investigation of undergraduates' usage and attitudes toward electronic books. *Reference & User Services Quarterly*, *47*(3), 266–73.

Gulliver, K. (2014, December 1). Digital natives like a good lecture, too. *Chronicle of Higher Education*. Retrieved from https://www.chronicle.com/article/Digital-Natives-Like-a-Good/150301

Gunnlaugson, O. (2009). Establishing second-person forms of contemplative education: An inquiry into four conceptions of intersubjectivity. *Integral Review*, *5*(1), 26.

Haas, C. (1996). *Writing technology: Studies on the materiality of literacy*. Mahwah, NJ: Lawrence Erlbaum Associates.

Haas, C., & Flower, L. (1988). Rhetorical reading strategies and the construction of meaning. *College Composition and Communication*, *39*(2), 167–83.

Hamdan, N. A., Mohamad, M., & Shaharuddin, S. (2017). Hypermedia reading materials: Undergraduate perceptions and features affecting their reading comprehension. *Electronic Journal of e-Learning*, *15*(2), 116–25.

Hanz, K., & McKinnon, D. (2018). When librarians hit the books: Uses of and attitudes toward e-books. *Journal of Academic Librarianship*, *44*, 1–14.

Harman, B. A., & Sato, T. (2011). Cell phone use and grade point average among undergraduate university students. *College Student Journal*, *45*(3), 544–55.

Harris, M. (2014). *The end of absence: Reclaiming what we've lost in a world of constant connection*. New York, NY: Penguin Group.

Hart, T. (2004). Opening the contemplative mind in the classroom. *Journal of Transformative Education*, *2*(1), 28–46.

Hartman, D. K., & Morsink, P. M. (2015). Reading at a million crossroads: Massively pluralized practices and conceptions of reading. In R. J.

Spiro, M. DeSchryver, M. S. Hagerman, P. M. Morsink, & P. Thompson (Eds.), *Reading at a crossroads? Disjunctures and continuities in current conceptions and practices*. New York, NY: Routledge.

Haskins, C. (2019, November 1). Gaggle knows everything about teens and kids in school. *BuzzFeed News*. Retrieved from https://www.buzz feednews.com/article/carolinehaskins1/gaggle-school-surveillance -technology-education

Hayles, K. N. (2010). How we read: Close, hyper, machine. *ADE Bulletin*, *150*(18), 62–79.

Head, A. J., DeFrain, E., Fister, B., & MacMillan, M. (2019). Across the great divide: How today's college students engage with news. *First Monday*, *24*(8). https://firstmonday.org/ojs/index.php/fm/article/view /10166/8057

Hendrickson, G. L. (1929). Ancient reading. *Classical Journal*, *25*(3), 182–96.

Hicks, T. (2011, October 22). Teach digital writing: Five paradigm shifts for K–12 education. *The Current*. Retrieved from https://thecurrent .educatorinnovator.org/collection/teach-digital-writing-five-paradigm -shifts-for-k-12-education

Hill, P. (2019, March 11). Instructure: Plans to expand beyond Canvas LMS into machine learning and AI. *E-Literate*. Retrieved from https:// eliterate.us/instructure-plans-to-expand-beyond-canvas-lms-into -machine-learning-and-ai/

Hobbs, K., & Klare, D. (2016). Are we there yet? A longitudinal look at e-books through students' eyes. *Journal of Electronic Resources Librarianship*, *28*(1), 9–24. doi:10.1080/1941126X.2016.1130451

Hobbs, R. (2018, March 10). Freedom to choose: An existential crisis. *Renee Hobbs at the Media Education Lab*. https://mediaedlab.com /2018/03/10/freedom-to-choose-an-existential-crisis/

Hobbs, R (2011). *Digital and media literacy: Connecting culture and classroom*. Thousand Oaks, CA: Corwin Press.

Hoeft, M. E. (2012). Why university students don't read: What professors can do to increase compliance. *International Journal for the Scholarship of Teaching and Learning*, *6*(2), 1–19.

Horning, A. S. (2019). Developing information literacy through critical reading and writing. In M. R. Lamb, & J. M. Parrott (Eds.). *Digital reading and writing in composition studies*. New York, NY: Routledge. 41–56.

Howard, N. (2009). *The book: The life story of a technology*. Baltimore, MD: The Johns Hopkins University Press.

Howard, R. M., Serviss, T., & Rodrigue, T. K. (2010). Writing from sources, writing from sentences. *Writing & Pedagogy*, *2*(2). doi:10.1558/wap .v2i2.177

Hwang, W., Wang, C., & Sharples, M. (2007). A study of multimedia annotation of web-based materials. *Computers in Education*, 48(4), 680–99.

Hyler, J., & Hicks, T. (2014). *Create, compose, connect! Reading, writing, and learning with digital tools.* New York, NY: Routledge.

Ignacio Madrid, R., Van Oostendorp, H., & Puerta Melguizo, M. C. (2009). The effects of the number of links and navigation support on cognitive load and learning with hypertext: The mediating role of reading order. *Computers in Human Behavior*, 25(1), 66–75. doi:10.1016/j.chb.2008 .06.005

Jackson, L. (2010). The talking book and the talking book historian: African American cultures of print—The state of the discipline. *Book History*, 13(1), 251–308.

Jaggars, S. S. (2014). Choosing between online and face-to-face courses: Community college student voices. *American Journal of Distance Education*, 28(1), 27–38.

Jajdelska, E. (2007). *Silent reading and the birth of the narrator.* Canada: University of Toronto Press.

Jhangiani, R. S., & Jhangiani, S. (2017). Investigating the perceptions, use, and impact of open textbooks: A survey of post-secondary students in British Columbia. *The International Review of Research in Open and Distributed Learning*, 18(4). https://doi.org/10.19173/irrodl.v18i4 .3012

Johns, A. (1998). *The nature of the book: Print and knowledge in the making.* Illinois: University of Chicago Press.

Johnson, T. E., Archibald, T. N., & Tenenbaum, G. (2010). Individual and team annotation effects on students' reading comprehension, critical thinking, and meta-cognitive skills. *Computers in Human Behavior*, 26, 1496–507.

Kalir, R., & Garcia, A. (2020). *Annotation.* Cambridge: MIT Press. Retrieved from https://mitpressonpubpub.mitpress.mit.edu/annotation

Kay-Shuttleworth, J. (1853). *Public education: As affected by the minutes of the committee of privy council from 1846 to 1852; with suggestions as to future policy.* London, United Kingdom: Longman, Green, Longman, and Roberts.

Keen, A. (2012). *Digital vertigo: How today's online social revolution is dividing, diminishing, and disorienting us.* New York, NY: Macmillan St. Martin's Press.

Keller, D. (2014). *Chasing literacy: Reading and writing in an age of acceleration.* Boulder, CO: Utah State University Press.

Kelly, M. (2020, March 6). As COVID-19 pushes classes online, some students are caught in the broadband gap. *The Verge*. Retrieved from https://www.theverge.com/2020/3/6/21168463/coronavirus -covid19-seattle-public-schools-networks-broadband

Kerr, M. M., & Frese, K. M. (2017). Reading to learn or learning to read? Engaging college students in course readings. *College Teaching, 65*(1), 28–31.

Kim, J. (2010, March 9). Laptop bans are a terrible idea. *Insider Higher Ed*. Retrieved from https://www.insidehighered.com/blogs/technology -and-learning/laptop-bans-are-terrible-idea

King, C. M. (2019). The reader in the textbook: Embodied materiality and reading in the writing classroom. *Composition Studies, 47*(1), 95–115.

Kirschner, P. A. (2017). Stop propagating the learning styles myth. *Computers & Education, 106*, 166–71. doi:10.1016/j.compedu.2016.12 .006

Kirschner, P. A., & Karpinski, A. C. (2010). Facebook and academic performance. *Computers in Human Behavior, 26*(1), 1237–45.

Knox, B. M. (1968). Silent reading in antiquity. *Greek, Roman, and Byzantine Studies, 9*(4), 421–35.

Kohn, A. (1993). *Punished by rewards: The trouble with gold stars, incentive plans, A's, praise, and other bribes*. Boston, MA: Houghton Mifflin.

Kress, G. (2003). *Literacy in the new media age*. New York, NY: Routledge.

Kretzschmar, F., Pleimling, D., Hosemann, J., Fussel, S., Bornkessel-Schlesewsky, I., & Schlesewsky, M. (2013). Subjective impressions do not mirror online reading effort: Concurrent EEG-eyetracking evidence from the reading of books and digital media. *PLOS One, 8*(2), 1–11.

Kulkarni, C., & Chi, Ed. (2013, April). All the news that's fit to read: A study of social annotations for news reading. Conference on Human Factors in Computing Systems—Proceedings. 2407–16. doi:10.1145/2470654.2481334

Lamb, M. R., & Parrott, J. M. (Eds.). (2019). *Digital reading and writing in composition studies*. New York, NY: Routledge.

Lang, J. M. (2016). *Small teaching: Everyday lessons from the science of learning*. San Francisco, CA: Jossey-Bass.

Lanier, J. (2010). *You are not a gadget: A manifesto*. New York, NY: Random House.

LaRose, R. (2010). The problem of media habits. *Communication Theory, 20*(2), 194–222.

Lederman, D. (2018, October 31). Conflicted views of technology: A survey of faculty attitudes. *Inside Higher Ed*. Retrieved October 23, 2019, from https://www.insidehighered.com/news/survey/conflicted-views -technology-survey-faculty-attitudes

Lei, S. A., Bartlett, K. A., Gorney, S. E., & Herschbach, T. R. (2010). Resistance to reading compliance among college students: Instructors' perspectives. *College Student Journal, 44*(2), 219–29.

Levine, L. E., Waite, B. M., & Bowman, L. L. (2007). Electronic media use, reading, and academic distractibility in college youth. *Cyberpsychology and Behavior, 10*(4), 560–66.

Library Journal Research (2018). Academic student experience ebook survey. Retrieved from https://s3.amazonaws.com/WebVault/research /2018_AcademicStudentEbookExperience.pdf

Licastro, A. (2019). The past, present, and future of social annotation. In M. R. Lamb & J. M. Parrott (Eds.), *Digital reading and writing in composition studies*. New York, NY: Routledge. 87–104.

Lieberman, M. (2017, August 9). The digital-native debate. *Inside Higher Ed*. Retrieved from https://www.insidehighered.com/digital-learning /article/2017/08/09/are-digital-natives-more-tech-savvy-their-older -instructors

Lin, L., Robertson, T., & Lee, J. (2009). Reading performances between novices and experts in different media multitasking environments. *Computers in the Schools*, *26*(3), 169–86.

Liu, Z. (2005). Reading behavior in the digital environment: Changes in reading behavior over the last ten years. *Journal of Documentation*, *61*(6), 700–712.

Locke, J. (1712). *Some thoughts concerning education*. A. & J. Churchill.

Lockhart, T., & Soliday, M. (2016). The critical place of reading in writing transfer (and beyond): A report of student experiences. *Pedagogy Critical Approaches to Teaching Literature Language Composition and Culture*, *16*(1), 23–37.

Mangen, A., Olivier, G., & Velay, J.-L. (2019). Comparing comprehension of a long text read in print book and on Kindle: Where in the text and when in the story? *Frontiers in Psychology*, *10*. doi:10.3389/fpsyg .2019.00038

Mangen, A., Walgermo, B. R., & Bronnick, K. (2013). Reading linear texts on paper versus computer screen: Effects on reading comprehension. *International Journal of Educational Research*, *58*(1), 61–68.

Manguel, A. (1996). *A history of reading*. London, United Kingdom: HarperCollins.

Mathews, M. M. (1966). *Teaching to read, historically considered*. Chicago, IL: The University of Chicago Press.

McIntosh, J. (2019). Clip, tag, annotate: Active reading practices for digital texts. In M. R. Lamb & J. M. Parrott (Eds.), (2019). *Digital reading and writing in composition studies*. New York, NY: Routledge. 176–88.

McKitterick, D. (2003). *Print, manuscript and the search for order, 1450– 1830*. Cambridge, United Kingdom: Cambridge University Press.

McLuhan, M. (1964). *Understanding media: The extensions of man*. Cambridge, MA: MIT Press.

Meyer, J., & Land, R. (2006). *Overcoming barriers to student understanding: Threshold concepts and troublesome knowledge*. New York, NY: Routledge.

Micciche, L. (2014). Writing material. *College English*, *76*(6), 488–505.

Mihailidis, P., & Cohen, J. N. (2013). Exploring curation as a core competency in digital and media literacy education. *Journal of Interactive Media in Education, 2013*(1), 2.

Miller, K., Lukoff, B., King, G., & Mazur, E. (2018, March). Use of a social annotation platform for pre-class reading assignments in a flipped introductory physics class. *Frontiers in Education, 3,* 8. doi:10.3389/feduc.2018.00008

Miller, R. E. (2016). On digital reading. *Pedagogy Critical Approaches to Teaching Literature Language Composition and Culture, 16*(1), 153–64.

Miller, T. P., & Leon, A. (2017). Introduction to special issue on literacy, democracy, and fake news: Making it right in the era of fast and slow literacies. *Literacy in Composition Studies, 5*(2), 10–23.

Mizrachi, D., Salaz, A. M., Kurbanoglu, S., & Boustany, J., on behalf of the ARFIS Research Group. (2018). Academic reading format preferences and behaviors among university students worldwide: A comparative survey analysis. *PLOS ONE, 13*(5). doi:10.1371/journal.pone.0197444

Monaghan, J. E. (2005). *Learning to read and write in colonial America: Literacy instruction and acquisition in a cultural context.* Amherst, MA: University of Massachusetts Press.

Morehead, K., Dunlosky, J., & Rawson, K. A. (2019). How much mightier is the pen than the keyboard for note-taking? A replication and extension of Mueller and Oppenheimer. *Educational Psychology Review, 31*(3). 753–80. doi:10.1007/s10648-019-09468-2

Morris, J. (2016). A genre-based approach to digital reading. *Pedagogy Critical Approaches to Teaching Literature Language Composition and Culture, 16*(1), 125–36.

Morris, J. (2019). Annotating with Google Docs: Bridging collaborative reading and writing in the composition classroom. In M. R. Lamb & J. M. Parrott (Eds.), *Digital reading and writing in composition studies.* New York, NY: Routledge. 116–29.

Mueller, P. A., & Oppenheimer, D. M. (2014). The pen is mightier than the keyboard: Advantages of longhand over laptop note taking. *Psychological Science, 25*(6), 1159–68.

Murawski, W. M., & Scott, K. L. (Eds.). (2019). *What really works with Universal Design for Learning.* Corwin: A SAGE Publishing Company.

Myatt, J. (2019). Reorienting relationships to reading by dwelling in our discomfort. In M. R. Lamb & J. M. Parrott (Eds.), *Digital reading and writing in composition studies.* New York, NY: Routledge. 161–73.

Myrberg, C., & Wiberg, N. (2015). Screen vs. paper: what is the difference for reading and learning? *Insights, 28*(2).

National Center for Educational Statistics (2017). Fast Facts. Enrollment: Do you have information on postsecondary enrolment rates? Retrieved August 30, 2020, from https://nces.ed.gov/fastfacts/display.asp?id=98

Nehamas, A. & Woodruff, P. (1997). Phaedrus. In Cooper, J. M., *Plato: Complete works*, Indianapolis IN: Hackett.

Nielsen, J. (2006). F-shaped pattern for reading web content (original study). Nielsen Norman Group. Retrieved from https://www.nngroup.com/articles/f-shaped-pattern-reading-web-content-discovered/

Noble, S. J. (2018). *Algorithms of oppression*. New York, NY: New York University Press.

Nokelainen, P., Miettinen, M., Kurhila, J., Floréen, P., & Tirri, H. (2005). A shared document-based annotation tool to support learner-centred collaborative learning. *British Journal of Educational Technology*, *36*(5), 757–70.

Novak, E., Razzouk, R., & Johnson, T. E. (2012). The educational use of social annotation tools in higher education: A literature review. *Internet and Higher Education*, *15*, 39–49.

Oldenburg, R. (1989). *The great good place: Cafes, coffee shops, community centers, beauty parlors, general stores, bars, hangouts, and how they get you through the day*. Cambridge, MA: Da Capo Press.

Ong, W. J. (1982). *Orality and literacy: The technologizing of the word*. London, United Kingdom: Methuen.

Ophir, E., Nass, C., & Wagner, A. D. (2009). Cognitive control in media multitaskers. *Proceedings of the National Academy of Sciences of the United States of America*, *106*(37), 15583–87.

Oswal, S. K., & Meloncon, L. (2014). Paying attention to accessibility when designing online courses in technical and professional communication. *Journal of Business and Technical Communication*, *28*(3), 271–300.

Pargman, D., Hedin, B., & Hrastinski, S. (2013). Using group supervision and social annotation systems to support students' academic writing. *Högre Utbildning*, *3*(2), 129–34.

Penny Light, T., Chen, H. L., & Ittelson, J. C. (2011). *Documenting learning with ePortfolios: A guide for college instructors*. San Francisco, CA: Jossey-Bass Publishers.

Pernice, K. (2017). F-shaped pattern of reading on the web: Misunderstood, but still relevant (even on mobile). Nielsen Norman Group. Retrieved from https://www.nngroup.com/articles/f-shaped-pattern-reading-web-content/

Perrin, A. (2016, September 1). Majority of Americans are still reading print books. Pew Research Center. Retrieved from https://www.pewinternet.org/2016/09/01/book-reading-2016/

Piper, A. (2012). *Book was there: Reading in electronic times*. Chicago, IL: University of Chicago Press.

Porter-O'Donnell, C. (2004). Beyond the yellow highlighter: Teaching annotation skills to improve reading comprehension. *English Journal*, *93*(5), 82.

Postman, N. (1992). *Technopoly: The surrender of culture to technology*. New York, NY: Vintage.

Prensky, M. (2001, October). Digital natives, digital immigrants. *On the Horizon, 9*(5). MCB University Press.

Protopsaltis, A. (2008). Reading strategies in hypertexts and factors influencing hyperlink selection. *Journal of Educational Multimedia and Hypermedia, 17*(2), 191–213.

Pryal, K. R. G., & Jack, J. (2017, November 27). When you talk about banning laptops, you throw disabled students under the bus. *HuffPost*. Retrieved from https://www.huffpost.com/entry/when -you-talk-about-banning-laptops-you-throw-disabled_b_5a1ccb4ee4 b07bcab2c6997d

Qadir, N. (2018). Tuning your pedagogical practice: Incorporate digital and social technology. *Inside Higher Ed*. Retrieved from https://www .insidehighered.com/blogs/gradhacker/tuning-your-pedagogical -practice-incorporate-digital-and-social-technology

Qualley, D. (2019). How digital writing and design can sustain reading, or Prezi is not just for presentations—Well, now, maybe it is. In M. R. Lamb & J. M. Parrott (Eds.), *Digital reading and writing in composition studies*. New York, NY: Routledge. 176–88.

Ravizza, S. M., Hambrick, D. Z., & Fenn, K. M. (2014). Non-academic internet use in the classroom is negatively related to classroom learning regardless of intellectual ability. *Computers & Education, 78*, 109–14. doi:10.1016/j.compedu.2014.05.007

Rea, A., & White, D. (1999). The changing nature of writing: Prose or code in the classroom. *Computers and Composition, 16*(3), 421–36.

Reed, J. M. (2018). The history of the textbook: The state of the discipline. *Book History, 21*, 397–424. doi:10.1353/bh.2018.0013

Rees, J. (2018, September 26). Preparing for the post-LMS world. (opinion). *Inside Higher Ed*. Retrieved from https://www.insidehighered .com/digital-learning/views/2018/09/26/role-faculty-post-lms-world -opinion

Reid, A. J. (2014). A case study in social annotation of digital text. *Journal of Applied Learning Technology, 4*(2), 15–25.

Richards, N. (2015, February 13). The Fifty Shades of Grey Paradox. *Slate Magazine*. Retrieved from https://slate.com/technology/2015/02/fifty -shades-of-grey-and-the-paradox-of-e-reader-privacy.html

Rodrigue, T. K. (2017a). Digital reading: Genre awareness as a tool for reading comprehension. *Pedagogy Critical Approaches to Teaching Literature Language Composition and Culture, 17*(2), 235–57.

Rodrigue, T. K. (2017b). The digital reader, the alphabetic writer, and the space between: A study in digital reading and source-based writing. *Computers and Composition, 46*, 4–20. doi:10.1016/j.compcom.2017 .09.005

Rose, D., & Dalton, B. (2009). Learning to read in the digital age. *Mind, Brain, and Education*, *3*(2), 74–83.

Rule, H. J. (2017). Sensing the sentence: An embodied simulation approach to rhetorical grammar. *Composition Studies*, *45*(1), 19–38.

Rule, H. J. (2018). Writing's rooms. *College Composition and Communication*, *69*(3), 402–32.

Salmerón, L., Kintsch, W., & Cañas, J. J. (2006). Reading strategies and prior knowledge in learning with hypertext. *Memory and Cognition*, *34*, 1157–71.

Schüll, N. D. (2014). *Addiction by design: Machine gambling in Las Vegas*. Princeton, NJ: Princeton University Press.

Schwartz, D., Tsang, J., & Blair, K. (2016). *The ABCs of how we learn*. New York, NY: W. W. Norton.

Scribner, S., & Cole, M. (1981). Unpackaging literacy. *Writing: The Nature, Development, and Teaching of Written Communication*, *1*, 71–87.

Seaman, J. E., & Seaman, J. (2019). *Freeing the textbook: Educational resources in U.S. higher education, 2018*. 1–48. Retrieved from https://www.onlinelearningsurvey.com/reports/freeingthetextbook2018.pdf

Seaman, J. E., & Seaman, J. (2020). *Inflection point: Educational resources in U.S. higher education, 2019*. 1–41. Retrieved from https://www.onlinelearningsurvey.com/reports/2019inflectionpoint.pdf

Sellen, A., & Harper, R. (2002). *The myth of the paperless office*. Cambridge, MA: MIT Press.

Seneca. (1917). *Epistles, Volume I: Epistles 1–65*. (Richard M. Gummere, Trans.). Loeb Classical Library 75. Cambridge, MA: Harvard University Press. https://www.loebclassics.com/view/LCL075/1917/volume.xml

Shapiro, L. (2011). *Embodied cognition*, 1st edition. New York, NY: Routledge.

Sharma, A., Van Hoof, B., & Pursel, B. (2013). An assessment of reading compliance decisions among undergraduate students. *Journal of the Scholarship of Teaching and Learning*, *13*(4), 23.

Sharma, S. A., & Deschaine, M. E. (2016). Digital curation: A framework to enhance adolescent and adult literacy initiatives. *Journal of Adolescent & Adult Literacy*, *60*(1), 71–78. doi:10.1002/jaal.523

Singer, N. (2017, May 13). How Google took over the classroom. *New York Times*. Retrieved from https://www.nytimes.com/2017/05/13/technology/google-education-chromebooks-schools.html

Smale, M. A. (2020). "It's a lot to take in"—Undergraduate experiences with assigned reading. *CUNY Academic Works*, 1–10.

Smale, M. A., & Regaldo, M. (2017). *Digital technology as affordance and barrier to higher education*. New York, NY: Palgrave Macmillan.

Smith, T. S., Isaak, M. I., Senette, C. G., & Abadie, B. G. (2011). Effects of cell-phone and text-message distractions on true and false recognition.

Cyberpsychology, Behavior, and Social Networking, 14(6), 351–58. doi:10.1089/cyber.2010.0129

Sosnoski, J. (1999). Hyper-readers and their reading engines. In G. E. Hawisher & C. L. Selfe (Eds.), *Passions pedagogies and 21st century technologies* (pp. 161–77). University Press of Colorado, Utah State University Press.

Sprouse, M. (2018). Social annotation and layered readings in composition. *Proceedings of the Annual Computers & Writing Conference, 2018*, 39–52.

Starcher, K., & Proffitt, D. (2011). Encouraging students to read: What professors are (and aren't) doing about it. *International Journal of Teaching and Learning in Higher Education, 23*(3), 396–407.

St Clair-Thompson, H., Graham, A., & Marsham, S. (2018). Exploring the reading practices of undergraduate students. *Education Inquiry, 9*(3), 284–98. doi:0.1080/20004508.2017.1380487

Stommel, J. (2017, June 5). If bell hooks made an LMS: Grades, radical openness, and domain of one's own [blog]. Retrieved from https://www.jessestommel.com/if-bell-hooks-made-an-lms-grades-radical-openness-and-domain-of-ones-own/

Stommel, J. (2018, March 11). How to ungrade [blog]. Retrieved from https://www.jessestommel.com/how-to-ungrade/

Sun, Y. & Gao, F. (2014). Web annotation and threaded forum: How did learners use the two environments in an online discussion? *Journal of Information Technology Education: Innovations in Practice, 13*, 69–88.

Supiano, B. (2019, July 19). Grades can hinder learning. What should professors use instead? *Chronicle of Higher Education.* Retrieved from https://www.chronicle.com/interactives/20190719_ungrading

Swartz, J. (2016, Jan 11). Apple loses more ground to Google's Chromebook in education market. *USA TODAY.* Retrieved from https://www.usatoday.com/story/tech/news/2016/01/11/apple-loses-more-ground-googles-chromebook-education-market/78323158/

Sweeney, M. A. (2018). Audience awareness as a threshold concept of reading: An examination of student learning in biochemistry. *Research in the Teaching of English, 53*(1), 58–79.

Sweeney, M. A., & McBride, M. (2015). Difficulty paper (dis)connections: Understanding the threads students weave between their reading and writing. *College Composition and Communication, 66*(4), 591–64.

Thornton, B., Faires, A., Robbins, M., & Rollins, E. (2014). The mere presence of a cell phone may be distracting: Implications for attention and task performance. *Social Psychology, 45*(6), 479.

Tobin, T. J., & Behling, K. T. (2018). *Reach everyone, teach everyone: Universal Design for Learning in higher education.* Morgantown: West Virginia University Press.

Tracy, R. (2015, June 17). A framework for content curation. E-Learning

Provocateur. Retrieved from https://ryan2point0.wordpress.com/2015 /06/17/a-framework-for-content-curation/

Turkle, S. (2011). *Alone together: Why we expect more from technology and less from each other.* New York, NY: Basic Books.

Turkle, S. (2015). *Reclaiming conversation: The power of talk in a digital age.* New York, NY: Penguin Books.

Twenge, J. (2017). *iGen: Why today's kids are growing up less rebellious, more tolerant, less happy—and completely unprepared for adulthood—and what that means for the rest of us.* New York, NY: Simon and Schuster.

Ulin, D. L. (2010). *The lost art of reading: Why books matter in a distracted time.* Seattle, WA: Sasquatch Books.

Ulmer, G. (2003). *Internet invention: From literacy to electracy.* London, United Kingdom: Longman.

U.S. Department of Education, National Center for Education Statistics. (2019). *Digest of Education Statistics, 2017* (NCES 2018–070), Chapter 3.

Van den Broek, P., & Kendeou, P. (2015). Building coherence in web-based and other non traditional reading environments: Cognitive opportunities and challenges. In R. J. Spiro, M. DeSchryver, M. S, Hagerman., P. M. Morsink., & P. Thompson (Eds.), *Reading at a crossroads? Disjunctures and continuities in current conceptions and practices.* New York, NY: Routledge.

Vocke, D. E. (1991). An artifact from the 19th century schoolhouse: The McGuffey Reader. *OAH Magazine of History*, *5*(3), 5–6. https://doi .org/10.1093/maghis/5.3.5

Wang, G. (2018). *Artful design: Technology in search of the sublime, A MusiComic manifesto.* Redwood City: Stanford University Press.

Watters, A. (2014, September 5). Beyond the LMS. Hack Education. Retrieved from http://hackeducation.com/2014/09/05/beyond -the-lms-newcastle-university

Weimer, M. (2015). How concerned should we be about cell phones in class? Faculty Focus. Retrieved from https://www.facultyfocus .com/articles/effective-classroom-management/how-concerned -should-we-be-about-cell-phones-in-class/

Wellmon, C. (2015). *Organizing enlightenment: Information overload and the invention of the modern research university.* Baltimore, MD: Johns Hopkins University Press.

West, J. (2018). Raising the quality of discussion by scaffolding students' reading. *International Journal of Teaching and Learning in Higher Education*, *30*(1), 146–60.

Wiley, D., Webb, A., Weston, S., & Tonks, D. (2017). A preliminary exploration of the relationships between student-created OER, sustainability, and students' success. *International Review of Research in Open and Distributed Learning*, *18*(4).

Williams, B. (2018). *Literacy practices and perceptions of agency: Composing identities*. New York, NY: Routledge.

Willingham, D. T. (2017). *The Reading Mind*. San Francisco, CA: Jossey-Bass.

Wineburg, S., & McGrew, S. (2019). Lateral reading and the nature of expertise: Reading less and learning more when evaluating digital information. *Teachers College Record*, *121*(11), 1–40.

Winnick, M. (2016, June 16). Putting a finger on our phone obsession [dscout blog post]. Retrieved from https://blog.dscout.com/mobile-touches

Wiradhany, W., & Nieuwenstein, M. R. (2017). Cognitive control in media multitaskers: Two replication studies and meta-analysis. *Attention, Perception, & Psychophysics*, *79*(8), 2620–41.

Wolf, M. (2016). *Tales of literacy for the 21st century*. United Kingdom: Oxford University Press.

Wolf, M. (2018). *Reader, come home*. New York, NY: HarperCollins Publishers.

Wolter, D. L. (2018). *Ears, eyes, and hands: Reflections on language, literacy, and linguistics*. Washington, DC: Gallaudet University Press.

Womack, A.-M. (2017). Teaching is accommodation: Universally designing composition classrooms and syllabi. *College Composition and Communication*, *68*(3), 494–525.

Woolley, S., Sattiraju, N., & Moritz, S. (2020, March 26). U.S. schools trying to teach online highlight a digital divide. *Bloomberg.com*. Retrieved from https://www.bloomberg.com/news/articles/2020-03-26/covid-19-school-closures-reveal-disparity-in-access-to-internet

Yeh, H., Hung, H., & Chiang, Y. (2016). The use of online annotations in reading instruction and its impact on students' reading progress and processes. *ReCALL*, *29*(1), 22–38.

Zimmerman, J. (2016, September 11). Welcome, freshmen. Look at me when I talk to you. *Chronicle of Higher Education*. Retrieved from https://www.chronicle.com/article/Welcome-Freshmen-Look-at-Me/237751

INDEX

....

TEACHING AND LEARNING IN HIGHER EDUCATION

Minding Bodies: How Physical Space, Sensation, and Movement Affect Learning
Susan Hrach

Ungrading: Why Rating Students Undermines Learning (and What to Do Instead)
Edited by Susan D. Blum

Radical Hope: A Teaching Manifesto
Kevin M. Gannon

Teaching about Race and Racism in the College Classroom: Notes from a White Professor
Cyndi Kernahan

Intentional Tech: Principles to Guide the Use of Educational Technology in College Teaching
Derek Bruff

Geeky Pedagogy: A Guide for Intellectuals, Introverts, and Nerds Who Want to Be Effective Teachers
Jessamyn Neuhaus

How Humans Learn: The Science and Stories behind Effective College Teaching
Joshua R. Eyler

Reach Everyone, Teach Everyone: Universal Design for Learning in Higher Education
Thomas J. Tobin and Kirsten T. Behling

Teaching the Literature Survey Course: New Strategies for College Faculty
James M. Lang, Gwynn Dujardin, and John A. Staunton

The Spark of Learning: Energizing the College Classroom with the Science of Emotion
Sarah Rose Cavanagh